40X

# STARS IN BLUE

# STARS ★ IN BLUE

## Movie Actors in America's Sea Services

James E. Wise, Jr., and Anne Collier Rehill

NAVAL INSTITUTE PRESS
*Annapolis, Maryland*

Library of Congress Cataloging-in-Publication Data
Wise, James E., 1930–
      Stars in blue : movie actors in America's sea services / James E. Wise, Jr. and Anne Collier Rehill.
          p.      cm.
      Includes bibliographical references and index.
      ISBN 1-55750-937-9 (alk. paper)
      1. Actors as sailors.     2. Motion picture actors and actresses—United States—Biography.      I. Rehill, Anne Collier, 1950–    .
      II. Title
      PN1998.2.W55    1997                            97-14333

Printed in the United States of America on acid-free paper ♾

04  03  02  01  00  99  98  97      9  8  7  6  5  4  3  2

Photos at chapter openings are from the following sources: pages 13, 33, 51, 61, 183, 245, 255, 259: U.S. Navy photos; pages 85, 93, 99, 113, 135, 149, 189, 207, 219, 241: Photofest; pages 159, 201, 227: U.S. Coast Guard photos; page 3: Eddie Albert collection; page 45: Dale Howard collection; page 77: Dept. of Special Collections Research Library, UCLA; page 81: Ed Begley, Jr., collection; page 107: Louise Tracy collection; page 117: Ernest Borgnine collection; page 123: Frank Coghlan collection; page 143: Tony Curtis collection; page 167: Mrs. M. Y. Tompkins collection; page 173: Fan*Fare; page 177: Copyright by Universal City Studios, Inc., courtesy of MCA Publishing Rights, a division of MCA, Inc., all rights reserved; page 197: Bridget Madison collection; page 213: Logan Ramsey collection; page 223: Army Air Forces photo; page 233: Robert Stack collection; page 265: John Gavin collection

*For our spouses, Carlotta and Brian,*
*the brightest stars of all*

# Contents

## Part 4: The Korean War and Afterward

## Appendixes

# Preface

The inspiration for this book came when I was doing research on World War II Pacific carrier operations, specifically the Battle of the Philippine Sea and the Great Marianas Turkey Shoot, and learned of the exploits of Wayne Morris. Morris, a movie actor who became a naval aviator and an ace during World War II, was a first-rate F6F Hellcat fighter pilot in Pacific aerial combat. As I looked deeper into Wayne Morris's life, I began to realize that a large number of stars wore Navy uniforms, during both world wars, throughout the Korean conflict, and afterward. A few stars chose the Coast Guard, which on 1 November 1941 was transferred to the Navy under Executive Order 8929.

Douglas Fairbanks, Jr., became a highly decorated naval officer who saw extensive action in the European theater. Henry Fonda enlisted in the Navy and became a quartermaster third class before attaining a commission and serving as an operations and intelligence officer on board a seaplane tender in the Pacific. For his exceptional performance of duty he was awarded the Bronze Star. Robert Montgomery, father of the *Bewitched* television star Elizabeth Montgomery, joined the American Field Service in April 1941, before the United States had declared war, and served in France before it fell to the German juggernaut. He eventually saw PT boat and cruiser duty in the Pacific and was aboard a destroyer that participated in the Normandy invasion.

Other actors served their country in equally impressive ways. Enlisting the skills of coauthor Anne Collier Rehill, I went to work on gathering as much information as I could find on each star's naval service. Details about the service of enlisted personnel were slim and in most cases available only from the National Personnel Records Center in St. Louis, Missouri. I also consulted other Navy records such as official biographies, logs, diaries, award citations, and wartime documents. I checked over oral histories and autobiographies and attempted to contact the stars themselves, or their families, in many cases with success.

I put all this together in preliminary write-ups, after which Anne dug deeper into the source material, rewriting and making additions, trying to convey a sense of who these people are (or were, in too many cases), and of how they got into the movies. While confirming and adding various anecdotes and details about the entertainment industry's history, Anne sometimes came across conflicting reports—perhaps not too surprising, since the very nature of movies is to create reality from illusion. We have nailed down the facts as best we could.

We have included an appendix on the contribution of one female movie star—Hedy Lamarr. Although she did not serve in the Navy, Lamarr invented frequency-hopping during World War II; today this antijamming device is used for communications throughout the military. Other actresses volunteered their services by entertaining the troops through United Service Organizations clubs and the famous Stage Door Canteen in Hollywood, and some toured the front lines with USO shows. Many helped out at home by visiting defense plants and boosting morale among plant workers.

It was not easy for well-known movie stars to find a place among experienced, career-minded Navymen. They were sometimes treated with disdain because of their notoriety and had to earn the respect of their shipmates through hard work and dedication to duty. Most did find their place, and all served their country with honor. We believe that you will find what follows to be a tribute to them.

James E. Wise, Jr.

# Acknowledgments

I t is impossible to list everyone who has helped in collecting information for this book. With apologies to those not mentioned and with deep thanks to all, we would like to acknowledge in particular a few people:

Frank "Junior" Coghlan, movie star, naval aviator, and one-time head of the film-cooperation program of the Navy's Chief of Information, led the way in reaching the stars. Natalie Hall was a tireless researcher who located material that seemed nearly impossible to find. Jack Green, photo archivist in the photographic section of the Naval Historical Center at the Washington Navy Yard, supplied illustrations rarely seen before.

As for the stars themselves, and their families, we are especially grateful to the following for their gracious support and assistance: Eddie Albert, Jackie Cooper, Tony Curtis, Kirk Douglas, Peter Duchin, Marjorie Ewell, Douglas Fairbanks, Jr., Peter Ford, John Gavin, Dale Howard, Bridget Madison, Pat Morris, Paul Newman, Logan and Mary Ann Ramsey, Beverly and Buddy Rogers, Edward Romero, Robert Stack, and Suzi Tracy.

Others we wish to thank include Obadia E. Armstrong, Joe Baltake, John W. Balzer, Joe Bitterly, Don Canney, Bernard F. Cavalcante, Evelyn M. Cherpak, Edith Correale, Wendy Davis, Mario DeMarco, Harry Flynn, Johnny Grant, David C. Graham, Albert Hansen, Dick Hansen, John Hodges, David M. Jaffe, Allan King, Brigitte Kueppers, Charles A. Lloyd, Helen McDonald, J. Daniel Mullin, Jules Posner, Scott Price, Capt. Rosario Rausa (USN, Ret.), Stanley H. Smith, Jennifer Walsh, Seldon West, Mary V. Yates, and James G. Zumwalt, as well as Paul Stillwell, Paul Wilderson, and their colleagues at the U.S. Naval Institute.

# STARS IN BLUE

★

## PART 1

# Above and Beyond

In wartime, there are always a few who stand out. Whether because they are braver than most, are exceptionally cool under fire, or have more bravado, or because the ideas they hatch to defeat or weaken the enemy turn out to be brilliant, such warriors deserve special recognition. The military does its best to honor all of them, even though inevitably, unfortunately, the courageous feats of many go unnoticed or unrewarded. Following are the stories of several whose exploits did not go unnoticed during World War II.

# Eddie Albert

In real life, Eddie Albert—Eva Gabor's costar in the TV series *Green Acres* (1965–71)—was a hero in World War II. On 21 November 1943, at Betio Island in the Tarawa atoll, Lt. (jg) Edward Albert Heimberger took command of several LCVPs (landing craft, vehicle and personnel) and sped to the rescue of thirteen wounded Marines who were trapped on an exposed reef offshore under enemy fire, the tide coming in. He had already saved the lives of at least three others.

Many of them recognized Albert, whom they had seen in *Brother Rat* (1938), *Four Wives* (1939), and other movies, always cast as a good, honest, regular American. Now he was here with them, picking them off a reef of death at Tarawa, and the image those young Marines had of him may have helped Albert live up to it. However they managed to pull it off, Eddie Albert Heimberger and his intrepid company saved men that day who would otherwise have drowned or been shot to death.

This regular American (born 1908) grew up in Minneapolis, where Frank Daniel and Julia Heimberger had moved their family from Rock Island, Illinois. Having attended Catholic school and the University of Minnesota while working at a variety of jobs, including a stint as master of ceremonies for a weekly magic show, the young entertainer decided to strike out on his own. Quitting school, he became part of a singing-and-dancing trio and performed first on a program broadcast by a local radio station, then in Cincinnati, Chicago, and New York. By the time he got to New York he had dropped his last name, now using just the first two.

The group split up in New York, and after some lean times living without electricity and singing in clubs for a few bucks a night, Albert found work singing on NBC radio programs. He also began acting in summer stock and even landed a brief Broadway role. Persevering, by 1936 he was playing the part of Bing Edwards in the Broadway play *Brother Rat,* which attracted enough critical attention to secure his next Broadway role, in *Room Service.* By this time Warner Brothers had noticed the young actor and signed him to a contract. His first movie was *Brother Rat,* and he continued to appear on both screen and stage, bicoastally.

He also made some independent forays into Mexico, having heard stories of Japanese and Nazi secret activities there. Under cover as a trapeze artist in a circus show, he traveled throughout the country gathering information and taking pictures, handing it all over to Navy intelligence.

On 9 September 1942, at age thirty-four, he joined the Navy and, thanks to his work in Mexico, was sent to Cornell University in Ithaca, New York, for officer's training. On 31 January 1943 he was honorably discharged to accept appointment on 1 February as a lieutenant (jg), USNR.

Lieutenant Heimberger was assigned to the amphibious attack transport USS *Sheridan* (APA-51), with Task Force 53. Commissioned on 31 July 1943, with Heimberger aboard as a "plankowner" (initial crew member of a newly commissioned ship), the *Sheridan,* after a shakedown cruise off San Francisco, sailed for the western Pacific on

1 October. After embarking Marines (Landing Team 1st Battalion, 8th Marines) and their equipment in New Zealand and delivering cargo at Noumea, the ship sailed for Efate Island in the New Hebrides. Her landing force underwent amphibious training there from 7 to 9 November, after which she sailed again, ready to participate in the invasion of the Gilbert Islands. The *Sheridan* was joining the savage battle for the island of Betio in the Tarawa atoll.

About three hundred acres in size, Betio was held by Japanese Special Naval Landing Forces *(Rikusentai)* who defended it fiercely to the end. As the American Marines approached the island, their landing craft could not make it over the fringing reef because of a low tide. The Marines were forced to wade the rest of the way in to shore completely exposed to enemy fire, and many of them drowned, weighed down by their bulky equipment. Many others were shot down. It took seventy-two hours to secure the island, at the cost of 3,407 American casualties. The dead numbered 997 Marines and 30 Navy; 88 Marines were missing; and 2,233 Marines and 59 Navy were wounded. Almost 30 percent of the men who were directly involved in the fighting were killed or wounded. Ninety out of 125 amtracs (tracked landing vehicles) were lost on the reefs, in deep holes under the water, or to enemy fire.

The USS *Sheridan* (APA-51) and other attack transports en route to Kwajalein to participate in the bloody January–February 1944 operations there. (U.S. Navy photo)

The 2d Marine Division's troops performed heroics that would later be recognized in a Presidential Unit Citation. There were also individual awards, including 4 Medals of Honor (3 of them posthumous), 46 Navy Crosses (22 posthumous), 4 Distinguished Service Medals, 248 Silver Stars, and 21 Legion of Merit awards. (The Bronze Star and the Navy Commendation Medal did not yet exist.)

As for the enemy, out of a garrison of 4,500 men, 146 remained alive. Nineteen of these were definitely Japanese; the others were Korean laborers who had been conscripted.

Operation Galvanic, as it was called, got under way during the early-morning hours of 20 November 1943, but not much progress was made that day. Among the assault craft that waited offshore for clearance to start toward the beach were twenty-six LCVPs from the *Sheridan*. They waited almost thirty hours, the ninety-five Marines they held getting seasick, tired, and, of course, wet. The minesweeper *Pursuit* (AM-108) offered meals, which assuaged matters only slightly.

Two LCP(L)s (landing craft, personnel, light) from the *Sheridan* supported the LCVPs, and a control boat (PA 51-14), under the command of Lt. John Fletcher, would guide them to their designated areas on the beach. A salvage craft (PA 51-13), the assistant control boat, skippered by Lieutenant Heimberger, was to repair boats, refuel, and transfer men from out-of-action boats. Both commanders' boats could move fast and were easy to maneuver. For crews, aside from their commanders they had a coxswain and a gunner armed with a .30-caliber air-cooled machine gun.

Finally they got their clearance—at 0616 on the second day of the assault. They were to land on Beach Red 2. But by now the tide was lower than it had been the previous day, and there was barely two feet of water, with parts of the reef already dry. The boats could not get over the coral, and the Marines left their landing craft five hundred yards from the shore, wide-open targets. They began dropping by the score, as artillery fire blew their disembarking craft out of the water.

Dead and wounded were all over the beach, and about 150 Marines were waist-deep in water, at least 100 of them wounded. More were getting shot up by the minute. Seeing the carnage, Fletcher and Heimberger both raced in, independently of one another, to aid the men. The boats made three or four trips back and forth, picking men up and

Along with the others who had picked men off the reef that day at Tarawa, Heimberger was cited for outstanding performance of duty during action against the enemy. (U.S. Navy photo)

ferrying them out to LCMs (landing craft, mechanized—large open flat-bottomed bargelike craft for carrying tanks and heavy vehicles ashore). From there the wounded could be transferred to ships. When Heimberger's boat suffered a damaged propeller, he sent it back to the *Sheridan* with the wounded, taking command of an LCVP for his next trip in to the reef. They came under fire while taking the wounded aboard, but no one was hit. By this time the tide had begun to come in, and enemy strafing was picking up.

Realizing that he could do more with several LCVPs, Heimberger decided that on his next trip he would try to get all the rest of the men at once. Leaving his coxswain with orders to keep up the excellent work, Heimberger now boarded a third boat and took over four others that were nearby. He had them transfer their extra passengers to LCMs, keeping only their crews. They were to follow him to the beach.

About halfway there (two thousand or so yards out) the bullets seemed to be hitting harder and faster. The Americans slowed down, trying to identify the guns' positions. Finally they had it: the gunfire was coming from a sunken hull that they had thought dive bombers had knocked out an hour earlier, and from a machine-gun nest at the end of the island's pier. There were also snipers and guns on the island.

The LCVPs fired on all of these positions, which silenced the enemy's gunfire for a while, and the rescuers got back to work. Heimberger decided to pick up the wounded using one boat at a time; the others were to lay to a hundred yards off and keep the enemy machine guns under control. Heimberger's boat went in first.

As they started to take men off the reef, knowing that their eight drums of gasoline would be set off if incendiaries hit it, they had to pause to take out a sniper in a wrecked LCVP about forty feet away. (Later, 13.2 mm armor-piercing bullets were found in the boat.) During all this the coxswain had to control the boat against a strong current, holding it away from the wounded but close enough to lift them up, while at the same time taking care not to ground the boat on the reef.

At last, thirteen men had been lifted into the boat, not always easily. They had to be grabbed in whatever way possible, which for some meant being pulled in by a badly broken arm or leg. Thirty-five unwounded were still in the water, and Heimberger said he could take some of them, but not all would fit. None of the Marines moved. They asked if he was coming back again, and would he bring them rifles. But the return trip, with requested rifles and ammo aboard, was too late for those Marines. Nearby gun nests had all been knocked out, but the Marines had never made it to shore. Heimberger delivered the rifles to the end of the pier, where Marines who could still fight immediately put them to good use.

Also on the return trip, Heimberger intercepted a boat that held Col. Elmer Hall, commander of the 8th Marines, who had been speeding toward the beach along with other boats. Heimberger told them about the enemy's increased firepower and where he thought it was coming from. Noting the information, the colonel transferred a medical officer to Heimberger's boat to tend to the wounded, ordering Heimberger to report to Commodore J. B. McGovern (primary control officer) on the

*Pursuit.* McGovern had him transfer the wounded to the nearest ship (the *Sheridan*), after which he was to return for further orders.

Heimberger asked the wounded what they had gleaned about the enemy's firepower and his position. With a freshly equipped salvage boat, he then returned to the *Pursuit* with two amtracs loaded with 37mm ammunition. Reporting to McGovern, he submitted the information he had obtained from the wounded, after which McGovern had him take the two amtracs to the beach.

By this time the Marines had secured the pier, so Heimberger reported to the chief beachmaster for his next orders. He tried to relieve Lieutenant Fletcher, who had also been directing rescue operations and had been without relief or rest for three days, but Fletcher would not leave his job. Heimberger worked on the pier for the rest of that day helping to move supplies, an operation that was slowed by the annoying snipers. Finally he was ordered to coordinate the delivery of much-needed ammunition to Marines still in the heat of close-in battle, in the course of which yet another sniper was picked off.

The last harrowing duty of Lt. (jg) Heimberger and company, including the cool-under-fire Texan Larry Wade, was to retrieve the bodies of those Marines who were left in the water off Tarawa. Heimberger, third from left, is in command of PA 51-13. (U.S. Marine Corps photo)

Unaffected, affable, and carrying out his orders with dispatch and daring, Eddie Heimberger was an appreciated addition to the war effort wherever he was sent. That night he stayed on the island with the Marines. Trying to catch a bit of rest proved a fruitless pursuit when, during a fire burst, somebody fell into his burrowed-out crevice, right on top of him. As they snuggled in, sharing the space head to foot, the Marine remarked calmly that he had been in the service for thirty-eight years and this was the worst he had seen yet. Gunfire continuing throughout the night above them, the Marine took off his trousers and folded them across his chest, commenting that at least he could still look sharp in the morning. Toward dawn, after cautioning Heimberger about a sniper he had spotted nearby, he put on his trousers and was up and out.

Minutes later Heimberger followed, noticing the Marine smoking a little pipe and helping the wounded. He asked someone who this remarkable man was; he turned out to be Lt. Col. Evans F. Carlson, founder and leader of the legendary Carlson's Raiders. (Surviving the war, Brigadier General Carlson died of a heart attack in 1947, at age fifty-one.)

After Tarawa, on 17 December 1943 Lieutenant Heimberger received orders detaching him from the *Sheridan* and transferring him to the Bureau of Aeronautics in Washington, D.C., where he reported on 10 January 1944. His next duty was in the Training Film Division, and he was sent on war-bond tours around the country as well, visiting factories, hotels, and shipyards, bringing firsthand information about how things were going on the front lines. His experience making training films was to provide an ideal background for the educational films he would soon be producing on his own. He made about six training films while in the Navy before he was released from active duty on 9 January 1946, a full lieutenant (as of 1 March 1944).

Along with the others who had picked men off the reef that day at Tarawa, Heimberger was cited for outstanding performance of duty during action against the enemy, in a 30 November 1943 letter from the commanding officer of troops, USS *Sheridan*, to the commanding officer of the ship. "Their boat handling and devotion to duty under machine gun fire was an important factor in the successful operation of Landing Team one-eight." Heimberger was entitled to wear the

On 21 September 1994, Eddie Albert received the Navy's Distinguished Public Service Award. At right is Commandant of the Marine Corps Gen. Carl E. Mundy, USMC. (U.S. Navy photo)

American Area Campaign Medal, the Asiatic–Pacific Area Campaign Medal, and the World War II Victory Medal.

Eddie Albert found it difficult to resume his acting career, but he and his wife, Margo—they were married in 1945—began performing their own nightclub act, packing the house not only at New York's Waldorf-Astoria but also in Hollywood, Miami, and Las Vegas. Albert also began producing documentaries for companies and educational films for children. Nor did he give up on acting, and by the early 1950s he had begun to find work as second leads and eventually in starring roles, consistently giving skilled performances, and no longer always as the good guy. He received a nod from the Academy of Motion Picture Arts and Sciences for his supporting role in *Roman Holiday* (1953) and another for playing Cybill Shepherd's father in *The Heartbreak Kid* (1972). Other major work has included *Attack* (1956), *The Teahouse of the August Moon* (1956), *The Sun Also Rises* (1957), and *The Longest Yard* (1974). Albert has also had plentiful television work.

He and actress, singer, and dancer Margo of *Lost Horizon* fame (1937) had two children. She passed away in 1985. Albert, a man of principle and action, became committed to environmental issues in 1969 and remains an outspoken activist, supporting as well several youth organizations. In 1994 he received the Navy's Distinguished Public Service Award.

# Douglas Fairbanks, Jr.

Douglas Fairbanks, Jr., like his swashbuckling father, had a penchant for the dramatic and a derring-do air about him. Adm. Horatio Nelson was his idol, and throughout World War II he saw himself alternately as a hero and as a dreamer who should (and could) have stayed at home. Instead he was trained by the British as a commando and flotilla commander in deception operations, and, carrying his skills back to the States, he developed a similar operation that U.S. commanders used during the war. He remained on active duty until 1946.

He hardly had a typical background for soldiering. Born in 1909, Douglas Fairbanks, Jr., grew up surrounded by famous, wealthy people, his father a legend, his stepmother Mary Pickford known as America's Sweetheart. His mother, socialite Anna Beth Sully, further widened his circle, and from infancy his companions were the elite of society. He befriended presidents, kings, admirals, generals, movie moguls, industry leaders, and diplomats worldwide. During his career he appeared in numerous movies, and by the time he joined the Navy, several months before the United States declared war, his was one of the most popular names in the country. This celebrity status would not always work in his favor in the military, and he would have repeated run-ins with various departments and personnel who were afraid he would expect special treatment.

Despite his father's disapproval, Fairbanks attended no college, instead making his film debut at age thirteen in Hollywood. His first effort bombed, but, undaunted, he discreetly visited his father's studio, where Douglas Senior was still making classics. The son watched and learned. Between 1925 and 1928 he made fifteen films; his first hit, *The Dawn Patrol,* came in 1930. Several films later, his interpretation of Sergeant Ballantyne in *Gunga Din* (1939) won him renewed international acclaim. The movie was no doubt helped by the timing of its release with respect to events in Europe, where the British and French were beginning to weaken. With its portrayal of British heroes valiantly fighting on, *Gunga Din* had great morale-boosting value.

By this time the actor had become involved in international politics, and he felt strongly that the United States should support the Allied cause. Knowing that President Franklin D. Roosevelt agreed, he offered to assist in any way it was thought he could. Herbert Bayard Swope, former publisher of the *New York World,* shared his sentiments; it was at Swope's Long Island home that Fairbanks met Mary Lee Hartford, whom he married in 1939 (having been married once before, to Joan Crawford, 1929–33).

In April 1941 Fairbanks was commissioned into the U.S. Naval Reserve, but first FDR gave him an assignment as special envoy to Panama, Argentina, Uruguay, Chile, Peru, and Brazil. Ostensibly his mission was to ascertain the impact of U.S. movies on Latin American public opinion, but the real purpose of his visit was to contact national groups in several countries thought to be harboring sympathy for the Nazi regime. Most important from a Navy perspective, he was to find out which countries would let U.S. naval forces use their ports for operational and repair facilities. Fairbanks met with artists, writers, and actors, picking their brains and letting it be known that the United States sympathized with the Allies. Completing his mission in a little over two months, he reported for active duty.

Fairbanks's initiation into the Navy was not greeted with warmth or enthusiasm. While undergoing training as a deck officer "under instruction" on board a supply ship out of Charlestown Navy Yard, Boston, he was teased continually and given a grimy cot all the way in the bow of the supply ship, though it turned out there was plenty of room amidships. Fairbanks took it all without complaining or becoming ruffled, prompting one of the officers to shake his hand and tell him, as he was leaving the ship, that they had all decided he was okay.

Upon his arrival in Newfoundland he reported to the new *Benson*-class destroyer USS *Ludlow* (DD-438), on convoy duty. The heavy North Atlantic seas made him so queasy that even reminding himself that his hero Lord Nelson frequently got seasick did not help. What did make life more tolerable was that on the *Ludlow* they started to teach him a few things about becoming a qualified deck officer.

Gradually the United States found itself edging into an undeclared conflict with Germany, establishing a wide neutrality zone around the Americas and ordering hostile forces not to operate within its boundaries. However, under the U.S. Lend-Lease/Cash and Carry policy, British ships were soon visiting U.S. ports to load war supplies, which later included munitions. Churchill and FDR met in Argentia, Newfoundland, in August 1941 to finalize arrangements for the use of U.S. Navy ships in protecting convoys, to work out details for the implementation of FDR's call for "all aid short of war," and to develop the Atlantic Charter establishing postwar goals.

In September the shooting phase of the undeclared war began when a German U-boat fired torpedoes at the American destroyer *Greer* (DD-145), which counterattacked with a depth-charge barrage. Both attacks missed their mark, but soon other incidents occurred. U-568 torpedoed the destroyer *Kearney* (DD-432) on 7 October, and a few weeks later U-552 sank the destroyer *Reuben Jones* (DD-245) while on convoy duty, with heavy loss of life. Later in the war the *Ludlow* would be credited with sinking U-960 in the western Mediterranean.

Fairbanks stood deck watches as the *Ludlow* escorted her convoy to Iceland. By now he was beginning to learn about radio, visual communications, gunnery, navigation, and antisubmarine warfare. The destroyer was often brought to battle stations, and Fairbanks grew accustomed to the alarm followed by seeming chaos, men shouting as they grabbed World War I–era helmets and life vests. The green officer was starting to get a little seasoning.

He was next ordered to the battleship *Mississippi* (BB-41), flagship of Task Force 99, assigned as watch officer. This time he was "under instruction" for gunnery and communications. Toward the end of November 1941 the *Mississippi* and other ships of the task force were ordered to Norfolk for repair and overhaul. While en route, one of the junior communications officers fell to seasickness, and Fairbanks assumed communications decoder duties.

It was while he was on watch that he decoded the 7 December All Navy (AlNav) message, "Air attack on Pearl Harbor. This is not a drill." The distribution header "AlNav" signified nothing to the substitute communications officer, nor did he recognize the importance of the message, which he tossed into the wastebasket. But a few minutes later, the words "This is not a drill" still gnawing at him, he pulled the message back out and took it up to the bridge, just in case.

The first night in Norfolk, all hands were ordered to stay on board ship, war having been declared. In order to ease the blow, the chaplain announced the showing of a movie that night on deck that no one would want to miss. To Fairbanks's chagrin, it was *The Corsican Brothers*, which he had finished filming before reporting for active duty, and he guessed—correctly—that he would never live this down.

After a brief tour at headquarters in Washington—unsatisfactory except for the fact that he was reunited with his family—Fairbanks was ordered to the post of executive officer of the minesweeper *Goldcrest* (AM-80), operating out of Staten Island. He was in no way qualified for such duty, possessing none of the knowledge of sophisticated electronics or the experience necessary for the job. However, it seemed, he had been rushed out of Washington, where his high-profile presence had again caused problems; there were those who feared his star status was attracting too much media attention.

He muddled through the cold, damp, boring Staten Island experience as best he could, looking forward to evenings with Mary Lee in their uptown hotel room and becoming friends with the ship's captain.

On the *Wasp*, which delivered Spitfires and Hurricanes to the Royal Air Force in Malta, Douglas Fairbanks, Jr., wrote the official naval record for historical purposes. (U.S. Navy photo)

Within weeks the Navy realized that a mistake had been made. The captain gave Fairbanks a better fitness report than Nelson himself would have received. Clearly this was wrong, and the Navy hustled the too-likable Fairbanks back to Task Force 99, aboard the brand-new battleship *Washington* (BB-56). The task force was now attached to the British Home Fleet and consisted of the aircraft carrier *Wasp*, the light cruisers *Wichita* and *Tuscaloosa*, and a number of destroyers and support ships. The force used Reykjavík and Scapa Flow, Scotland, as its operating bases.

Fairbanks made his way to Montreal, from where the United States was delivering bombers to the Royal Air Force and the Royal Canadian Air Force in Britain. But there was no room left on board his assigned aircraft; the brass had taken it all. Fairbanks had to get on that flight, but there was only one way to do it. He made the fourteen-hour flight lying down and strapped into the frigid metal-ridged bomb bay. They laid a few blankets over the ridges for padding and told him to dress in numerous layers, goggles on. When the sleeping pill they had given him wore off, he was still there, freezing, unable to go to the bathroom, and afraid someone would accidentally hit the wrong button.

In London, upon learning that his ship was out on patrol off Norway and Iceland, Fairbanks enjoyed an unexpected opportunity to visit with old friends such as "Larry" Olivier, Vivien Leigh, and Noël Coward. Then he flew off to Scapa Flow, boarded a shore boat, and reported aboard the *Washington* on 22 April 1942. He was assigned to Rear Adm. Robert "Ike" Giffen's flag staff as assistant staff gunnery and communications officer, eventually becoming the admiral's flag lieutenant. Taking as always the expected ribbing without complaint, Fairbanks won the friendship of two officers in particular, under whose knowledgeable guidance the still-green Hollywood émigré began to learn the ropes in earnest. He took courses in Navy correspondence, in international law, and in rifle and pistol shooting, passing the expert pistol-shot test. This qualified him for close-combat shooting and won him the bronze medal for pistol marksmanship.

Fairbanks was finally beginning to feel a sense of belonging. But when Admiral Giffen said he had some unique tasks in mind for his flag lieutenant, all he felt was a sense of foreboding.

His first temporary duty was to go aboard the carrier *Wasp* (CV-7), which, along with the British carrier HMS *Eagle,* was about to deliver Spitfires and Hurricanes to the Royal Air Force in Malta. Fairbanks's job was to write up the official naval record of the operation for historical purposes. Positioned in the Mediterranean Sea south of Italy, Malta in 1942 was directly in the path of resupply for Rommel's forces in Africa. Stubborn island forces were holding out against continuous air-bombing attacks by Italian and German aircraft, RAF losses were heavy, and replacement aircraft were desperately needed. It was Fairbanks's first time aboard an aircraft carrier, and the sight of small planes taking off heroically and then landing on a short midocean runway did not inspire in him any desire to become a pilot. The junior officer scribbled away, recording the precarious aircraft landings.

Operation Bowery got under way in early May, and the *Wasp* and *Eagle* proceeded to flyoff positions east of Gibraltar, after making their way through fearful seas. Fairbanks stood communications watches on the bridge of the *Wasp* as well as assuming communications duties and participating in gunnery exercises. Flyoff of the aircraft started on 9 May. Fifty launches would be needed to complete the mission, including U.S. Navy fighters to patrol the operating area as the British planes took off. The day was long and nerve-wracking, with one fatal accident on takeoff and a narrowly successful emergency Spitfire landing. At 2400 the ship received her first message from Malta: the first three flights had landed at 1010, during an enemy air raid. Another message reported that all the Spitfires had landed safely on Malta, had quickly been refueled, and were back in the air fighting the raiding aircraft.

On the morning of 10 May six Swordfishes landed from Gibraltar, collecting guns, equipment, and ground crew for the Malta planes, and mail. Then they and the Spitfire that had emergency-landed the previous day took off for the island. Malta had been under continuous air attack since the arrival of the first Spitfires, but the Allied planes had fared well and brought down thirty enemy planes while losing only three Spitfires. Next day, as the task force sailed westward through the Straits of Gibraltar, the ship received a personal message from Prime Minister Winston Churchill, thanking the captain and crew of the *Wasp* for timely assistance.

Later in the war both the *Wasp* and the *Eagle* were sunk by enemy action. The *Wasp* went down after being torpedoed by the Japanese submarine I-19 in the Pacific, and the *Eagle,* while on her ninth aircraft-ferry trip to Malta, was struck by four torpedoes fired by U-73 sixty-five miles south of Majorca. She sank in eight minutes.

Back in Scapa Flow aboard the *Washington,* Fairbanks was ordered off on another special mission. This time he was to sail aboard the powerful cruiser USS *Wichita* (CA-45), which, along with other task-force warships, would provide escort for the next large convoy going to Archangel, in Russia. The convoy was PQ-17, which would suffer the most devastating losses of the war.

With temporary additional duty orders in hand, Fairbanks reported to the *Wichita* in June 1942. On the last day of the month, the cruiser and her force weighed anchor and sailed to join PQ-17 off Iceland. The doomed convoy consisted of thirty-three merchant ships and twenty-one close-escort vessels and, at a distance, additional cover forces consisting of the battleships HMS *Duke of York,* the American battleship *Washington,* the carrier HMS *Victorious,* and the cruisers *Cumberland, Nigeria,* and *Manchester,* plus several American and British destroyers. The reason for the large covering force was the Admiralty's concern that a powerful German naval group—the battleship *Tirpitz,* pocket battleship *Scheer,* and heavy cruiser *Hipper*—had recently shifted their position to Alten Fjord near North Cape, which would put them within striking distance of the convoy.

PQ-17 left Iceland on 2 July, and by that afternoon the Luftwaffe and U-boats had begun their attack. The cover force was ordered to stay in waters between Iceland and Spitsbergen. Its responsibilities included protecting a westbound convoy and acting as a deterrent to German surface combatants should they sortie from the Norwegian Fjord. Fairbanks's report describes the mounting German attack on PQ-17:

> 1655: The USS *Tuscaloosa* two blocks a signal saying "S to port." Then a sudden emergency blast on her foghorn, she hauls off at flank speed to starboard. She later flashes: "3 torpedoes fired at us on port side." We dispute among ourselves whether or not it was all a false alarm. Some swear they saw a strange wake just before the signal came. Others say it was a school of fish, and even more say there was nothing there at all. In any case the whole force picked up its skirts and ran. . . .
>
> Fifteen minutes later: No results. "Resume Formation."
>
> At 1712 we hear again from the convoy. "Air bombers coming in to attack!" Then comes a running account of the battle. The first report is that two torpedoes are headed for the convoy. Then another one. We think we can hear the roar of engines and the firing of guns over the radio. Reports of torpedoes and bombers are coming through intermittently but sometimes with such a rush that we lose all count. We know of at least fifteen but have not heard yet of any hits. There is a lull and now suddenly "Jerry" is returning. We all wish we could go back in and help out as we are so close, but the overcast sky and our families' prayers have so far, we think, kept us hidden. No use telling the enemy what they *may* not know. Our job is to wait on the sidelines for enemy surface warships.

The Germans continued to hammer the convoy throughout 3 and 4 July, British and American ships signaling various messages regarding the

Americans' national anniversary. Fairbanks's report continues:

> At 0805, Admiral Hamilton sends a general signal to all U.S. ships in
> the squadron: "On the occasion of your great anniversary it seems
> most uncivil to make you keep station at all but even today freedom
> of the seas can be read two ways. It is a privilege for us all to have
> you with us and I wish you all the best of hunting."
>
> Captain Hill replied, "It is a great privilege to be here with you
> today in furtherance of the ideals which July Fourth has always rep-
> resented to us and we are particularly happy to be a portion of your
> command. Celebration of this holiday always requires large fireworks
> displays. I trust you will not disappoint us."
>
> A short while later the captain of the *Norfolk* also sent us felici-
> tations: "Many happy returns of the day. The United States is the only
> country with a known birthday."
>
> To this our Captain answered, "Thank you. I think it is only fit-
> ting that you should celebrate Mother's Day!"

As the *Wichita*, along with other ships of the cruiser force, engaged
the enemy, Nazi planes fell from the skies, and destroyers darted in
and out of the convoy formation, attacking U-boat contacts. Some
were on fire, but they pressed their attacks, smoke billowing high over
the battle area as merchant ships exploded, the victims of enemy
bombers and U-boats.

In the midst of the slaughter, during which the cruiser force felt help-
less and wanted to assist, a shocking message was received, quoted in
Fairbanks's official report: "1911: From Admiralty to CS-1: Cruiser
Force must withdraw to westward at high speed!" Admiral of the Fleet
Sir A. Dudley Pound, noting that the convoy was about to come opposite the Alten Fjord and suspecting that the *Tirpitz* would sortie out and
attack the Allied ships, was ordering the support force to withdraw and
the merchant ships to proceed independently to Russian ports.

Abandoning the convoy made the men "feel ashamed and resent-
ful," Fairbanks wrote, adding that the next day Admiral Hamilton
sent the following message: "I know you will be feeling as distressed
as I am at having to leave that fine collection of ships to find their own
way to harbor. The enemy under cover of his shore based aircraft, has

succeeded in concentrating a vastly superior force in this area. We are therefore ordered to withdraw. We are all sorry that the good work of the close escort could not be completed. I hope we shall all have a chance of settling this score with them soon."

PQ-17 lost twenty-five of thirty-six ships. The *Tirpitz* did sortie out on the fifth, but she returned to the fjord when German reconnaissance planes were unable to locate the *Victorious*. Churchill was later to refer to the PQ-17 tragedy as one of the saddest of the war.

Arriving back on board the *Washington,* Fairbanks, by now a full lieutenant, had a new set of orders awaiting him. He had written to his friend Adm. Lord Louis "Dickie" Mountbatten requesting, in veiled terms, that he be transferred to Mountbatten's Combined Operations Command in London. Now he was to report to U.S. Naval Headquarters in London and join other U.S. officers on the staff. When they gave him a farewell celebration, Lieutenant Fairbanks finally felt like a real U.S. Navy officer.

The mission of Mountbatten's staff was to develop all aspects of amphibious war plans while at the same time executing raids on specific Nazi-held territories in Europe; the Americans were present to learn how the operations were carried out. Military volunteers who executed the daring raids were called commandos.

Fairbanks was still "under instruction," and thus was not made to take commando training. However, he did learn the trade during the summer of 1942, becoming familiar with the equipment and tactics used by special units such as Britain's Long-Range Desert Group and the special boat and air units. He proved himself particularly innovative in the art of deception, possibly due to his natural flair for the dramatic.

He also, of course, took advantage of another opportunity to catch up with old London pals, but this relatively pleasant time was again spoiled by the fact that he was a celebrity. After explaining to Fairbanks that his presence brought to the command more visibility than security advised, Mountbatten presented his idea: Lieutenant Fairbanks could introduce to the U.S. Navy and Army the British special-operations deceptive techniques and new equipment. But first, obviously, he would have to learn all about amphibious raiding. He should learn to command a flotilla of small landing craft.

Mountbatten was quite excited by the proposal and assumed that his friend would be, too. Hiding his fear and dread, Fairbanks tried to get out of it by reminding Mountbatten that he was an American with no authority over the British men, but the admiral mistook this for modesty and told him not to worry, he was sure it would all work out. Thus a very nervous Douglas Fairbanks, Jr., was trained to be a naval commando and flotilla commander in the English Channel. While dodging E-boats (German motor torpedo boats) and Luftwaffe planes, the Combined Operations flotillas made selected hits, designed primarily to unnerve the Germans, on the enemy-held French shores.

It was decided that the best way for Fairbanks to learn would be good old on-the-job training, and he made his first sortie as an observer. His Higgins boat (a high-speed landing craft) was one of several in a flotilla of about thirty boats that also included British LCF(L)s (landing craft, flak, large) and LCS(M)s (landing craft, support, medium). They picked up seven hundred or so Royal Marine commandos at the Isle of Wight and made their way into the nighttime channel accompanied by two destroyer escorts, Fairbanks having no idea of the nature of their mission. By now he had mostly learned to conceal his terror, which sharpened into total alertness at dawn, when alarms signaled the presence of E-boats in the area. Falling silent, the commandos heard above the commotion of the sea a radio message that the destroyers had chased the enemy away. Later they were alerted again, this time about some Luftwaffe planes that were searching for them. Thankfully, two RAF fighters scared these off. Finally they got back to the safe shores of England, where Fairbanks learned that the mission had simply been part of their training; it would be repeated several times before they made an actual raid.

The real raid came weeks later, by which time Fairbanks felt comfortable in command of a small flotilla that was part of a larger group. One early morning, with his mentor in charge of the lead flotilla, Fairbanks awaited the order to head out. They were facing heavy gales, and it took them several tries to make it out into the channel. Finally, soaked, they arrived at an island unknown to Fairbanks, waking up the guards. Undaunted, the commandos shot at them anyway, as the enemy returned fire, and headed back to sea. Picking up an RAF survivor at sea in a raft, they made it safely back to England.

In October 1942 Fairbanks was ordered back to the States to report to Adm. H. Kent Hewitt, Commander Amphibious Force, U.S. Atlantic Fleet Headquarters, in Norfolk, Virginia. He was to develop a proposal for deception operations similar to those being used by the British. After convincing the appropriate people that the idea should at least be tried, Admiral Hewitt authorized Fairbanks to recruit a number of volunteers who had been thoroughly trained in electronics, sonics, and the visual sciences. He established his unit near Virginia Beach at an island waterway called Camp Bradford. Some of his suggestions met with predictable resistance, but many were approved, including night goggles for infrared light and fluorescent smoke for the operations. An amphibious diversionary training manual was also written.

By May 1943 Hewitt's command had been transferred to Algiers after the Allied landings in North Africa, in preparation for the invasion of Sicily. Hewitt was now Commander U.S. Naval Forces, North West African Waters. Fairbanks's group—seventy young officers and four hundred sailors—was given the name Beach Jumpers. Based at Bizerte and Ferryville in Tunisia, the unit had at its disposal all types of seagoing equipment, PT boats, LSTs, and air-sea rescue craft (ASRCs), plus electronic gear, loudspeakers, smoke-laying devices, recordings of sounds such as British and American voices giving orders, and a wide assortment of weapons. Fairbanks also had a new title: special operations planning officer.

Operation Husky, the invasion of Sicily, finally got under way during the early-morning hours of 10 July 1943. Fairbanks was on board the USS *Monrovia* (APA-31), Admiral Hewitt's flagship. He kept in touch by radio with his Beach Jumper units, designated Task Group 80.4, and kept track of their deception operations, which had been scaled disappointingly down to mere nuisance status.

The Beach Jumpers followed frogmen who swam in first, signaling the way. Then the Jumpers landed and marked each beach with a colored panel. The idea was to assist the landing-craft commanders in discharging troops on their assigned beaches while under fire. At one point the staff operations officer noticed that one of the marked spots remained deserted. Annoyed, because the other beaches were getting crowded, he ordered Fairbanks to go in and see what was going on. With the British staff liaison officer, Fairbanks took a standby landing

When the Beach Jumpers landed on the Pontine island of Ventotene in September 1943, Fairbanks chased a German up the beach and then witnessed the surrender of the Fascisti as other Allied forces were landing. After a day's standoff, the remaining Germans surrendered. Fairbanks (standing, right) and company captured a Nazi flag from a German gunboat. (Douglas Fairbanks, Jr., collection)

craft in, unbothered by enemy fire. Once ashore, they searched up and down for a Beach Jumper, finally spying one. Indignant, they marched over to chew him out, shells exploding all around them. As they reached him, the young officer shouted above the din that they had just walked over a minefield. Needless to say, Fairbanks and the other officer had little to add.

Within a few weeks Sicily fell to Allied forces, and planning began for the invasion of Italy—Operation Avalanche. On 8 September 1943 an American invasion force consisting of four divisions of the Fifth Army landed on the beaches of Salerno, a city just south of Naples. The British Eighth Army had already crossed the Messina Strait and was fighting its way north to join up with the Fifth. Once they had joined up, the Fifth would move north to capture Naples. Task Force 80.4, Fairbanks's Beach Jumpers, strengthened by the addition of a destroyer, the USS *Knight* (DD-633), and two Dutch sloops, the *Soemba* (N1) and *Flores* (HX-I), moved along the western coast north of Naples to neutralize the small islands of the Pontine group and to preoccupy with deception operations a reserve German division at Gaeta. The Germans stood ready to move south, should the need arise, to provide reinforcements at Naples.

The ragtag fleet broadcast over loudspeakers the announcement that Allied ships were offshore ready to invade the Pontine island of Ventotene. This was followed up with the prerecorded sounds of air-craft engines, shouting, and other battle-preparation noises. Within fifteen minutes the island forces signaled their surrender.

As the captain was deciding who should go in first, Fairbanks spoke up to make a suggestion, and the captain immediately took it that he was volunteering. Thus Fairbanks, with three Beach Jumpers, manned a whaleboat and landed ashore. He wound up chasing a German up the beach and managed to avoid being shot. Eventually he found himself back at the shoreline, where the Fascisti were surrendering and other Allied support forces were landing. Though most of the Italian soldiers surrendered, there remained about four hundred German troops on the northern end of the island who intended to fight it out with the invaders. After a day's standoff, however, the Germans surrendered.

Using hit-and-run tactics, the small fleet next successfully harassed the Germans in and around the Gaeta area. Thanks to the Beach

Jumper tactics, the Germans defending Gaeta were now forced to worry about countering an attack from the sea while they waited for orders to join the fight at Naples. Fairbanks was awarded the Silver Star for his role in the capture of Ventotene.

On 1 October 1943 the Fifth Army occupied Naples, Lieutenant Fairbanks (to become lieutenant commander on 7 October 1943) and the Beach Jumpers having contributed their usual deception-and-diversion efforts. As the months passed, fierce German resistance and continuous rain and snow made roads impassable. It took eight months for the Fifth and Eighth armies to fight their way from Naples to Rome, a distance of just over one hundred miles. While Allied forces struggled up the Italian boot, Fairbanks and his Beach Jumpers were busy providing support for the assault on the island of Elba and the Anvil operation against southern France.

Fairbanks led his squadron of PT boats to the northern side of Elba, hoping to draw some of the island defenders away from the southern beaches where the French were to land. The PTs maneuvered in as close as they could, then the rubber boats paddled in the rest of the way. The Beach Jumpers signaled an all's-well and began climbing the hill. So alerted, the PTs let loose a barrage of rockets and machine-gun fire, laying smoke and blaring forth the prerecorded sounds of troops preparing to come ashore. Because of their heavy smoke cover, the enemy fire all this attracted missed its mark, and they were able to continue their deception until they heard by radio that the French main force had landed on the southern beaches.

For his part in this operation, Fairbanks was awarded the French Croix de Guerre with Palm (equivalent to the U.S. Distinguished Service Medal), signifying that the medal had been earned in combat.

Operation Anvil, later renamed Dragoon for security reasons, was planned to be a diversionary assault on the southern coast of France to coincide with the Normandy invasion. Task Group 80.4 conducted its own diversionary missions on 14–17 August 1944. Commanded by Capt. H. C. Johnson, the force consisted of the USS *Endicott* (DD-495), commanded by Comdr. John Bulkeley (the Medal of Honor PT commander who took General MacArthur and his family out of the Philippines as Japanese forces closed in), HMS *Scarab,* eighteen PTs, thirteen ASRCs, and several smaller support craft. The group was to create the impression of a large invasion in the Marseille-Toulon area, thus diverting attention from the actual assault area in the vicinity of Cannes. Fairbanks's subcommand, Task Group 80.4.1, consisted of two Royal Navy gunboats, a squadron of U.S. PT boats, a few ASRCs, and several amphibious raiding boats.

During the early-morning hours of 17 August, Fairbanks was in the command PT boat as the group began firing its arsenal at Baie de la Ciotat, close by the large Toulon naval base. Their salvos were answered immediately with a heavy enemy barrage, leading Fairbanks and his men to believe that their ruse was working: the enemy forces evidently thought they were warding off the main Allied invasion. Concerned about not having experienced guidance close at hand, Fairbanks transferred his command to HMS *Aphis* at the first opportunity. This way, he reasoned, not only could he better coordinate his boats, but he would benefit from the presence of the *Aphis*'s seasoned captain. At 0540 one of the ASRCs radioed that it had an engine breakdown and was under attack by two large ships. Fairbanks promptly ordered a PT boat to the rescue and ordered his ship and the HMS *Scarab* to engage the enemy. There were not supposed to be any big enemy ships in the area, according to the obviously faulty intelligence they had received.

Upon arriving at the scene they sighted the ASRC, which was partially on fire but still firing its guns at the warships. Fairbanks radioed the *Endicott* for help, and at 0610 he began firing on the enemy. A U.S. naval air scout had identified the two ships as a formerly Italian (now German) corvette, the *U-Jäger 60-81,* and a large converted armed yacht, the *U-Jäger 60-73* (ex-Egyptian). The firing between the ships was intense, and Fairbanks and company were out of their league.

The radars on the *Aphis* and *Scarab* had been destroyed. The little squadron laid a cloud of thick smoke all around them, inside of which they circled continually, hiding from the enemy. Fairbanks and the captain of the *Aphis* realized that further resistance was futile, and the best they could hope for was to avoid enemy fire while awaiting help. In desperation, Fairbanks again radioed the *Endicott*. Where was she? For that matter, where were they?

Admiring the composure of the captain, Fairbanks tried to hide his own terror and kept inventing reasons to lean down and pick

In the August 1944 invasion of southern France, Fairbanks led a squadron of PT boats to the northern side of Elba, hoping to draw some of the enemy away from the beaches where the French were to land. (Douglas Fairbanks, Jr., collection)

something up off the deck, hoping to avoid the next blast of hot metal. The men, he noted, were magnificently cool in the heat of battle, joking as they went about getting their jobs done. Fairbanks was later told that he too had joked and appeared calm, but the only thing he remembered feeling was hysteria.

When the gunnery officer shouted that his main battery was cool enough to fire again, Fairbanks and the captain decided that they might as well try to find their way out of the cloud and do some shooting while awaiting rescue. By some miracle they came into the clear, capping the "T" to the enemy's advancing line. They fired once and hit the *U-Jäger 60-81* dead-on. All parties seemed shocked into a momentary lull as the ship began to sink. Just then the *Endicott*—finally—came steaming into the foray with all guns blazing. In short order both enemy ships were on fire and sinking. The ships of the task group picked up forty German survivors.

For his exceptional performance of duty in the French invasion operation, in July 1945 Fairbanks was made a Knight of the French Legion of Honor (military division). For his diversionary operations carried out with British forces, he received the Royal Navy's Distinguished Service Cross.

Toward the end of August 1944, Fairbanks was ordered back to the States and assigned to the Strategic Plans Division, which worked closely with the Psychological Warfare Division. While on this new assignment, he was honored by the U.S. Navy with the Legion of Merit.

Fairbanks's final wartime act was to hatch an idea that he hoped would put an end to Japanese hostilities. Presented in a top-secret memo in January 1945, the plan was to convince the dowager empress, rumored to be sympathetic to the notion, that further resistance was pointless. She could be reached through a network of contacts and old friendships. She would convince the emperor, who would surrender. By then a final coup d'état would be in place.

The idea was considered but ultimately rejected as too risky and perhaps slightly wacky; the military, of course, had other top-secret plans. By now promoted to commander, Fairbanks was on the verge of being ordered to join Lord Mountbatten at Ceylon, to assist in various deception operations against Japan. These plans also were overridden, though, when the atomic bombs were dropped on Japan in early August 1945, ending the war.

Fairbanks extended his service, unsure of whether he would find work in Hollywood. He seriously considered staying in the Navy and volunteered for another six months while he thought about it. During this time he befriended President Harry S. Truman, who suggested that he become a foreign diplomat. Fairbanks was intrigued by the idea, but nothing came of it, perhaps because such posts were low-paying and thus were typically awarded to candidates far more wealthy than he.

Just as his six months were about to run out, RKO Studios called and asked if he would be interested in the lead role in a new movie, *Sinbad the Sailor* (1947). His acceptance would once again secure his place in Hollywood, but before long he relocated to London and has been back and forth ever since. His films have included *That Lady in Ermine* (1948), *State Secret* (1950), *Chase a Crooked Shadow* (1958), and *Ghost Story* (1981).

Assistant Secretary of the Navy for Air Artemus L. Gates presented Lieutenant Commander Fairbanks with the Legion of Merit on 29 December 1944. Mary Lee Hartford Fairbanks accompanied her husband. (U.S. Navy photo)

Fairbanks went on inactive reserve on 5 February 1946. He was promoted to captain on 1 October 1954 and retired at that rank on 1 July 1969. Mary Lee passed away in 1988; they had three children. Douglas Fairbanks, Jr., maintains an active schedule and continues to travel.

# Henry Fonda

Henry J. Fonda approached everything he did with a seriousness of purpose. After Pearl Harbor he registered for the draft right away, and on 24 August 1942 he walked into Naval Headquarters in Los Angeles to enlist. His hope was to serve as a gunner's mate, since this was a shooting war and Fonda, as always, intended to give it his all and get the job done right. He was already an established star, having made his screen debut in 1935 in *The Farmer Takes a Wife,* and having played the lead, in 1940, in what many still consider his masterpiece, *The Grapes of Wrath* (for which he was nominated for an Academy Award).

In 1942, at age thirty-seven, Fonda was exempt from the draft. He was not exempt from the objections of his wife, but Frances Seymour finally relented and sent him off with her blessing. She would wait with their children in their Pennsylvania Dutch–style house (complete with walk-in fireplace, it sat on nine acres of gentleman's farmland amid flagstone walkways, flowers, vines, haystacks, chickens, rabbits, and a Victory Garden grown under the guidance of *Organic Gardening and Farming* magazine). Fonda felt that he must do his duty as an able-bodied American man. What would his fans say, he asked Fran, if they saw his face up there on the screen instead of out there with the rest of his compatriots? His place was with them, for now.

Born in 1905 in Nebraska to a printer father and a mother who woke him up in the middle of the night at age five so he would not miss Halley's Comet, Henry Fonda was brought up a Christian Scientist and taught to be honest, hardworking, and forthright.

He went through boot camp, with its physical training, questionnaires, and tests, at San Diego. Previously always skinny—he and buddy Jim Stewart had tried muscle-building exercises at MGM to get some meat onto their scrawny arms—on the boot-camp diet Fonda gained weight for the first time in his life. He earned his white cap after eight weeks' training. His plan of becoming a gunner's mate was fouled, though, by a chief petty officer who gave him what-for about wanting so badly to go out and get himself all shot up. After seeing the results of Fonda's tests and recognizing the young fool's high intelligence, the chief cut orders for him to attend sixteen weeks of quartermaster training. This meant that Fonda would be a navigator's assistant—not good news. Math had never been his forte, and during his training he would not only have to improve his math skills, he would also have to master trigonometry and navigation equipment. His primary duty as quartermaster would be communications—signaling with blinkers and flags. He stayed up nights and studied as he had never done before, after which newly rated Quartermaster Third Class Fonda was on his way to his first ship, the USS *Satterlee* (DD-626), a *Benson/Gleaves*-class destroyer.

The *Satterlee* was the second U.S. destroyer to be so named. The original was a World War I four-piper, part of the destroyers-for-bases deal reached between Britain and the United States. The British were desperate for more "small boys" after their staggering losses early in World War II, and the U.S. destroyers were turned over for Royal Navy service in September 1940. The original *Satterlee*, renamed HMS

Quartermaster Third Class Henry Fonda's first ship was the *Benson/Gleaves*-class destroyer *Satterlee* (DD-626). Before reporting aboard he put in some late nights trying to master the Navy's complicated signaling techniques, blinkers, and flags. (U.S. Navy photo)

*Belmont,* was torpedoed and sunk by the German U-boat U-82 on 31 January 1942 in the mid-Atlantic.

Fonda reported to the second *Satterlee* in May 1943, as she stood almost completed in the builder's ways at the Seattle-Tacoma Shipbuilding Corporation. The ship's executive officer, Lt. Charles Cassell, reported around the same time, and when he boarded the ship, Fonda was one of those already aboard. Cassell later told Capt. Alexander G. Monroe, USNR, in an interview for *Naval History* magazine, that Fonda "had already, on his own, set up shop in one of the ship's offices and was hard at work checking inventory against allowance . . . and beginning the endless task of making corrections. He also checked regularly on shipyard work in the bridge area and took custody of the navigation equipment when it arrived. I should have done that work, but my XO duties kept me busy. As soon as possible we selected a QM striker, but Fonda *was* the Navigation Department." This was typical behavior for the focused, steady Fonda. At times aloof, even unapproachable, Fonda brought to each task the same powers of concentration. (But he also knew how to have a right good time when the occasion called for it; after the war he and Jimmy Stewart partied for almost a year.)

The *Satterlee*'s sea trials began in May 1943 and ended with commissioning on 1 July. As the ship left port and headed for San Diego, it was discovered that one crewman was missing, a signalman third class. Fonda accepted those responsibilities as well, meaning that he had to stand double watches and work twice as long and hard as the others. But when the *Satterlee* arrived in San Diego, Fonda was able to celebrate by hitching a ride to Hollywood and the farm.

He returned a week later to a new set of orders. He was to report to Naval Headquarters, 90 Church Street, New York City, for officer's training. Meanwhile, the *Satterlee* was to get under way the following day bound for Norfolk, Virginia. Because of Fonda's departure, there would be no quartermaster third and no signalman third. Fonda promptly volunteered to stay with the ship during the transit. If he was going to be an officer, he needed all the Navy experience he could get.

The *Satterlee* departed as planned, in company with three destroyers, escorting the British aircraft carrier *Victorious*. The group ran south to the Panama Canal, transited the canal, and sailed north to the naval base at Norfolk. During this transit Fonda had a hellish time with the signalman's part of his duties. Standing on a small perforated platform off the bridge behind the surface lookout, he had to read the signals from the *Victorious* and relay them to the striker, below him. A chain running across the front of the platform kept them from falling overboard. All this was tricky enough business under normal conditions, but when they hit stormy weather on their way to the Panama Canal, the lookout got seasick. Worse, the winds blew it straight into Fonda's face and telescope, making it all the more difficult—and unpleasant—for him to decipher the flagship's messages.

Shortly after their arrival in Norfolk, a relieved Fonda got shore leave along with the signalman first, whom he had befriended, and the two of them went out and got pie-eyed. The party went on until daybreak. Later that morning Fonda reeled onto the northbound train with his seabag and his orders to report to Naval Headquarters, New York. The ship's logbook notes recorded his departure: "Fonda, H.J. 562-62-35, QM3/c, USN transferred to local receiving station for further transfer to Commandant 3rd Naval District for assignment by Bureau of Naval Personnel."

Fonda reported to his new command in New York and was discharged as an enlisted man. Moments later he was sworn in again, as a lieutenant (jg). He was ordered to Washington to make training films at Naval Air Station Anacostia. But a bitterly disappointed Fonda managed to convince his new boss at Anacostia that he could best serve in air combat intelligence (ACI). The officer, who would have preferred to be anywhere but behind a desk himself, evidently was an understanding man and ordered Fonda to Naval Training School (Air Combat Intelligence), Naval Air Station Quonset Point, Rhode Island.

Fonda found his new training much to his liking. His schoolmates were mayors, district attorneys, young judges—bright people with interesting backgrounds. In their company he learned coding, photo interpretation, and other requisite skills, finishing the course in the upper quarter of his class. Finally granted his wish to join the fighting Navy, the newly designated ACI officer was ordered to the seaplane tender USS *Curtiss* (AV-4) to serve as assistant air operations officer under Vice Adm. John Howard Hoover, Commander Forward Area Central Pacific.

Before Fonda's departure, a fellow ACI officer spoke to the green men about what to expect in the Pacific. Among other admonishments, he advised them confidentially to bring along as much liquor as they could carry. It would come in handier than anything else when they needed to bargain for boats, vehicles, or whatever their admirals told them to get.

After a week's leave with his family, Fonda traveled north to San Francisco and boarded a Dutch freighter that took him and several other ACI officers to Pearl Harbor. In a parachute bag he carried fourteen bottles of top-grade bourbon, carefully wrapped.

A two-week cram course in antisubmarine warfare at Kaneohe, Hawaii, was followed by temporary assignment to the staff of Vice Adm. Chester W. Nimitz, the U.S. naval commander in the Pacific. As an additional duty, Fonda was made an officer-courier and soon found himself en route to the Kwajalein atoll delivering dispatches to Admiral Nimitz (whose flagship was the carrier *Essex* [CV-9]). He made the mistake of leaving his parachute bag in a Quonset hut while taking a launch out to the *Essex*. Upon his return, he discovered that the bag had undergone a series of mishaps culminating in its being tossed out

Vice Adm. George D. Murray, USN, Commander Marianas, congratulates Lt. Henry J. Fonda, USNR, after presenting him with the Bronze Star with citation in recognition of his service as an assistant operations officer and air combat intelligence officer on the staff of Commander Forward Area, Central Pacific, and Commander Marianas. (U.S. Navy photo)

of a departing plane onto the runway. At least four bottles had been smashed. Dripping with bourbon, Fonda reported to his new home, where the executive officer ordered him to hand over all of his clothes for early, emergency-only laundering, normally done once and only once a week.

The *Curtiss* provided maintenance and general support for the PBM seaplanes of Patrol Bomber Squadron (VPB) 216. The PMB "Mariners" collected intelligence that was processed by Fonda and his small group of photo interpreters and analysts. Information gathered from numerous frames of aerial film and postmission debriefings were dispatched to higher command for use in tactical planning, and Fonda routinely briefed and debriefed squadron crews.

The *Curtiss*'s wartime patrols "lasted most of the daylight hours," remembers VPB-216 commanding officer Capt. Harry E. Cook, "and most landings were made in the late afternoon." Cook's account (from the *Naval History* interview with Captain Monroe) continues:

Because we had to refuel from tenders, it was well after dark before we secured to a mooring buoy for the night. The real problem was that shortly after dark the Japanese began their nightly bombing attacks. . . . [This] went on until Commander Forward Area Central Pacific arrived, embarked in USS *Curtiss*. . . . [Then] things started changing fast, and soon there was an antisubmarine net around the whole anchorage, and we no longer were able to have movies on the weather decks because darken ship and other regulations were more tightly enforced.

Fonda's conscientiousness made a lasting impression on Cook, in particular once in late 1944, when one of his patrolling aircraft reported the sighting of a Japanese submarine. Fonda, who was staff watch officer at the time, received the report and knew he had to move immediately to alert naval forces in the area. "Action on his part was necessary," Cook says, "and he left to issue the warning to alert all units present. He was in such a hurry that he stumbled as he started down a ladder . . . with the result that he suffered a bad laceration . . . . [He] continued full tilt until he had completed his duty and only then did he get to sick bay for treatment."

Later that day Fonda served as master of ceremonies for a shipboard entertainment program featuring renowned banjoist and Naval Reserve officer Eddie Peabody. As he took the makeshift stage, Fonda received a standing ovation—his shipmates' demonstration of their approval of Lieutenant Fonda.

Shortly after Fonda reported aboard the *Curtiss,* the ship moved on to Eniwetok. The general-quarters alarm went off regularly, and all hands grabbed life preservers and helmets and rushed to the deck. Fonda was assigned to battle stations only a few times during the war.

The *Curtiss* moved with the fleet as it mounted campaigns against Guam, Saipan, and Iwo Jima. With Americans now within striking distance of their home islands, the Japanese initiated kamikaze operations, which took a heavy toll on U.S. combatants and their crews. When the ship was off Saipan in December 1944, Tokyo Rose broadcast information about the seaplane tender, including the fact that actor Henry Fonda was on board. She promised that Japanese forces would soon sink the ship, and within a few days the *Curtiss* was indeed attacked, narrowly missing being hit by kamikazes.

Fonda first saw one of these suicide planes when the *Curtiss*'s guns shot it down and it crashed into the water some twenty-five yards from the ship. Fonda believed that his duty was to collect whatever intelligence he could from the downed aircraft, and the next day, after things had quieted down, he and two sailors climbed into shallow-water diving gear. They dove down to the plane, about thirty feet below the surface, finding the bodies of the pilot and bombardier still strapped into their overturned aircraft. Fonda and his mates recovered maps, flight plans, and other valuable documentation.

ACI officer Fonda, now a full lieutenant, studied it all and concluded that the kamikazes were being launched from tiny Pagan Island in the middle of the Marianas chain. On his recommendation, Admiral Hoover ordered air strikes against the island, and for the next few weeks the Japanese attacks stopped.

In addition to the kamikaze attacks, the fleet was faced with increasing Japanese submarine activity, and Fonda was able put to good use the ASW training he had received at Kaneohe. Since naval intelligence had broken the Japanese code, forces afloat knew the date of departure, speed, and course of enemy subs operating in their area. Using

The *Curtiss* was hit by a Japanese kamikaze but survived, after fifteen hours of firefighting. (U.S. Navy photo)

this information, Fonda would plot a sub's course on a sheet of Plexiglas and devise a search pattern. On one occasion, naval forces were deployed to an area in which Fonda had estimated a sub's position. An attack was made, and the Japanese sub was destroyed.

In late June 1945 the *Curtiss* put into Guam, and Fonda and his cabin mate went ashore on liberty. While they were enjoying their brief respite, the *Curtiss* headed back to sea, and on 22 June the ship was hit by a Frank kamikaze off Okinawa on the starboard forward at the third-deck level. This was the last attack of the Floating Chrysanthemum/Kikusui 10 kamikaze operation and the end of the Divine Wind that had been planned to save Japan. Aboard the *Curtiss*, it took fifteen hours to bring the fires under control, by which time the forward magazine had been flooded and only half the ship was livable. The seaplane tender lost forty-one men, with twenty-eight wounded. When the *Curtiss* staggered back to port at Guam, Fonda and his cabin mate went aboard and found their quarters destroyed.

Admiral Hoover shifted his flag to Guam, and it was there that Fonda learned of V-E Day. The event brought home a grim reality to the Hoover command: even though it would mean more men and ships available for Pacific duty, taking Japan would still be a bitter struggle. There would be massive casualties.

At the beginning of August, Fonda and his boss, the air operations officer on Hoover's staff, flew to Tinian and met the crew of the *Enola Gay*. They were among the few intelligence officers who had access to what was being planned. Fonda did not know precisely what the B-29's effect would be, but he did recognize the significance of its presence. Upon their return to Guam the officers kept the secret, which was revealed to the world when, on 6 August 1945, the atomic bomb was dropped on Hiroshima.

A week later Fonda pulled the 2300–0700 communications-desk watch, which meant he had to sort through the dispatches that were brought at regular intervals from the communications Quonset hut. About midwatch, he came across a message for him that sent him into a fury. He was ordered to report to Washington, on a Priority Two basis, to participate in the *Naval Radio Hour* program. Fonda had successfully avoided such duty thus far, but a Priority Two meant he was to leave posthaste. While fuming over these orders, he heard a commotion in the communications hut. Finally a guard came in carrying the latest batch of dispatches, wearing the biggest smile Lieutenant Fonda had ever seen: Japan had given up, he announced. At first Fonda did not believe him, but then, left alone again and smoking a cigarette, he knew it was really over.

With his Priority Two in hand and not minding at all now, Fonda was on his way the day after the dispatch had arrived. Hung over but still continuing the celebrations that had begun the previous day, he attended a brief ceremony before boarding a plane that would take him to the States. Vice Adm. G. D. Murray, USN, Commander Marianas, in the name of the President of the United States awarded Lieutenant Fonda the Bronze Star with the following citation:

> For distinguishing himself by meritorious service in connection with operations against the enemy as an Assistant Operations Officer and Air Combat Intelligence Officer on the Staff of Commander Forward Area Central Pacific and Commander Marianas from 12 May 1944 to 12 August 1945. He contributed materially to the planning and execution of air operations which effectively supported the Marianas,

Western Carolines, and Iwo Jima Campaigns, neutralized enemy installations on nearby enemy-held islands and atolls, and which subsequently developed into search missions in Empire waters and strikes on the Japanese mainland. His keen intelligence, untiring energy and conscientious application to duty were in a large measure responsible for his successful contribution to the Central Pacific campaign.

Henry Fonda had been proved right: he had had a very important contribution to make to the war effort. After a brief tour in Navy Public Affairs in Washington, he left active duty, remaining in the Naval Reserve until November 1953.

In Hollywood, after celebrating extensively along with the rest of the country, Fonda got back to work. The first film in which he appeared was the Western *My Darling Clementine*, touted by the *New York Times* as one of the ten best pictures of 1946. Among the numerous movies he made subsequently was *Mister Roberts*, Thomas Heggen's timeless war story set in the Pacific. Fonda was able to bring firsthand experience to his outstanding performance as the leading character on both the stage (1948) and screen (1955; the picture was saluted by the Academy as one of the year's best). The officer's cap he wore during these performances was the same one he had worn during the war in the Pacific.

Fonda's association with the Navy was to last for many more years, if sporadically. On 4 July 1957 he and fourth wife Afdera were living in a villa on the Riviera, near Villefranche. A U.S. cruiser was anchored in the harbor, and Fonda decided to treat the boys to an Independence Day celebration. He had stashed away several hundred dollars' worth of fireworks. As the daylight faded, he blasted a rocket off the terrace, over the water in the direction of the ship. The cruiser responded immediately in kind, alternating with Fonda and continuing to send up colorful displays long after his supply had run out.

During the Vietnam War, at age sixty-two, Fonda served again. Although the actor did not approve of U.S. involvement in the conflict, the United Service Organizations executive who called him was able to convince him that he owed it to the American servicemen to help boost their morale however he could; the war was not their fault. Fonda participated in the Handshake Tours of April 1967, flying all over South Vietnam and out to the carriers *Ticonderoga* (CV-14), *Kitty Hawk* (CVA-63), and *Bennington* (CV-20). He had taken the precaution of bringing along a Polaroid camera and plenty of film, fearful that he would not be able to think of anything to say. Neither standup comedy nor light chatting had ever been his bent. But the camera was a hit, and everyone seemed to want to be photographed with Henry Fonda.

He disapproved as well of his daughter Jane's later actions in Vietnam but understood that her motivation was pure; she simply failed to grasp the big picture. In perhaps an encapsulated version of their country's heartbreaking division over the ill-fated U.S. involvement in Vietnam, father and daughter disagreed, fought, and later came to terms with what became history.

Henry Fonda's many memorable plays and movies include *The Caine Mutiny Court Martial* (Broadway, 1955), *War and Peace* (1956), *Advise and Consent* (1962), *In Harm's Way* (1965), and *On Golden Pond* (1981). He won the 1981 Academy Award for best actor for his performance in the latter (and had won an honorary Academy Award the previous year for his accomplishments in his field); and that same year the Los Angeles Drama Critics Circle honored him with a lifetime achievement award. He died in 1982.

Fonda was married five times and "damned ashamed of it," he told biographer Howard Teichmann, but at least he got it right the last time with Shirlee Mae Adams, with whom he lived for seventeen years. The marriages produced three children, two of whom caught the acting bug.

# John Howard

During the August 1944 invasion of southern France, while the task group commanded by movie star Lt. Comdr. Douglas Fairbanks, Jr., was firing at the enemy at Baie de la Ciotat in Operation Dragoon, another actor was nearby in an equally hazardous operation. Lt. (jg) John Richard Cox, Jr., known on-screen as John Howard, was executive officer on board the USS YMS-24. His minesweeper was clearing offshore waters for the safe passage of incoming Allied troops and supplies.

Having participated in the landings on the coast, YMS-24, in company with YMS-63 and YMS-200, was engaged in a magnetic and acoustic sweep some sixty miles eastward in the Gulf of Frejus. The sixteenth of August 1944 would prove to be a fateful day for Cox and his shipmates. "At 1220B, YMS 24 started a turn to port in response to a signal from OTC [the officer in tactical command] in approximate position 43-24-15N and 06-45-30E, in 29 fathoms of water," Cox wrote in his action report, continuing:

Immediately thereafter, there was an underwater explosion either directly under the stem or slightly on the port bow. There was a resultant complete destruction and loss of the forward third of the ship up to the middle of the bridge topside, and to the bulkhead between the forward and after crew's compartments (frame 43) below. . . .

There was no plume following the explosion, nor was it accompanied by any unusually loud sound. The midship part of the ship was lifted some distance out of the water, and the ship afterwards submerged to the main deck level before righting herself and settling down. Thereafter she remained on an even keel, with gradually increasing draft toward the bow. A ring of debris and greasy water surrounded the forward part of the ship for some 30 yards. The force of the explosion as evidenced by the falling debris seems to have been concentrated upward and toward the stern. Two men standing on the forward gun deck were blown to a distance of 100 to 150 yards on the starboard quarter. From these observations, and from actual sighting of moored mines before and after the explosion, it is probable that the damage and loss can be ascribed to contact with one or more horns of an enemy moored mine of five feet or less depth.

Shortly after the explosion, it was ascertained that the ship would remain afloat for a while due to the buoyancy of her after compartments, though she was leaking forward, and all effort was made to treat wounded, check on missing and dead, destroy all secret equipment and salvage publications. The Executive Officer [Cox] assumed command after it was discovered that the Captain had been killed instantly at his station on the bridge.

About ten to fifteen minutes after the explosion, USS YMS-63 and HMS ML-563 maneuvered alongside to assist in rescue operations. YMS-63 tied up with her port beam to the stern of YMS-24, and ML-563's bow to her port quarter. About twenty minutes thereafter, another explosion occurred under the stern of ML-563, destroying approximately the after third of the ML. This undoubtedly resulted in further springing of the underwater hull of YMS-24 and more

Lt. (jg) John Cox (center of photo) was executive officer on board the minesweeper YMS-24 during the August 1944 invasion of southern France. (Dale Howard collection)

rapid flooding of her compartments. YMS-63 then sighted two mines beneath the surface and apparently in line of drift, and cast off with what wounded and survivors had been placed aboard her. . . . About forty minutes later, an LCVP was brought through the minefield and evacuated the remaining wounded and survivors of both ships. Order was given to abandon YMS-24 after it was seen that she was leaking badly forward.

In the ship's war diary Cox added, "The Captain [Lt. (jg) Samuel R. Pruett, USNR] and four enlisted men of this vessel were killed. Fifteen men were injured. Ship sank approximately six hours after striking mine."

What acting commanding officer Cox did not mention, in the loss-of-ship reports that he submitted on 26 August and 1 September 1944, were his own heroic efforts. But the citation accompanying his Navy Cross helps to tell the rest of the story. Awarded at the Navy Pier in Chicago on 30 November 1944, it reads:

For extraordinary heroism in action as Executive Officer of the U.S.S. YMS-24 during the amphibious invasion of Southern France on 16 August 1944.

During minesweeping operations to clear the heavily mine infested waters of the Gulf of Frejus for the landing of reinforcements and vital supplies in support of the Allied Armies in Southern France, the U.S.S. YMS-24 struck an enemy mine which blew off the bow causing her subsequent sinking, the loss in action of her Commanding Officer, and other casualties. Lieutenant (junior grade) Cox, exercising prompt, fearless and deliberate action, instituted all possible, though futile, measures to save the ship from sinking and later to remove the wounded to the care and safety of rescue vessels which had come alongside. He entered every compartment in search of missing or trapped men. Following a second mine explosion under the stern of one of the rescue vessels alongside, with complete disregard for his own safety, he unhesitatingly jumped into the water between the two foundering craft and removed a critically injured man who had been dropped during the transfer of the wounded and was in immediate danger of drowning. His gallant, self-sacrificing and untiring efforts contributed materially to the prompt care of the wounded and to the probable saving of many lives.

The exceptional heroism, cool and determined action, and outstanding devotion to duty displayed by Lieutenant (junior grade) Cox were in keeping with the highest traditions of the naval service.

Cox was also awarded the French Croix de Guerre for his part in this action.

Before entering the naval service, Cleveland-born (in 1913) John R. Cox, Jr., was the handsome actor John Howard, cast in the leading roles of mostly B-grade films. Self-effacing, intelligent, and hardworking, he had been a top student in high school, winning a scholarship to continue his studies at Case Western Reserve University, where he graduated Phi Beta Kappa.

When the Depression hit his family, Cox helped out by going to work at the local radio station, where he played piano. After a reading of *John Brown's Body*, performed with others from the drama department of his school, a studio scout noticed him. This eventually

Minesweepers like this (YMS-21) cleared offshore waters for the safe passage of incoming Allied troops and supplies. (U.S. Naval Historical Center)

led to a contract with Paramount Pictures and seventy-five dollars a week, which no doubt seemed a fortune at the time.

It was certainly enough motivation to move to Hollywood, and in 1934 John Cox, now Howard, began his movie career. After several unremarkable films, he was cast in Frank Capra's classic *Lost Horizon* (voted by the Academy one of 1937's best pictures), costarring with Ronald Colman and Jane Wyatt. A few years later George Cukor directed him in *The Philadelphia Story* (1941, with Cary Grant and Katharine Hepburn). But Howard may be best remembered for his starring role in several films in the Bulldog Drummond sleuth series (1937–39). After the war he appeared in many other movies, notably *The High and the Mighty* (1954, with John Wayne).

He worked in the film industry into the 1970s, appearing as a regular in the television soap opera *Days of Our Lives*. He also decided to work his way out of the acting field and became a private-school teacher at Highland Hall, one of the prestigious Waldorf schools. He stayed on for eighteen years, becoming head of the high school and chairman of its board.

Howard embraced his new Southern California life outside of the acting world. He was a devoted teacher and the father of four children, married to former actress and prima ballerina Eva Ralf (they had met on Broadway in the 1950s, in a show in which she was dancing and he was acting). A superb celestial navigator, he often taught navigation to private yachtsmen. He also made wooden furniture and toys, especially for his grandchildren. John Howard died in 1995.

# Robert Montgomery

Robert Montgomery, né Henry Montgomery, Jr. (1904), grew up in financial security. He and his parents, Henry and Mary Weed Bernard Montgomery, enjoyed the life of the privileged—Henry Senior was a rubber-company executive—and young Henry was tutored privately, attended prep schools, rode horses, and traveled in Europe. But when the lad was still a student at New York's Pawling School for Boys, his father died suddenly, leaving the family with insufficient means for the sixteen-year-old to finish school.

The future movie star had to find whatever work he could. Fortunately, working would turn out to be his forte. Wherever there was action, movement, change, or speaking out on issues, Robert Montgomery would frequently be a presence. But all that would happen later. Right now the teenager just needed a job, and he landed one as a mechanic with the New York, New Haven, and Hartford Railroad. His next stop was Standard Oil, in whose employ he shipped out as a deckhand on an oil tanker in the early 1920s.

Upon his return from the sea, having decided to become a writer, he moved to Greenwich Village. Ensconced in that culturally rich environment, he was offered bit parts in plays, including *The Mask and the Face.* It was but a small taste of what would become a career, but all Henry Montgomery knew at the time (1924) was that this acting thing was for him.

Success came quickly, and by 1928 the handsome six-foot-tall actor had appeared in several Broadway plays, as the lead in four of them, and had begun going by the name Robert. His killer blue eyes, energy, clever talk, charm, and natural sophistication had universal appeal, and he was cast repeatedly as a society playboy. But who was complaining? The previous mechanic and oiler was becoming a known face, and a great deal of money was to follow.

In 1929 came his first speaking film appearance, in *So This Is College,* after which he starred with Joan Crawford in *Untamed* (also 1929). By now Montgomery was under contract with MGM. But he did not just rake in the acting roles; he became a spokesman for actors, at the risk of his career, helping to shape the fledgling Screen Actors Guild into a powerful organization. He and other determined, change-oriented actors joined the recently formed union in 1933, and a year later Montgomery was elected its vice president. For three years after that, a critical period in the establishment of the guild's presence and influence in Hollywood, he served as its president.

In the meantime, he continued to work at making movies, at which he excelled both artistically—of particular note was 1937's psychological drama *Night Must Fall,* which earned him an Oscar nomination for best actor—and financially. In 1940 his reported income was over two hundred thousand dollars. Gradually he became known for his versatility and desire to portray new character types, which critics especially applauded in *Yellow Jack* (1938) and *The Earl of Chicago* (1940). The box office was not suffering either, and 1941 profits piled up with films such as *Rage in Heaven* and *Here Comes Mr. Jordan* (for which he got another Academy nomination).

Nineteen-forty found Montgomery actively supporting the presidential campaign of Wendell Willkie and serving as chairman of the Hollywood Republican Committee. He also traveled to London to make the RKO film *Haunted Honeymoon* (1940), and while there he volunteered for duty in the American Field Service, becoming one of the first Hollywood stars of the World War II era to enlist in the armed forces.

He drove an ambulance in France until the Americans were forced out after Dunkirk fell. The actor escaped the onrushing German juggernaut through Spain and Portugal, but his withdrawal was temporarily delayed by a side trip to fly to the rescue of fellow thespian Madeleine Carroll, trapped on the Riviera. The beautiful international star had been at her country home in France when the Germans invaded. She made it as far as Biarritz before it began to look as if she might be spending more time in France than she now wanted to, but Montgomery, by this time already in Portugal, chartered a plane and flew to her, bringing her back to Lisbon. From there they steamed to America.

With the war on, Montgomery felt the need to help out and applied for U.S. naval service in early 1941. While he waited for the response he made several movies in quick succession, no doubt anticipating the lost income that acceptance into the military would mean. He and his wife (since 1928), Elizabeth Bryan Allen, also scaled down their lifestyle, dismissing servants and selling their estate and fancy cars.

News from the Navy came several months later, as a result of which Lt. (jg) Henry Robert Montgomery was commissioned in the U.S. Naval Reserve on 28 April 1941. After a one-month assignment with the Office of the Chief of Naval Operations in Washington, he reported as assistant naval attaché at the U.S. embassy in London. His duties as an intelligence officer there included running the Naval Operations Room, which tracked the location of all British ships.

In September 1941 he was designated special naval observer, in which capacity he remained with the British fleet until January 1942. During this brief additional-duty tour he served aboard British anti-submarine destroyers. One other temporary assignment was to report back to Washington with the mission of setting up a Naval Operations Room in the White House similar to the one in London.

Robert Montgomery's first sea duty was at the Melville, Rhode Island, Torpedo Boat School. Ordered to Motor Torpedo Boat Squadron 5 in the Panama Canal Zone, he served as executive officer and division commander of the squadron and as commanding officer of PT-107. (U.S. Navy photo)

While in the nation's capital, the star had to defy reporters' tireless efforts to get him to spill war stories. The Hollywood refugee remained tight-lipped per strict military regulations, committed to carrying out his wartime service as ordered and to the best of his ability. His three-year active-duty service to his country would place him in harm's way routinely, but he remained reluctant to discuss details about it even after the war.

Having requested sea duty, Montgomery was next ordered to the Melville, Rhode Island, Torpedo Boat School. Before heading out from Washington, he broadcast the radio program *This Is War,* which would be the first in a series designed to heighten Americans' awareness of the war.

After qualifying in all phases of PT boat operation, he was ordered to Motor Torpedo Boat Squadron 5, which operated in the Panama Canal Zone. There he served as executive officer and division commander of the squadron, and as commanding officer of PT-107.

While attached to the *Columbia* (CL-56) in the Pacific, Montgomery saw action during the first raid on the Japanese stronghold at Munda. (U.S. Navy photo)

Following his PT boat tour, in November 1942 Robert Montgomery was ordered to the 10,000-ton light cruiser USS *Columbia* (CL-56), which had joined the Pacific Fleet in the Solomons. While attached to the cruiser, he saw action during the first raid on the Japanese stronghold at Munda. Next he became assistant operations officer and intelligence officer on the staff of Commander Destroyer Squadron 5, and for his exemplary service he received a Letter of Commendation, with authorization to wear the Commendation Ribbon. The Commander in Chief, U.S. Pacific Fleet, made the presentation:

> For excellent service . . . as Assistant Operations Officer and Intelligence Officer on the staff of Commander Destroyer Squadron five in the Solomons area during January and February 1943. While his unit was assigned the task of preventing the enemy from supplying and reinforcing his forces on Guadalcanal, he skillfully assisted the commander in his planning and execution of operations. This was accomplished while in almost continuous combat with the enemy, including bombardment of enemy troops and installations and engagements with enemy aircraft. He contributed materially to the hampering of enemy operations and furnishing gunfire support and screening during landings of our forces.

Montgomery was promoted to lieutenant commander in early March 1943 while still in the South Pacific, after which he was flown back to the States to recuperate from the jungle fever he had contracted, leaving him more than twenty pounds lighter. A month later he reported to the chief of the Operational Training Command, Pacific Fleet. In May he was assigned duty with the Operational Training Command, Subordinate Command, with headquarters in Seattle. He remained there until August, at which time he was transferred to the Naval Small Craft Training Command, Roosevelt Base, Terminal Island, San Pedro, California.

During this tour Lieutenant Commander Montgomery contributed to the ongoing development of dronettes for Navy use. Small radio-controlled, pilotless aircraft used by the Army and Navy for antiaircraft training, dronettes had been developed by another actor, Reginald Denny, whose hobby had been radio-controlled model planes. At Roosevelt Base, Montgomery had the idea of experimenting with catapult-launching the dronettes from speedboats that were being used as aircraft rescue boats. The concept was eventually adopted, greatly facilitating the use of dronettes for antiaircraft practice afloat, and contributing as well to the big picture: the gunners who practiced on the small ghost planes ultimately downed more than twenty-eight hundred Japanese and German pilots.

In February 1944, now forty-one years old and known in the Navy as an outstanding officer, storyteller, and mimic, Montgomery joined the staff of Commander Destroyer Squadron 60, which was embarked on the USS *Barton* (DD-722). The *Barton* was one of the hundreds of Allied vessels that were preparing for Operation Overlord, the Normandy invasion. Destroyer Squadron 60 played a critical role in the battle for the German-occupied French port of Cherbourg during the days following the invasion. The *Barton,* along with eleven destroyers, three American battleships, two American cruisers, and two British cruisers, relentlessly pounded strong coastal defense forces in an effort to open the port for use in supporting Allied invasion armies. After a fierce three-day battle the Germans finally were overcome, assuring the success of Operation Overlord.

For his "meritorious achievement" while in action against the enemy "during the approach, landing and assault on the Continent of Europe by the Allied Expeditionary Force from June 3 to 23, 1944," Montgomery was awarded the Bronze Star with Combat V. His citation went on:

> By his cool and courageous performance of duty in the face of frequent devastating enemy aerial attacks throughout the entire assault period, Lieutenant Commander Montgomery contributed essentially to the success of his unit during this critical period of vital combat operations, and his gallant conduct was in keeping with the highest traditions of the U.S. Naval Service.

On 19 August 1944 Montgomery reported for duty in the Navy Department's Washington administrative office; later that month he was assigned additional duty at Astoria, New York, for work in connection with the Army Photographic Section, Army Signal Corps. On 5 October 1945 he was released from active duty. Two years later he was made a Knight of the French Legion of Honor. In addition to these awards, by-now Commander Montgomery wore the American Defense Service Medal, Base Clasp; the American Area Campaign Medal; the Asiatic–Pacific Area Campaign Medal; the European–Africa–Middle Eastern Area Campaign Medal; and the World War II Victory Medal.

He wasted no time resting on his laurels, and shortly after leaving active duty, Robert Montgomery reported back to show business. In 1945 he appeared in *They Were Expendable* (shot the previous year, while he was still on active duty), with John Wayne and Donna Reed. Based on the true story of a PT boat squadron skippered by then-Lieutenant John D. Bulkeley (Robert Montgomery) during the U.S. retreat from Bataan, the script was written by World War I naval aviator Frank "Sprig" Wead, from the book by William L. White. The film was enthusiastically supported by the Navy, always interested in a positive image for the taxpayers, especially at a time when the Pacific war was raging on against a stubborn foe.

Shot around an island off Florida, the movie was directed by Comdr. John Ford (on leave) until he fell ill during the last few weeks of filming. At that point Montgomery took over the direction, Ford having assured the nervous MGM producers that the actor could handle the job. That assessment proved correct: *They Were Expendable* was not only a huge box-office and critical hit, it also became a turning point in Montgomery's career. It was as a result of this demonstrated directing ability that the studio agreed to let him do it again, notably in the 1946 adaptation of Raymond Chandler's thriller *Lady in the Lake* (in which he also starred). They also let him try out a new technique he had been advocating for some time, a method wherein the action would be viewed chiefly through the eyes of one of the characters, in the form of the camera lens.

Wealth, fame, and successful new professional directions had not dimmed Montgomery's interest in the Screen Actors Guild, and in 1946 he served his fourth term as president. His political activities also remained on the front burner; in 1933 and 1937 he had supported the New Deal, but by 1940 he had become a Republican. During the grim blacklist period of the 1950s, Montgomery stood by his convictions, if not in a way that Wisconsin senator Joseph R. McCarthy would have chosen for him.

The Academy of Motion Picture Arts and Sciences had been founded in 1927, due largely to the efforts of MGM studio chief Louis B. Mayer. The original idea had been to provide a forum in which to deal with issues affecting the film industry. But in 1957 the Academy went too far, instituting a rule that made ineligible for an Academy Award any avowed communist or anyone who refused to respond to a subpoena to appear before a committee. This McCarthy-inspired witch-hunt edict was officially revoked as "unworkable" in 1959, but in the meantime the House Committee on Un-American Activities had conducted scores of inquiries, ruining or putting on hold hundreds of careers. Many actors had refused to participate. Montgomery's position was that communist influences could more effectively be opposed from within the industry than by official U.S. government policy.

His political commitments kept him more than busy, but Montgomery's career in show business was far from over. He made seven postwar movies; produced the 1950–57 TV series *Robert Montgomery Presents,* directing, hosting, and sometimes appearing in the programs; and co-produced, directed, and narrated *The Gallant Hours* (1960, with James Cagney as Admiral Halsey). Later his focus shifted primarily to the business world, and he worked as a communications consultant and served on the board of several prominent institutions, among them the Lincoln Center for the Performing Arts.

As always, Robert Montgomery found plenty to keep him out of trouble, and his industrious, no-nonsense approach never flagged. He remained in the Naval Reserve, eventually achieving the rank of captain. He and his first wife were divorced in 1950. They had two children (one of whom, Elizabeth, starred in the TV series *Bewitched;* she passed away in 1995). In 1950 Montgomery was married again, to Elizabeth Grant Harkness. He died in 1981.

# Wayne Morris

One Hollywood star not only got into the action but became an air ace: Bert DeWayne Morris, Jr., popularly known as Wayne Morris. Flying F6F-3 Hellcats off the aircraft carrier USS *Essex* (CV-9) with Navy Fighter Squadron 15, Bert Morris, as he insisted on being called in the Navy, downed seven Japanese planes and survived the war. Three of the Hellcats he flew had to be pushed over the side because they were too shot up to be of further use. Morris is probably the only movie-actor air ace in the history of U.S. warfare.

Before his Navy years, Morris's most notable role was that of a boxing champion in the movie *Kid Galahad* (1937, with Humphrey Bogart, Bette Davis, and Edward G. Robinson). Critics touted him as a rising star, but in subsequent films he never made it beyond secondary roles, albeit with promise. Even so, after the war his fine performance in *Paths of Glory* (1957), his last film, would win praise as his best.

The tall, blond, good-natured actor was born in Los Angeles in 1914. He graduated from Los Angeles High School, where he starred as a running back on the Los Angeles City College football team. Between high school and college, while pondering his future, he worked for a year as a forest patrolman in Los Angeles National Park. He went on to study acting at Los Angeles Junior College and then at the Pasadena Playhouse School of the Theater. Soon after completing his studies he was signed by Warner Brothers, which cast him in *Kid Galahad* because of his rugged, all-American looks and athletic prowess. In his last movie before going AWOL on Hollywood, Morris played an Army Air Corps pilot in *I Wanted Wings* (1941, with Veronica Lake). He had begun taking flying lessons during the shooting of *Flight Angels* (1940); perhaps his make-believe air-combat roles inspired him to fly for the Navy. Whatever the case, Morris was commissioned an ensign in the U.S. Naval Reserve in May 1941.

His first assignment was to the Naval Aviation Cadet Selection Board, Long Beach, where he remained for almost a year—until April 1942, when he began his flight training at Naval Air Station Pensacola. After receiving the coveted designation of naval aviator, he was sent to Naval Air Station Hutchinson, Kansas, there to serve as a primary flight instructor.

But Ens. B. D. Morris wanted to get into fighters. He resisted the prospect of never moving beyond U.S. borders, the fate of many in his profession who had donned a uniform. In this pursuit he was fortunate to have a close connection to Lt. Comdr. David McCampbell, who was to be skipper of Fighter Squadron 15, and later commander of Carrier Air Group 15—and who was his wife's uncle. McCampbell understood and responded to his in-law's pleas. He asked the young thespian to write requests (twice) for assignment to a fighter squadron, and he hand-delivered them to the Bureau of Naval Personnel in Washington.

The first letter got Morris transferred to Jacksonville (June 1943), not for fighter duty but for PBY (Catalina) training. A hefty man, the actor was thought too much so to fit into fighters. The second request did the trick, though, and in July 1943 Morris was ordered to join VF-15, known as Fighting Fifteen, in Melbourne, Florida.

There, along with the other fighter pilots undergoing McCampbell's rigorous, thorough training, Morris enthusiastically got to work. At

David McCampbell (left) was skipper of Fighting Fifteen and later commander of Carrier Air Group 15. (U.S. Navy photo)

twenty-nine, he was older than most of the others and wanted to be just one of the guys. He went by the name Bert, reserved for friends and family, rather than Wayne, his stage name.

Carrier Air Group 15 comprised VF-15 (fifty-four F6F-3 Hellcats), VB-15 (thirty-six SB2C-3 Helldivers), and VT-15 (twenty torpedo-bomber Avengers). The Hellcat, manufactured by Grumman Aircraft Engineering Corporation on Long Island, was the U.S. response to the dreaded Japanese A6M Mitsubishi Zero fighter, responsible for the deaths of so many American pilots in the early Pacific air war. Designed specifically to challenge the Zero, the Hellcat became known for its superior flight characteristics, eventually outperforming its nemesis. In less than two years, the Hellcat destroyed more than five thousand Japanese aircraft.

As the squadron headed toward the Pacific battle area aboard the *Essex* in April 1944, Morris—as of March 1943 a lieutenant—was a

Grumman Hellcats taxi up the *Essex*'s flight deck during the Marcus Island raid, 20 May 1944. (U.S. Navy photo)

section leader, and later he would be assigned to lead his own division. A team player, he proudly displayed a large squadron insignia across the back of his flight jacket.

The squadron went into action 11 June 1944, with a forty-one-fighter sweep over Guam. The Hellcats downed eight enemy aircraft; one of their pilots and his plane were lost. During the action, Morris and his division were flying below an overcast at fourteen thousand feet when they spotted a Japanese Kawanishi H6K5 Mavis flying boat. Morris made his run from the starboard side of the fleeing aircraft, sending bursts of fire into it as it lost altitude. He finally broke off his attack at two hundred feet and watched as the lumbering aircraft crashed and burned on a reef below.

On 19 June, the day of the Marianas Turkey Shoot, VF-15 scored sixty-eight kills, but Morris and his division found no bandits along their vector line. The next day, though, Morris scored a probable. During a dawn sweep over Orote Field, eighteen *Essex* fighters encountered four low-flying Mitsubishi Zekes on a reciprocal heading. Two of them ducked into clouds while a third safely evaded its enemies. The fourth Zeke continued to come straight at the Hellcats, and Morris's wing-man fired a head-on shot. Meanwhile, Morris fired a deflection shot that sent the enemy aircraft spinning and smoking into the clouds below. The Hellcats followed the Zeke down and sighted an oil slick and a dye marker. Morris was credited with a probable kill.

On 23 June four Zekes attacked VF-15 as it escorted *Essex* dive bombers to Orote Field. During this action Morris made three runs on one of them, scoring hits on each pass. He stayed with the stricken Zeke until it crashed into the sea.

After that, *Essex* fighters stayed out of trouble, mostly, until 8 September, by which time Adm. William F. Halsey, Jr., was ready to hit the Philippines. The *Essex*, as part of Task Force 38, prepared for air strikes on bases that could be used to help defend Palau.

On 9 September the carrier's mission was to attack the Mindanao airfields. After shooting down a Japanese patrol plane during the first strike, the fighters were assigned to lead twelve dive bombers and eight torpedo planes as they went after the enemy's shipping and airfields.

A Mitsubishi Topsy transport was tally-hoed at thirteen thousand feet flying straight and level. One team of Hellcats drew smoke, but the Topsy attempted no evasive action. Bert Morris then made one high-side run, sending bursts into the starboard wing tank from four o'clock up. The Topsy burst into intense flames and spun off to the left in what became a tight spiral to the ground. No one was observed parachuting. There had been no apparent protection of fuel tanks and no armament.

Several days later, on 13 September, Morris got his fourth kill while his squadron was strafing Bacolod airdrome on Negros Island. Morris saw a lone Zeke make a single pass at four Hellcats, then start to flee at eight thousand feet. Having a slight altitude advantage, Morris tightened his turn as the Zeke dove into a wide spiral. He was able to stay with the enemy, firing throughout, as the Zeke for some reason continued its spiraling dive. At four thousand feet, it exploded.

Enemy fighters showed little organization, it was noted in the action report, apparently preferring individual tactics. They outnumbered the Americans but never pressed home coordinated attacks, and Morris and his squadron mates were able to pick them off one by one.

On 10 October, while escorting dive bombers and torpedo planes in an attack on Okinawa, the Fighting Fifteen Hellcats quickly found themselves in a dogfight with twenty enemy fighters and fighter bombers north of Yontan airfield. Morris pounced on the first one that got within range, a Kawasaki Tony fighter that successfully evaded his fire by turning inside him. Morris held his altitude, fell back, and attacked the fighter from astern. Carrying his run down to three hundred feet, he shot the enemy into the sea—but not before it had cartwheeled, smoking, on the water.

Later that month the *Essex* and her air group joined in the Battle of Leyte Gulf. On 24 October, Morris was launched with two divisions as the enemy attacked Task Force 38 with fighters, dive bombers, and torpedo bombers. The carrier *Princeton* (CV-37) was hit and erupted into flames, smoke pouring from her. Four Hellcats flew combat air patrol over the stricken ship; meanwhile, Morris and his squadron mates were vectored toward an incoming raid. The official action report (of Commander Air Group 15, 27 October 1944) tells the story thus:

> The 3 VFs intercepting the raid were vectored out on course 030 degrees while they climbed to 20,000'. The bogeys were tallyho'd 4 to 5 o'clock at 30 to 40 miles distance. They consisted of about 30 planes, VF [fighters], VB [dive bombers] and VT [torpedo-bombers]. The Rats [all Zekes] formed a Lufberry Circle [a defensive maneuver used to distract American fighters away from enemy dive bombers and torpedo planes that would attempt to slip through the protective screen] at about 16,000', while approximately 4 Hawks [dive bombers] or Fish [torpedo bombers] dove for the deck and escaped, later reaching their targets but accomplishing no damage. Attacks were made on the remaining bandits, 7 were destroyed and the rest of the raid dispersed. The enemy fighter pilots were the most aggressive encountered since the fleet action of 19 June. They flew excellent formation, kept good sections and traded head-on shots. They evidently were part of the No. 1 Team. Undoubtedly many E/A [enemy aircraft] were damaged but the speed of the action and the constant aggressiveness of the E/pilots prevented an accurate tally. Individual details of the aerial combat follow.
>
> Lieut. Morris made a high side run from about 3 o'clock on the leader and it crashed (1 Zeke). Morris continued on down and made

During the May 1944 raids on Marcus and Wake islands, Morris returns to the *Essex* after his third mission of the day and his fifth combat mission against the Japanese. (U.S. Navy photo)

a steep climb back up above the overcast (his wingman on this run had shot down a Jill), to rejoin. He then attacked 2 Zekes from 9 o'clock up; however he missed on his first pass, and the Zekes started shooting. He tried to turn with the Zekes, but after picking up numerous pieces of Jap lead, he was discouraged and ducked into a cloud. He made a 360 degree turn on instruments, and came out above these two Zekes circling the cloud. He made a pass at the Zeke astern from 5 to 6 o'clock and it burst into flames (1 Zeke). A couple of 20mm slugs in his engine were causing trouble, the cockpit was full of smoke and the hydraulic system was shot up, so he continued on down in his dive and headed for base.

In addition to his aerial heroics, Morris was credited with sinking and damaging a number of enemy ships. During the action on 9–10 September 1944 off Mindanao, he sank two small enemy cargo ships and damaged three others, and a few days later he and a squadron mate sank an enemy escort vessel and an antiaircraft barge. On 22 September he and another pilot attacked and probably sank an enemy submarine. The following month Morris scored hits on a Japanese cruiser and later damaged an enemy minelayer.

Air Group 15 completed its only tour of combat duty (six and a half months) on 14 November 1944 and headed back to the States. Fabled Fifteen, as the unit was by then known, was one of the most highly decorated naval air groups of the war. It boasted the most air combat kills (318); the most enemy aircraft destroyed on the ground (348); the most aircraft destroyed in one day (68); the most aircraft destroyed by a two-plane section during a mission (15); and the most enemy aircraft destroyed by a pilot in a single mission (9). These records were—and remain—unequaled in the history of naval aviation. The air group saw combat in the Marianas, at Iwo Jima, in the Palaus and the Philippines, and at Formosa and Nansei Shotos, and took part in the battles of the Philippine Sea and Leyte Gulf.

Morris flew fifty-seven missions and was one of twenty-seven aces in his air group. His record of shootdowns (all during 1944) was:

1 Mavis (11 June)
1 Zeke (23 June)
1 Topsy (9 September)
1 Zeke (13 September)
1 Tony (10 October)
2 Zekes (24 October)

He was awarded three Distinguished Flying Crosses and two Air Medals. His uncle-in-law, Commander McCampbell, was credited with thirty-four kills and was awarded the Medal of Honor. (David McCampbell passed away in 1996 at age eighty-six.)

While the aerial combat that merited all this recognition was raging in the Pacific, in California Morris's wife, Patricia Ann O'Rourke, was dealing with another aspect of the war, which she described in an article for the magazine *Photoplay*. Her story illustrates the daily,

Fighting Fifteen. Morris is fourth from left, bottom row. McCampbell is fourth from right, bottom row. (U.S. Navy photo)

glamourless courage and strength of those who were waiting at home. At night, with no phone and up in the country alone with their new daughter, Pat played solitaire and listened to the radio. One night she was surprised to hear the voice of her husband, speaking live from Hawaii about his air group's exploits in the skies. After the broadcast Pat felt certain that he would survive and return home, but she kept her feeling to herself. She got ahead on the housework and gardening, cutting back on expenses so that she could hire a housekeeper when her "boyfriend" got home.

And in December 1944, Bert made it home. The Morrises knew how lucky they were, even more so when their baby was sent a gift by one of the other air group wives whose husband had not made it back. Morris was ordered to the Naval Ordnance Test Station at Inyokern, California, and then to the Receiving Station, Terminal Island, California, where he remained until being released from active duty on 17 October 1945.

Morris's wife, Patricia Ann O'Rourke, held her position in their telephone-less country home with their daughter, Pam, whom Morris met only after returning from his Pacific tour. (Mrs. Bert DeWayne Morris collection)

After his rather eventful tour in the Navy, Morris went back to making movies. He worked steadily, appearing in many films including *Deep Valley* (1947), *The Time of Your Life* (1948), and *Paths of Glory*. In *Task Force* (1949, with Walter Brennan, Gary Cooper, and Jane Wyatt) Morris played a combat Navy pilot, a role in which acting must have felt more like déjà vu. He also appeared as a character actor on television. He continued to wear the Navy blue as a Naval Air Reserve officer, eventually attaining the rank of lieutenant commander and returning for short periods of active naval flying duty to maintain his proficiency.

## Hellcat Pilot Survived by Famous Brother

Ens. Robert "Bugs" Beedle, USNR, was shot down on 4 January 1945 while flying his Navy Hellcat against the enemy off Kavieng, New Ireland, in the Pacific. As a member of Fighter Squadron 18 aboard the carrier *Bunker Hill* (CV-17), Bugs had bagged a Japanese torpedo plane in earlier action during the Tarawa campaign and shot down an enemy fighter on the day he was downed himself. He was awarded an Air Medal for each victory and a Purple Heart for injuries sustained during aerial combat. His family and friends would feel the loss for the rest of their lives, but to the rest of the world Bugs Beedle was an unknown casualty.

His brother, Lt. William Holden, Army Air Corps officer, was one of many actors who grieved for relatives lost in wars far from home. In a twist of fate, ten years later Holden played a Navy pilot who was downed and killed in Korea in *The Bridges at Toko-Ri* (1955).

Morris died in 1959, while on board a Navy ship. By that year Pat's Uncle McCampbell had reached the rank of captain and been given command of the carrier USS *Bon Homme Richard* (CVA-31). While the ship was at Oakland, McCampbell invited Bert and other ex–squadron mates for a short cruise and breakfast. After enjoying the hearty meal, the forty-five-year-old actor climbed the five ladders up to the bridge as the ship passed under the Golden Gate. Upon reaching the top, he collapsed. He was immediately flown ashore by helicopter to Oakland Naval Hospital, where he was pronounced dead of a massive coronary.

Bert Morris had been married once before, briefly, and he and Pat remained good friends with Bubbles Schinasi. Morris had three children. He rests with many other World War II heroes in Arlington National Cemetery. His weather-worn white grave marker reads:

Bert DeWayne Morris, California

LCDR, USNR, World War II

February 17, 1914–September 14, 1959

DFC & 2 GS—AM & 1 GS

★

## PART 2

# The Early Years

The Great War, or the "War to End All Wars," had been in the making for decades before Serbian patriot Gavrilo Princip assassinated Archduke Franz Ferdinand, heir apparent to the Austro-Hungarian throne, at Sarajevo. For centuries before the war, empires and nations had been competing for territorial control in Europe and the colonies, and alliances were formed that would oppose each other during the war. In 1882, Germany, Austria-Hungary, and Italy formed a triple alliance known as the Central Powers. To resist any aggression from them, in 1907 Great Britain, France, and Russia formed the Triple Entente. The Balkans, called the powder keg of Europe, were in continuous turmoil as Greece, Serbia, and Bulgaria fought to end Turkish control of their territories. Nationalism was on the rise, and the powder keg was ready to blow, but the beginnings of the war were complicated.

*1914*

28 June    Archduke Franz Ferdinand and his wife, Sophie, are assassinated at Sarajevo.

28 July    Austria-Hungary declares war on Serbia after the latter rejects ultimatum. Russia begins to mobilize, and Germany delivers an ultimatum to Russia.

1 Aug.  Germany declares war on Russia, and on France two days later. The next day Britain declares war on Germany, and Germany on Belgium. World War I begins. The British Expeditionary Force (BEF) arrives in France on 21 August. Eight days later the Germans defeat the Russians at the Battle of Tannenberg.

14 Sept.  The Germans are turned back at the first battle of the Marne. Trench warfare begins.

11 Oct.  Russians battle Germans in Poland. The first battle of Ypres, Flanders, is fought 15 October.

2 Nov.  Russia declares war on Turkey. Four days later Great Britain and France do the same. The western front is stuck in trench warfare.

8 Dec.  The Battle of the Falkland Islands is fought. German naval combatants shell British towns along the English Channel on 16 December. The western front becomes stagnant.

The war raged on for almost three more years before the United States entered (6 April 1917), shortly after Czar Nicholas II abdicated his rule of Russia on 15 March.

*1917*

4 May  U.S. destroyers arrive in Ireland. On 10 May, Gen. "Black Jack" Pershing takes charge as commander of American Expeditionary Forces in Europe.

25 June  The first contingent of U.S. soldiers arrives in France. Greece goes to war with the Central Powers the next day.

14 Aug.  China goes to war against the Central Powers. The pope pleads for peace.

7 Nov.  The Russian Revolution begins. The Allies establish the Supreme War Council.

3 Dec.  The Russian Bolshevik government signs a peace pact with Germany, and fighting ends on the eastern front. Civil war continues in Russia.

The desire for peace was by now nearly universal, but nearly another year would pass before it would be accomplished. On 3 November 1918, Austria-Hungary surrendered to the Allies, and Germany signed an armistice on the eleventh. The Treaty of Versailles was signed on 28 June 1919.

It is estimated that 70 million men were in uniform. Of these, 9 million (116,000 of whom were Americans) were killed. About 9 million civilians also lost their lives. Bombings and shellings took a heavy toll, and an influenza epidemic killed nearly 20 million people worldwide between 1918 and 1919.

# Wallace Beery

In late October 1929, every student pilot's nightmare came true: the instructor nearly died, leaving the trainee to his own devices. The instructor was Wallace Beery, the well-known screen actor, who suffered a stroke while flying a Travel Air A600A six-place cabin aircraft with fellow actor Al Roscoe, who at the time was learning to fly. Roscoe must have been a good student, because he wrested control of the spinning plane from his stricken teacher, landing successfully without his guidance.

Wallace Beery remained in the hospital in serious condition for over a week, but he survived and went on to live another twenty years, albeit with a chronic heart condition. A flying enthusiast, Beery logged thousands of hours in his privately owned fleet of aircraft; in the late 1920s and 1930s he owned a Travel Air, a Bellanca CH400 Skyrocket, and a Bellanca 31-50.

Actors, and three real naval aviators, strike a pose in front of a Curtiss O2C during the shooting of *Hell Divers*. From left: Cliff Edwards; Lt. (jg) J. S. Thach, USN; Clark Gable; Wallace Beery; Lt. H. S. Duckworth, USN; and Lt. (jg) T. D. Southworth, USN. "Jimmie" Thach would become the famous World War II fighter pilot who developed the Thach Weave, in which fighters flew across the path of others to provide better protection to one another. Thach survived the war and went on to attain the rank of admiral. In 1956 he was assisted in carrying out his duties by one of the authors of this book, then-Lt. Jim Wise, who served as Thach's aide and flag lieutenant. (U.S. Naval Historical Center)

Beery received his Navy wings and commission in 1934, drilling out of the Naval Reserve Aviation Base at Long Beach, California. It was the movie *Hell Divers* (1931)—in which he starred with Clark Gable and Cliff Edwards, and with real-life naval aviators Lt. (jg) Jimmie Thach, Lt. H. S. Duckworth, and Lt. (jg) T. D. Southworth—that first aroused Beery's curiosity about naval aviation. The film let the public in, for the first time, on what went on inside aircraft carriers. And aside from these fascinating operational activities, Beery also learned something of the dive-bombing tactics the Navy's air arm had developed in the late 1920s. He was smitten; he had to be part of it. His Navy service would always remain one of the achievements Wallace Beery was proudest of, though he was never called to active duty.

Beery was born in 1885 in Kansas City, Missouri, the younger brother of actor Noah Beery. The kid brother found his way into show business by joining a circus as a teenager, soon joining Ringling Brothers, where he was charged with handling the elephants. Eventually he moved from the tent to the stage, appearing in the 1904 chorus line of *Babes in Toyland,* and next he began singing in musicals and playing in summer stock. It was while he was working with a Kansas City stock company, in 1913, that a Chicago film company, Essanay, signed him.

In 1915 he moved to California, where he worked for Essanay's West Coast studio near San Francisco. He directed a few silent films and acted in the likes of *The Last of the Mohicans* (1920), *The Four Horsemen of the Apocalypse* (1921), and *Robin Hood* (1922). At first he was usually cast as the heavy, but his interpretation of *Richard the Lion-Hearted* (1923) pointed the way for more sympathetic characterizations. From that point on Beery no longer always had to play the bad guy, though he usually played the blustery, sort-of-good bad guy.

Moving on to Paramount and then MGM, he made movies in the 1930s that included *The Big House* (1930; his work won him an Oscar nomination), *The Champ* (1931, with Jackie Cooper; this time he won the year's Academy Award), *Grand Hotel* (1932), *The Bowery* (1933, again with Jackie Cooper), *Treasure Island* (1934), and *Viva Villa* (1934). The hit parade continued into the 1940s, and the last picture he made was *Big Jack* (1949).

When he was not making movies, flying, or carrying out his Navy duties, Beery often headed up to Jackson Hole, Wyoming, where he kept a lodge and enjoyed hunting. He was married (and divorced) twice, first to Gloria Swanson and then to Rita Gilman. He had one child. Wallace Beery died in 1949.

★

# Ed Begley

Considered one of the finest character actors of the 1950s and 1960s, Ed Begley had planned to become an actor since age eleven. It was then that the Irish-issued lad began chatting with actor Edmund Elton, who performed at the Poli Theater in Begley's neighborhood. This was in Hartford, Connecticut, where Ed (born 1901) was one of three offspring in the family of Michael and Hannah Clifford Begley.

Smitten, young Begley began hanging around the theater, helping out, running errands, serving as an extra whenever possible. At age fifteen he competed in and won an acting contest for beginners, but his performing career would not go further until after his Navy service.

He enlisted in 1919, serving first as a musician, then as a hospital corpsman, and finally as a fireman stationed at Newport, Rhode Island.

He was ordered to the coal-burning transport USS *Hancock* (AP-3), where he remained until the ship was taken out of service. His next assignment was to the U.S. Naval Radio Station at Tuckerton, New Jersey. When it was sold to the Radio Corporation of America, orders came for Begley to report to the destroyer USS *Stewart* (DD-224), docked at the Philadelphia Navy Yard. Upon his discharge, he stayed and settled in Philadelphia, with no idea that his future would be so illustrious.

Begley's former ship was also to become notable, in a bizarre way. After a series of mishaps the *Stewart* was scuttled in 1942 at Surabaja, Java. But the Japanese invaders raised and salvaged the destroyer, combining the forward two stacks into one raking funnel and replacing the former pole mast with a tripod mast. The crossbreed ship puzzled U.S. aviators, and in the early days of the Pacific war they reported the possible presence of an American ship deep in Japanese-dominated territory.

The Japanese redesignated the modified *Stewart* Patrol Boat 102, attaching her to the Imperial Fleet. On 24 August 1944, while operating in the South China Sea, the 102 and another Japanese warship, Coastal Defense Ship 22, made sound contact with the American submarine *Harder* (SS-257). After numerous depth-charge attacks by the two Japanese combatants, the *Harder* was sunk with all hands.

After the war the destroyer was found at anchor at the Kure Naval Base; small American flags remained painted on the sides of the bridge, each one signifying a kill. Recommissioned DD-224 in Hiro Wan, Honshu, on 29 October 1945, she was struck from the Navy list in April 1946. Decommissioned, she was sunk shortly thereafter while being used as a target ship for aircraft.

Ed Begley's fate was far cheerier. After his Navy service he worked at a variety of jobs, including milkman, before getting a job in 1931 as a broadcaster at radio station WTIC, Hartford, Connecticut. He worked as another station's announcer from 1940 to 1942 and then moved to New York City. There his career continued to move in a desirable direction. Gradually Ed Begley became a well-known radio actor, playing roles in programs such as *Mr. Keen, Tracer of Lost Persons, The Kate Smith Show, The Philip Morris Playhouse, Charlie Chan, The Aldrich Family,* and the *Fat Man* broadcasts.

He made it onto both stage (beginning in 1943, in Broadway's *Land of Fame*) and screen (starting with 1947's *Boomerang*) and became a renowned actor on both coasts, commuting between the two. The films in which he appeared include *Sitting Pretty* (1948), *Dark City* (1950), *On Dangerous Ground* (1951), and *Lone Star* (1952). In 1957 he played Juror No. 10 in the classic film *Twelve Angry Men,* and he won the 1962 Academy Award for best supporting actor for his rendition of Boss Finley in *Sweet Bird of Youth.*

Begley was married three times, first (in 1922) to Amanda Hoff, the mother of actor Ed Begley, Jr. (who started out in the television series *My Three Sons,* starred in TV's *St. Elsewhere,* and played John "Stumpy" Pepys in 1984's *This Is Spinal Tap*). One of his preferred pastimes was spending time on his Van Nuys, California, ranch with Ed Junior and his three other children. Ed Begley died in 1970.

# Jack Benny

Even before flunking out of high school, Benjamin Kubelsky was not an inspired student. Nothing seemed to motivate him, and his parents despaired that they had raised a loser. Still, he was their child and they loved him, and they helped him as best they knew how. In the end, though, Meyer Kubelsky had to ask Benny not to help out in the family haberdashery business any more, because his dreamy, distant, haphazard way of taking the customers' money was wreaking havoc on the bookkeeping.

A Valentine's Day baby (1894, Chicago), Benny would have been born in Waukegan, just north of the Windy City, but Emma Sachs Kubelsky wanted to give birth in a big city. Benny was the issue of a hard-working immigrant Jewish couple who believed in caring for their own. The one thing the boy could do and loved to do was play the violin—

not masterfully, but competently. Achieving truly fine-musician status would have required much more practice. But Benny hated practicing.

Thankfully, the adolescent was able to land a job playing violin in a pit orchestra at the Barrison, one of two theaters in Waukegan. When it closed, the eighteen-year-old Kubelsky was invited to team up with Cora Salisbury, a pianist. After convincing the senior Kubelskys that she was not going to lead their son down the road to moral degradation and ruination, the pair joined the vaudeville circuit.

The act was well received, and it seemed that Benny had finally found his calling—the entertainment business. About a year later Cora left due to a family illness, but Benny stayed in the business, teaming up with pianist Lyman Woods until 1917. Again the act worked, by now with a bit of comedy added. The only problem was the name Benjamin Kubelsky, which Benny thought too similar to that of an established concert violinist. Accordingly, he changed his name to Ben Benny. This worked until just after World War I, when he realized that once again the name was too close to that of another violinist—Ben Bernie, a longtime entertainer. By this time Benny had been in the Navy, where sailors commonly called each other by the name of Jack. Jack Benny it was.

But the Navy gave him more than just a first name; it was during his military service that Jack Benny discovered he could hold his own onstage as a solo comedian. This happened purely by chance.

He enlisted on 29 May 1918. During his free time at boot camp—Great Lakes Naval Training Station, some thirty miles north of Chicago along Lake Michigan, near Waukegan—Benny and other former show-business sailors would join in playing ragtime music for their shipmates. Saturday-night sessions became a regular event in the base recreation hall. Benny was burdened with a terrible case of stage fright when it came to speaking onstage, an affliction he would never completely overcome, so he would stick to playing the violin and leave the talking to the other entertainers.

One night he launched into a solo he had always had good luck with on the road, "The Rosary." But this straight performance was not going over well with the more raucous audience he now faced, and he was soundly booed almost immediately. He continued playing nevertheless, highly embarrassed. A fellow performer walked out onto the

ADMINISTRATION BLDG. AND DRILL GROUNDS
GREAT LAKES NAVAL STATION, GREAT LAKES, ILL.

(U.S. Naval Historical Center)

### Great Lakes Naval Training Station

Opened in 1911, the Great Lakes Naval Training Station started out with just six hundred recruits, a number that by 1917 had grown to fifteen hundred. At the end of the First World War, the station had been the first stop for more than one hundred thousand recruits.

By March 1944 it was handling sixty-seven thousand. That April the station became Recruit Training Command Great Lakes, processing fresh catches in just ten weeks by the time World War II came to an end. A year later the RTC's population had dropped to ten thousand, only to shoot up again during the Korean War (one hundred thousand from 1951 to 1952).

New construction has regularly spruced the place up and allowed for expansion. Still going strong today, RTC Great Lakes provides the first eight weeks of Navy training to thousands of inductees each year. Following the attainment of their basic skills, about a third of the graduates take advantage of the RTC's Apprentice Training Program, which offers four weeks more of practice and instruction for those who are rated as firemen, seamen, and airmen.

stage, as if it were part of the act, and whispered into Benny's ear that he should put down the fiddle and talk to them.

What could he do? Here he was right on the stage in front of everybody; no place to hide. Benny began to talk. The first thing that came into his mind was some banter from earlier in the day, about the relative size of the Irish navy as compared with the Swiss and Jewish navies. The house exploded in laughter in what would become the beginning of a new, and rather profitable, direction in his career.

The base commander at this time was Capt. William A. Moffett (who later became chief of the Naval Bureau of Aeronautics and met his end on board the Navy dirigible *Akron,* lost off New Jersey amid nighttime thunderstorms on 3–4 April 1933). The Great Lakes Revue was being put together for the purpose of raising money for Navy Relief, which was organized and headed by the captain's wife. Benny and a pianist named Edward Elzear Confrey, or Zez—later a famous performer and the writer of such popular tunes as "Kitten on the Keys"—responded to the Moffetts' call for performers, auditioning for the show as a twosome. They were selected to do a fifteen-minute ragtime routine, which fit in nicely with their plans to put together a postwar vaudeville act; they needed as much practice performing together onstage as they could manage while still in the service.

During rehearsals for the revue, Benny also stumbled into a small part in a sketch, playing the role of the admiral's "disorderly" Izzy There. The part grew as the director became inspired by the violinist's flat, understated delivery, and by the time the show went on the road, Benny was the main comedy feature of the show.

For two weeks Midwesterners were entertained by the Great Lakes Revue, which traveled to several cities and finally to the New Majestic Theatre in Benny's hometown, Waukegan. Benny was acclaimed in the local paper, and Meyer and Emma must have celebrated with at least an extra cup of coffee.

The signing of the Armistice meant to Zez and Benny the beginning of their own vaudeville touring, but that vision of their future was dashed when the Navy would not let Zez go, apparently because there was no other ragtime pianist in the Navy. Benny could not wait forever. Discharged on 30 September 1921, he took the plunge and went onstage by himself, bolstered by his Navy performing experience.

Jack Benny does business with atoll executive officer Commander W. J. Wicks, USNR, in front of a Japanese-constructed building on Majuro atoll, September 1944. Benny is officially agreeing to appear in the "beautiful post-war Biltmore" in the event that it is ever actually built. (U.S. Navy photo)

Benny visits Naval Auxiliary Air Station Twenty-nine Palms, California, in April 1945. (U.S. Navy photo)

He enjoyed steady work throughout the 1920s, including performing at New York's Palace Theater. Already a popular entertainer by 1932, he achieved universal recognition with his weekly radio program, *The Canada Dry Ginger Ale Program* (which underwent several more name incarnations, including *The Jello Program,* before becoming *The Jack Benny Program* in 1944—sponsor, Lucky Strike). Millions of Americans huddled around their sets every week, relishing Benny's unfailingly superb comedy routines. The series lasted for twenty-three years and went on to become a television program, by which time its host had become an American institution.

The violin stayed with him, mostly as a prop; he rarely played it during his monologues and comic routines. A better-than-average player, he often took a ribbing from some of the country's foremost violinists, which did not stop him from joining concert violinist Isaac Stern and the New York Philharmonic Symphony Orchestra in a 1956 fund-raising effort for Carnegie Hall. Even before that enormously successful evening, Jack Benny had given concerts for charity, something he continued to do throughout his life. He also appeared in a number of films; among his hits were *Buck Benny Rides Again* (1940), *Charley's Aunt* (1941), and *To Be or Not to Be* (1942).

When the United States went to war in 1941, Benny was forty-seven, too old for military service. Anxious to contribute in some way, he joined the USO. He toured throughout the States beginning in 1942, flying back to Hollywood once a week to rehearse and do the radio show, and keeping in mind that military humor was based mostly on grousing; he had learned this from his own time in the World War I Navy.

After being asked one time to visit an Army hospital ward, Benny was struck by how much the men there seemed to appreciate the attention. Thereafter he made it a point to request permission to visit a hospital wherever he was, and he would put on a spontaneous show or just walk around, talking, laughing, and visiting with the patients.

His first overseas USO tour started in July 1943. He and a group of performers such as harmonica player Larry Adler, singer Wini Shaw, actress Anna Lee, and pianist Jack Snyder blazed in ten weeks through the European and African theaters on a thirty-two-thousand-mile trip, often putting on four shows a day. The next summer Benny and another troupe, which included actress Carole Landis, went island-hopping in a seventy-thousand-mile jaunt across the Pacific, giving performances at outposts, bases, airfields, and hospitals. Benny continued to contribute his professional services until the war ended, doing the same during the Korean conflict.

He was married to Sadye Marks in 1927. Under the name Mary Livingstone, she joined her husband on the radio and television as the needling but adoring secretary. She stayed for the next twenty years and became as integral a part of the show as the character of Rochester (played by costar Eddie Anderson) and the theme of Benny's long-running feud with another radio-show star, Fred Allen. Jack and Mary's was a lifetime union that produced one child, Joan, who provided them with several grandchildren. Jack Benny passed away in 1974.

# Humphrey Bogart

Far from growing up a street tough and even more famous today than when he was alive, Humphrey DeForest Bogart was the product (in 1899) of prominent New Yorkers Belmont DeForest Bogart, a surgeon, and Maud Humphrey, a magazine illustrator whose teachers included Whistler in Paris. The Bogarts' Upper West Side home was not all ease, though the family was comfortable financially. Maud was emotionally distant, a workaholic with little time for love; Dad had troubles too, and would eventually (after his son was grown and independent) end up addicted to morphine and in debt.

At age thirteen the future Bogie was sent to Trinity School, one of New York's institutions for gentlemen-in-training. There he showed early evidence of his penchant for flouting authority; he insisted on wearing a frowned-upon hat to school every day, imposing his own touch of individuality on the dress code. For this and other offenses, such as refusing to study German, Latin, and other subjects that were not of interest to him, the young rebel was invited regularly into the headmaster's office for mostly fruitless discussion.

Destined in his parents' master plan to go to Yale, in 1917 he was shipped off to the prep school Phillips Academy in Andover, Massachusetts, where his father had gone before him. The budding troublemaker did not much care for it there either, and of course he made no effort to hide his feelings. By the end of his first year it was suggested that he might be happier with another school's curriculum.

What to do next? It was spring 1918 when Humphrey arrived home in New York, and the country was at war. Many young men were anxious to join the fighting overseas and show the Huns a thing or two; to Humphrey Bogart, it sounded like a grand adventure. He would probably get to go to Paris, meet some French girls. . . . Soon after returning from school, Humphrey went down to the receiving ship USS *Granite State* and joined the Navy, officially ending his formal schooling.

He did not have to travel far for his training; he was ordered to the Naval Reserve Training Station in Pelham Park, New York. Graduating with a coxswain rating, he was next ordered to the USS *Leviathan* (SP-1326), the largest American troopship. The brand-new sailor reported on 27 November, more than two weeks after the war had ended.

The *Leviathan* was an ex-German passenger liner, Germany's largest, built by Blohm and Voss in Hamburg and originally named *Vaterland*. She was launched on 13 April 1913. When the United States entered World War I, on 6 April 1917, the U.S. Shipping Board seized her at Hoboken, New Jersey. The ship was turned over to the Navy in June and commissioned in July. Renamed in September, the *Leviathan* operated between Hoboken, Brest, and Liverpool. Until the Armistice was signed on 11 November 1918, the ship steamed back and forth across the Atlantic, ten round trips in all, carrying more than 119,000 troops.

It may have been while Bogart was attached to the *Leviathan* that an incident occurred that was to affect his image on the screen after

Humphrey Bogart's World War I ship was the USS *Leviathan* (SP-1326), but the young sailor missed the war. (U.S. Naval Historical Center)

leaving the service. As anyone knows who has watched his time-honored performances, Bogart talked as if his upper lip was paralyzed, and there was always a slight lisp. There are many explanations for this mannerism.

According to one story, a piece of shrapnel cut his mouth when he was at the wheel of the *Leviathan,* under fire from a U-boat. This would have been an interesting occurrence more than two weeks after the Armistice. In another version of events, Bogart was ordered to take a U.S. Navy prisoner to Portsmouth Naval Prison, New Hampshire. The two traveled side by side, with the prisoner handcuffed. As they changed trains in Boston, the con asked Bogart for a Lucky Strike, a supply of which Bogie always had and was happy to share. As he dug for matches, suddenly his ungrateful companion smashed him in the mouth with his manacles and jumped up to escape. Bogart, his upper lip badly torn and bleeding, reacted quickly, drawing out his .45 automatic and dropping the prisoner. Initial Navy surgery on the lip was badly botched, and subsequent plastic surgery did not help.

However it really happened, the sailor was permanently scarred. But he was also left with a distinctive screen trademark that made him appear especially sinister in his numerous gangster roles.

His rebellious spirit got him into other scrapes of his own making: he talked back to officers (with predictable results), took unauthorized leave (which landed him in the brig), and complained about his sentence (which increased it). Tales of the feisty Bogart abound, not without a firm foundation in fact.

In February 1919 he was transferred from the *Leviathan* to another transport, the USS *Santa Olivia* (SP-3125). For reasons unknown—late-night partying, probably—he missed his ship when she sailed from Hoboken for Europe in April. Bogart promptly surrendered to the port's naval authorities and was ordered to New York, to report to the receiving ship. He thus avoided being listed as a deserter, and his offense was recorded as a mere AWOL, for which he was awarded three days' solitary confinement on bread and water.

The spunky enlistee finally got out of the Navy with an honorable discharge on 18 June 1919. He had made it to seaman second class, with performance reports rating him above average in proficiency (3.0 on a scale of 1.0 to 4.0) and superior (4.0) in sobriety and obedience.

What to do next? Back in New York, Maud complained about his lack of direction, as usual. His father, with friends in various businesses including the National Biscuit Company and a Wall Street brokerage firm, tried to help. But Humphrey disliked business. He tried, but he did not last long at any of the jobs that were found for him. He preferred hanging out with his pals, riding horses, sailing, drinking, and smoking. He was a fun-loving socializer and a mischievous prankster and would remain one for the rest of his life. But this did not keep him from also loving his work, once he finally found it, or from becoming a professional, devoted, hardworking actor.

One day he hatched the idea of approaching the father of a friend for a job, because he was fed up with his current position—running messages around New York City on the subway. The friend's father, William S. Brady, owned a stage company and a film studio, and Humphrey Bogart's work for him represented the beginning of his acting career.

After being promoted to assistant stage manager, Bogart's performing debut came during a rehearsal, when he filled in for the indisposed juvenile lead. Despite the poor quality of this first attempt, he was hooked. In 1920 he landed his first part, in a Brady road production of *The Ruined Lady*. He first appeared on a New York stage two years later in *Drifting*, and he continued to perform in plays for the next thirteen years.

He began getting small parts in movies only in the late 1920s, and the general public became aware of his existence when he appeared as vicious killer Duke Mantee in the 1936 film version of *The Petrified Forest*. After more than fifteen years of working full-time in the business, Humphrey Bogart's name was known in Hollywood.

In 1943 he and third wife Mayo Methot traveled to North Africa with the USO in an effort to do their bit for the boys overseas, but the couple's performances were apparently not as entertaining as their offstage fights. Although they shared a genuine affection, the hard-drinking duo frequently fell into disharmony. Their disagreements were loud and sometimes featured displays such as door-banging and object-throwing. The USO's enthusiasm for husband-and-wife teams may have dwindled after the Bogart experience.

Back in California, Humphrey continued to do his bit by joining the Coast Guard Auxiliary and reporting for duty once a week, in Balboa. It was here that he began meeting secretly with Lauren Bacall, whom he met on the set of *To Have and Have Not* in 1944, when his alliance with Mayo had suffered through all but the final battles. He and Bacall were married in 1945, his fourth and final marriage. They had two children.

Bogart and Bacall were liberal Democrats, supported both FDR and Harry Truman, and initially opposed the efforts of the House Committee on Un-American Activities to identify communists within the movie industry, although they later recanted. Like his character Rick in *Casablanca* (which won him a 1943 Academy nod), Bogart was in no way a political activist or the advocate of any particular cause, but he spoke up and took sides when he felt it had to be done.

At the time he made *Casablanca,* his only affiliation with the military was chess games that he played with servicemen through the mail. But the Moroccan story would have lasting significance to its countless viewers as an anti-Nazi statement. It opened not more than two weeks after the Allies had landed in North Africa; and just as the movie's circulation increased, FDR, Churchill, and Gen. Charles de Gaulle were attending a well-publicized summit meeting in Casablanca. Good timing for the studio, this sequence of real-life wartime events also established Bogart as a lasting symbol of resistance to fascism.

He will always be remembered for classics such as *High Sierra* (1941), *The Maltese Falcon* (1941), *Casablanca* (1942), *To Have and Have Not* (1944), *The Big Sleep* (1946), *The Treasure of the Sierra Madre* (1948), and *The African Queen* (1951, for which he won the Academy Award for best actor). Among his most memorable roles was that of the unstable Captain Queeg in *The Caine Mutiny* (1954; it won him another best-actor nomination).

Cracking jokes almost until the end, Humphrey Bogart died in 1957.

★

# Pat O'Brien

"I'm going to tell you something I've kept to myself for years. None of you ever knew George Gipp. He was long before your time, but you all know what a tradition he is at Notre Dame. And the last thing he said to me, 'Rock,' he said, 'some time when the team's up against it, breaks are beatin' the boys, tell them to go out there with all they've got, win just one for the Gipper. I don't know where I'll be then,' he said, 'but I'll know about it, and I'll be happy.'"

With these words Pat O'Brien, in the role of the famous Notre Dame coach in the 1940 film *Knute Rockne, All American,* urged his team at halftime to charge out onto the field.

The real-life George Gipp, a standout player for Notre Dame, succumbed to complications from pneumonia in 1920. Eight years later, when his team faced what they feared was an invincible Army team, coach Rockne delivered his famous locker-room speech. The final score was Notre Dame 12, Army 6, and the next day the *New York Daily News* ran the headline, "Gipp's Ghost Beat Army." (Ronald Reagan played Gipp in the movie, hence his later well-known presidential slogan "Win one for the Gipper.")

After his portrayal of Rockne, O'Brien was in constant demand for talks at dinners and public affairs, where he gladly reenacted his scene. A leading actor of the 1930s and 1940s, he may always be best remembered for this performance, but his film career spanned nearly four decades, during which he appeared in scores of movies. O'Brien played Irishmen—priests, cops, reporters, politicians, servicemen. But before he broke into the film world, he served in the Navy at the close of World War I. And though he never left the Great Lakes Naval Training Station, O'Brien was a hardworking sailor.

William Joseph Patrick O'Brien was born in Milwaukee, Wisconsin, on 11 November 1899. An only child, he was raised by loving parents who sent him to parochial schools and made their home a favorite place for the kids to come for visiting and for some of his mother's famous doughnuts. The boys were also drawn to O'Brien Senior, who was a regular participant in their games and played baseball with them on weekends. In an ironic harbinger of days to come, the adolescent O'Brien worked on the grounds crew that marked the football field at Marquette University, and among the games played in 1913 was one with Notre Dame—starting end, Knute Rockne.

Bill O'Brien also served as an altar boy, which was no casual commitment. Altar boys had to be proven devout Catholics and could never arrive late; their hands had to be clean, and they had to know their Latin by heart. All of this was probably useful training for his later life, when O'Brien the actor had to learn lines and became known for his agreeable, highly professional comportment, not to mention his ability to rattle off dialogue faster than almost anyone else.

The high school of choice for Milwaukee Catholics was the local, costly, Marquette Academy, and O'Brien was certain he would never be able to pass the test qualifying him for a scholarship. But as luck had it, the year he was to apply, the scholarship was being sponsored by the Ancient Order of Hibernians. This gave the crafty O'Brien the idea of appealing to a common heritage, and in an earnest scholarly attempt

Ex-Navyman and actor Pat O'Brien and President Ronald Reagan greet each other at the May 1981 commencement exercises at Notre Dame University. In 1940, they costarred in the movie *Knute Rockne, All American,* with O'Brien as Knute and Reagan as George Gipp ("the Gipper"), standout Notre Dame football player. (Bettman)

(which was also calculated to have emotional impact) he made the voyage to the town library and composed a lengthy treatise on Irish history, concluding with the observation that the Ancient Order of Hibernians had been critical in helping kids like himself to get an education.

It did the trick, much to his friends' surprise. Bill O'Brien not only went to high school, he did well there. He also went out for baseball and football, and while not becoming exactly a star player, he did continue to enjoy the games, despite a few mishaps such as hitting a friend in the head with a baseball while pitching. The friend eventually came to, apparently none the worse for the experience, but O'Brien would never agree to pitch again.

In 1917 Spencer Tracy enrolled in the academy, and he and O'Brien became buddies as World War I raged on in Europe. American lives had been lost on the British merchant ship *Lusitania,* sunk by the German submarine U-20 on 7 May 1915; American ships had been lost to U-boats in 1917. On 6 April 1917, President Woodrow Wilson asked a joint session of Congress to declare war on Germany, which was promptly enacted.

A patriotic fervor swept the country, with Liberty Bond drives under way, bands playing, and soldiers and sailors marching through the streets en route to the war in Europe. Many who enlisted were just seventeen years old and had to get their parents' consent to join up. This consent did not often come easily, as one might imagine, but usually the forms were signed, even if also splashed with tears. O'Brien enlisted on 5 August 1918 and was on his way to war—or so he thought.

He was ordered to boot-camp training at the Great Lakes Naval Training Station. At the time there were about eighty-two thousand boots going through the camp, and the young enlistees soon learned through rumors that they might never see the war: it could all be over before they had even completed their training. But even without the promise of combat, the boys applied themselves assiduously to their tasks, learning to be gunner's mates and gunners, and carrying out whatever other chores they were ordered to do. They also spent their fair share of time swabbing office decks and shining brass. There was plenty of singing as well. In those days, both in and out of the military, people would commonly sing together in their spare time. In the Navy, someone might pull a harmonica out of his pocket, and soon others would join in on songs such as "Over There," "Good-bye Broadway, Hello France," "Pack up Your Troubles," and "Tipperary."

Meanwhile, the world around them was in the process of painful, complicated, and permanent change, as a growing global awareness increasingly affected everyday lives. In this environment, Bill O'Brien began to mature. He earned a spot on the Navy football team and quickly found that participating in sports got him more liberties, which he gladly took. But one Christmas he discovered that he had already taken too much time off—no going home for the holidays. Fortunately he had a good friend with extra leave time, and the commandant agreed to let him give it to O'Brien.

The end of World War I came on his nineteenth birthday, 11 November 1918, but O'Brien stayed in the Navy until 1921. Honorably discharged, his first task was to finish high school. During his absence, Marquette Academy had organized an ROTC, and students went to class in uniform. But the stubborn O'Brien refused to wear it, insisting that he be allowed to continue wearing his seaman second-class blues. After a predictable commotion, the school granted permission for O'Brien to attend classes in his U.S. Navy uniform. Wearing his blues, he proudly accepted his high-school diploma. He next attended Marquette University, but his heart was not in his studies. He made the university football team and played behind Red Dunne, the first all-American at Marquette. He participated actively in sports and fraternities (of which he joined two), but what held his interest most was the theater.

With no clear idea whence sprung this ambition, O'Brien nonetheless knew clearly that the stage was where he wanted to be, and visits to New York City only fueled his excitement over the idea. As a child he had practiced in front of the mirror, creating expressions for various characters he had invented, trying to imagine how an actor remembered all the words he was supposed to say. Later he entered elocution contests and acted in school plays, all the while developing an inkling that he might be more talented than the others. But now his dramatic interest took on a whole new grown-up dimension. He starred in the university's production of *Charley's Aunt*, his first lead role, working in whatever theater productions he could and looking for a way to get back to New York. With the help of his parents, who contacted and coaxed their congressman, he found a way in the form of a servicemen's educational allowance that paid for his enrollment in New York's Sargent's School of Drama.

Rooming with Spencer Tracy, who had also come to New York to pursue the acting profession, O'Brien joined the throngs of unknowns waiting for bit-part auditions while surviving on the cheapest food they could find, comforting each other with their mere presence. In the end, most would settle for other, more secure work, but O'Brien and Tracy never gave up. After his studies, O'Brien found work in a New Jersey stock company, the Plainfield Players, at fifty dollars a week. By 1925 he was appearing on Broadway, and in 1930 he was offered a role in *The Front Page* (1931), which took him to Hollywood. He remained

After the final 1965 curtain call for their performances in the play *Mister Roberts,* Hugh O'Brian and Pat O'Brien present a two-thousand-hour certificate and a C-130 model to Lt. Comdr. Frank Achille. Achille was the first West Coast naval aviator to spend that much time flying the aircraft; he had logged the hours carrying supplies to South Vietnam for the Military Air Transport Service. (U.S. Naval Historical Center)

in show business throughout his professional life, appearing—often as the star—in some eighty-five movies, including *Devil Dogs of the Air* (1935), *China Clipper* (1936), *Having Wonderful Crime* (1945), *Man Alive* (1945), *The Last Hurrah* (1958, starring Spencer Tracy), and *Ragtime* (1981). In 1960–61 he starred in the television sitcom *Harrigan and Son*.

During World War II, O'Brien traveled with the USO in the Caribbean and to North Africa and the Far East. By the 1950s he had moved his parents and his wife's parents to California, where he supported all three homes. A man of strong religious convictions, Pat O'Brien took great pleasure in his family, relaxing with athletic games such as handball. His lifetime marriage to actress Eloise Taylor (whom he married in 1931) produced four children; he died in 1983.

# Spencer Tracy

S pencer Tracy—winner of two Academy Awards (for *Captains Courageous*, 1937, and *Boys' Town*, 1938) and nominated nine times for his brilliant performances in films such as *Bad Day at Black Rock* (1955), *Inherit the Wind* (1960), *Judgment at Nuremberg* (1961), and *Guess Who's Coming to Dinner* (1967)—served in the Navy during World War I. Along with his brother Carroll and pal Bill (Pat) O'Brien, Tracy signed up to give the kaiser a thrashing, but he wound up getting not much farther than boot camp at the Great Lakes Naval Training Station.

He enlisted on 14 May 1918. Like the other boots, Tracy drilled, stood watches, scrubbed pots and pans, polished brass, and diligently learned all there was to know about the Navy. Since childhood he had had a gift for memorizing the written word, so remembering Navy rules and regulations was a breeze for him. His aptitude was to prove an invaluable asset during his acting career: he could memorize an entire script overnight.

Seaman Tracy was eventually transferred away from his buddies to the Norfolk Navy Yard, where he spent several months performing the same mundane duties. He may have been bored, but there was no getting out of this adventure, and he faced for perhaps the first time in his life the sobering reality that he was in it until his tour of duty was up.

At the time, his problems with alcohol may not yet have begun to interfere with his job. Later in his career, though, if he was off the wagon Tracy might disappear for weeks in the middle of shooting a movie. During these binges he could become violent, and in any case was often not the same man as when sober (he was known for moodiness even when not drinking, though generally people loved working with this consummate professional, who disliked rehearsals but never missed a beat, working mistakes into the performance). He was fully aware of the nature of his disease and fought it throughout his life with increasing success, managing, on his own, to stay away from spirits for years at a time. By the time Alcoholics Anonymous was in its fledgling stages (1935) he could have sought support there, but to attend one of those meetings would have meant public exposure, which was out of the question from a professional point of view and still taboo socially, and AA may not have been Tracy's kind of place anyway.

Secrecy came naturally to Tracy, who allowed not even those closest to him—including his longtime unofficial partner, Katharine Hepburn—to see whatever demons tortured his soul. He was born in 1900 in Milwaukee to John and Carrie Brown Tracy. A feisty boy who always seemed to be fighting, both in and out of school, Spence mellowed slightly as he grew up. He got involved in baseball and boxing; he joined the Boy Scouts and served in the Catholic church as an altar boy. But the anger was still there, and he continued to pull periodic disappearing acts on his fretting parents.

The complex young man eventually enrolled in Marquette Academy. There he became close friends with fellow student Bill O'Brien, who regaled him with tales of actors' lives. There also he became seriously involved for the first time in his religion. He seemed to be on a clear-cut path to the priesthood when he put all career plans on hold and enlisted in the Navy.

Following his 23 February 1919 release from active duty—he was honorably discharged as a seaman second class on 30 September 1921—Tracy enrolled at Northwestern Military and Naval Academy at Lake Geneva, Wisconsin. From there he went on to Ripon College, also in Wisconsin, where he lasted just long enough (year and eighty-nine days) for his future profession to take hold of him. This happened via the school's one and only acting teacher, who noticed Tracy because he looked more mature than the usual children he was forced to cast in men's parts. The professor invited him to audition. Tracy memorized the script and auditioned without reading, delivering his lines in an effortlessly projected adult voice. He played the lead, was applauded immediately by the school's newspaper, and of course appeared in other school productions.

Spencer Tracy was off to a good start, with the enthusiastic assistance of his professor, who wrote to New York City's American Academy of Dramatic Arts recommending that they interview this exceptional student. Another scriptless performance got Tracy accepted forthwith. He quit Ripon and moved to New York in April 1922. O'Brien was also in New York studying acting, and the two pooled their scanty resources.

After his course, Tracy found work with a stock company and was on his way, but nearly ten years would pass before he rose to fame. In 1930 his performance as a convicted killer on death row in the play *The Last Mile* caused a critical flurry. This propelled him to Hollywood in the company of director John Ford, who had been on a New York scouting tour. In California Tracy appeared with another newcomer, Humphrey Bogart, in *Up the River* (1930); it was the beginning of an enduring friendship. Fox Film Corporation offered him a long-term contract, which he turned down, saying he had to return to New York to finish the run of *The Last Mile*. After that he returned to Hollywood and signed with Fox, in the start of a career that took him on to MGM in 1935.

By the time the United States entered World War II in 1941, Spencer Tracy, now forty-one years old, was a giant among Hollywood stars and the father of two children. He and actress Louise Treadwell had

Tracy (second from left, front) supported the World War II effort through activities such as visiting naval bases. After making the rounds of the naval hospitals on Oahu, he relaxed with men of the fleet who were on R and R after months at sea. (U.S. Navy photo)

married in 1928 and were to remain lifelong friends, even after their marriage had disintegrated. Tracy did not serve in the military, but he supported the war effort through activities such as working at the Hollywood Canteen, visiting hospitals and naval bases, making radio broadcasts (including for the show *Command Performance*), and narrating short films for the Office of War Information. In 1944 he toured naval bases in Wisconsin and became the mascot of the submarine *Icefish* (SS-367), which sank two Japanese cargo ships that same year. Spencer Tracy went on to live out a prolific career, known for his strong presence and his versatility as an actor. He was able to enjoy being acclaimed during his lifetime as a great American actor. Tracy performed in over seventy movies before his passing in 1967.

★

## PART 3

# World War II

After World War I, Americans were anxious not to become embroiled in another conflict that would take away their boys and sap their national resources. But isolationism was no longer possible, especially for one of the world's greatest industrial powers. The globe had already become more of an international community, and what happened in one part of it inevitably impacted all of the others. When the United States officially entered World War II on 7 December 1941, it had already been committing money, materiel, and manpower to the Allied cause in the European theater.

# Harry Belafonte

A New York City native (1927), Harold George Belafonte, Jr., moved at age five to Jamaica, then still part of the British West Indies. His mother, Melvine Love Belafonte, had been born there—his father, Harold, a chef, was originally from Martinique—and Harry Junior was sent to live with relatives for seven years. There he became immersed in the colorful West Indian culture, with its close community spirit and its swaying, pulsing, melodic folk music.

Returning to New York in 1940, Harry was sent to a Catholic elementary school and then on to George Washington High School. In the city he had to defend himself more than once, living as he did in an area of Harlem that had its share of ruffians. He got into fights easily but would never carry a weapon, perhaps partly because of his deep sense of spirituality.

In 1943 he quit school and enlisted in the Navy. Because of his high IQ scores, Belafonte was sent to a Navy V-12 officers' training program. This program offered an accelerated college curriculum followed by a commission in the U.S. Navy. Officially put in operation on 1 July 1943, its purpose was to ensure a constant stream of highly qualified officers who could meet Navy and Marine Corps requirements. There were 131 colleges and universities selected for the V-12 program, and by 1946, sixty thousand men had completed it. Depending on how much college one had already completed, commissions were awarded anywhere from eight months to two years after beginning the program.

However, during World War II black Americans were generally not allowed to do much. Racism was still rampant and openly accepted, in the Navy as elsewhere, and Belafonte suffered from its unfairness along with other servicemen who were of African lineage. By the time he enlisted, blacks no longer had to serve only as cooks or waiters, but they were commanded by white officers who for the most part looked upon their assignment as some sort of punishment. Profoundly disturbed by the racial prejudice he repeatedly encountered, both in the Navy and in civilian life, Harry Belafonte was honorably discharged after twenty-eight months of service.

Two positive changes resulted from his time in the Navy: he met future psychologist Marguerite Byrd, who in 1948 would become his first wife, and he benefited from the GI Bill. After his naval service he returned to New York, where he worked in an apartment building as a maintenance man. One of the tips he received was in the form of two theater tickets, to a Negro Ensemble Theatre Company. He had seen countless movies but never before a theater performance. Even though this turned out not to be a good one, it was enough to convince the young Belafonte that this was what he should be doing. He joined the theater group and the Dramatic Workshop, the training ground of others such as Tony Curtis and Walter Matthau. He also continued to work, pushing a cart through the streets of the garment district.

Belafonte worked hard, both at his acting and at his job. Relaxation time often found him at a jazz club on Broadway called the Royal Roost. It was here that he made his professional debut. Remembering hearing Belafonte in a Dramatic Workshop production, the owner asked him if he would like to audition. This led to a two-week engagement,

(U.S. Naval Historical Center)

## The USS *Metha Nelson*

The *Metha Nelson,* a 156-foot wooden-hulled schooner, built in 1896 by H. D. Hendrixsen in Eureka, California, was never paid for her on-screen work, even though she played a critical role in numerous movies. Charles Laughton walked her decks as Captain Bligh, who made life a relentless hell for Mr. Christian (Clark Gable) and the ship's crew in the 1935 version of *Mutiny on the Bounty.* In other films, pirates manned her guns and slashed at enemies from her masts and riggings. Errol Flynn commanded her as an Irish physician forced to become a pirate in *Captain Blood* (1935, with Olivia de Havilland and Basil Rathbone). The movie proved to be a star-making showcase for the swashbuckler Flynn, but what did the ship get out of it? She went to war.

Originally the *Metha Nelson* had hauled cargo, mostly lumber, from Maine to Singapore. Later outfitted for a treasure-hunting cruise, she was eventually laid up with many other aging schooners in a backwater of the Los Angeles harbor, until movie studios expressed the need for an old-time sailing vessel. In 1942 MGM purchased the ship, after which the Navy bought and overhauled her at Craig Shipyard in Long Beach.

Complete with engine room, signal bridge, and magnetic compass, the *Metha Nelson* (IX-74) was placed in service in September 1943. Her wartime responsibilities were to act as a pilot ship and to identify all ships that trafficked in and out of Los Angeles. On 25 September 1945 she was placed out of service; the next month she was struck from the Navy Register and turned over to the War Shipping Administration. The *Metha Nelson* was resold to her former owner, having well served both the silver screen and her country.

which went on for twenty weeks more, followed by a tour around the country and then two years of singing in clubs nationwide.

By the time he opened in Los Angeles, the sensual, princely-looking, deep-voiced singer was a hit. His became a phenomenal success story. He was seen in movies including *Bright Road* (1953), *Carmen Jones* (1954), and *Island in the Sun* (1959), and on Broadway in the musical *John Murray Anderson's Almanac* (1953–54; he won several awards for best male supporting performance). He appeared in the television series *Sugar Hill Times* (1949) and in several TV specials, including *Tonight with Harry Belafonte* (1959). His records sold in ever-increasing numbers as the strains of Harry Belafonte's Calypso ballads grew in popularity and crossed oceans.

He and his second wife, Julie—formerly a dancer, she later turned to designing costumes—moved to New York's Upper West Side in 1957. This relocation was no easy feat; at the time, their interracial marriage raised such a ruckus, even in the allegedly more broadminded city, that only Eleanor Roosevelt's newspaper-column public appeal in their behalf was able to get results.

Aside from singing, Belafonte has spent the years lending his support to people in whom he has believed, such as the Rev. Martin Luther King, Jr., and to organizations such as UNICEF. He has also continued to star in movies, including *Saturday Night* (1974), *White Man's Burden* (1995, with John Travolta), and *Kansas City* (1996). And Harry Belafonte enjoys the company of his four children, one of whom runs his production company.

# Ernest Borgnine

E rnest Borgnine's universally acclaimed characters have included the cruel Sergeant Fatso in *From Here to Eternity* (1953, with Burt Lancaster, Frank Sinatra, and Montgomery Clift); the vicious goon in *Bad Day at Black Rock* (1955, with Spencer Tracy); the lonesome Bronx butcher in search of love in *Marty* (1955, with Betsy Blair), a performance that won him an Oscar as best actor of the year; and the cunning general in *The Dirty Dozen* (1967). He has dozens of superb films to his credit as well as television shows, notably as the star of the popular series *McHale's Navy* (1962–66).

Born Ermes Effron Borgnino in January 1917 in Hamden, Connecticut, the actor is the son of Italian immigrants and the grandson of Count Paolo Boselli, who shared his apparently abundant financial wisdom with King Victor Emmanuel of Italy. Borgnine graduated

In the 1930s, Ernest Borgnine served on board the USS *Lamberton* (DD-119), which towed targets out of San Diego. This photo of the ship's company includes Seaman Borgnine in the fourth row, second from the left. (Ernest Borgnine collection)

from New Haven's high school in 1935 and worked a stint selling vegetables off the back of a truck before enlisting. It was while he was pondering his future as a vegetable salesman (at the same time fully aware of how lucky he was to have a job in these lean years) that Borgnine's gaze fell upon a U.S. Navy recruiting poster. Not long thereafter he was in the Navy, an experience that he still credits with making a man out of him. It also provided a fertile atmosphere for the development of his future character in television's *McHale's Navy*.

The apprentice seaman remained in the Navy for ten years (including one hiatus), from October 1935 to October 1941 and then from January 1942 to September 1945. His first tour was served on board the four-stacker USS *Lamberton* (DD-119). During the 1930s the *Lamberton* operated out of San Diego, towing targets for surface combatants, submarines, and aircraft, a role that was to serve her well during World War II. She also participated in experimental minesweeping exercises and was redesignated DMS-1 (minesweeper, destroyer) in November 1940.

In 1941 Borgnine left the Navy, only to reenlist after Pearl Harbor. From January 1942 until the end of the war he served in the USS *Sylph*

Borgnine's World War II ship was the USS *Sylph* (PY-12), which patrolled for U-boats and tested new equipment. (U.S. Naval Historical Center)

(PY-12), a converted yacht devoted to antisubmarine-warfare activities throughout the war. Operating first out of Tompkinsville (New York) and then New London (Connecticut), the *Sylph* patrolled for German U-boats during 1942, a devastating year for American merchantmen off the East Coast. In the fall of 1943 she was assigned to Quonset Point, Rhode Island, and a year later to the naval base at Port Everglades, Florida, along with her unit, the surface division of the Atlantic Fleet's Antisubmarine Development Detachment. She was used mainly for training sonarmen and testing and researching new sound and antisubmarine equipment. The *Sylph* and her unit contributed greatly to the U.S. victory over Germany's vaunted undersea gray wolves.

During his naval service Borgnine rose in rank from seaman to gunner's mate first class. Upon his discharge in 1945, he was allowed to wear the American Campaign Medal, the Good Conduct Medal, the American Defense Service Medal with Fleet Clasp, and the World War II Victory Medal.

He returned to New Haven but could not muster any enthusiasm for the life of factory work that seemed to loom before him. He seriously considered reenlisting in the Navy, but finally, encouraged by his mother, he decided to give show business a whirl. A logical choice, he concluded, as he had always liked to ham it up.

A friend of the Blue Angels, Borgnine was honored with a plaque from the team in 1957, aboard the *Boxer* (CVA-21). (U.S. Naval Historical Center)

The GI Bill gave Borgnine the means to pursue his education, and he studied for six months at the Randall School of Dramatic Art in Hartford. Next, in the spring of 1946, he was off to the Barber Theater in Abingdon, Virginia, for some real-life experience. He wound up staying there for four years, working at whatever was needed at the moment—driving, scenery-painting, various stagehand chores. At last he persuaded his higher-ups to let him get on the stage during a performance, and there he remained. After appearing in numerous plays throughout the following few months, the budding actor decided it was time to move on to New York.

The city greeted him with its customary indifference, and Borgnine had his share of tough times before getting a part on Broadway in the play *Harvey,* in the role of a hospital worker. This led to other theater work, including the role of Guildenstern in a production of *Hamlet* that traveled to Denmark and Germany to entertain U.S. servicemen.

After appearing in several more plays as well as television programs, one of which was *Captain Video,* Borgnine landed his first work in movies, *China Corsair* (1951). Now it was time for Hollywood, but by now he had also been typecast as a villain. Several fine roles resulted, including *From Here to Eternity* (1953), before his performance in *Marty* (1955) proved definitively that Ernest Borgnine was a versatile actor. After winning the Academy's best-actor award in 1955, his future was secure. His work in *All Quiet on the Western Front* (1979, costarring Richard Thomas) helped win that movie an Emmy nomination.

Big, friendly, and endowed with a Latin gusto for everyday life, Borgnine is known for his amiability and lack of pretention. The father of three children, he has been married since 1972 to Tova Traesnaes. He was wed four times previously; his renowned 1964 third marriage was to Ethel Merman.

Borgnine continues to make movies and television shows; in 1995–97 he played a doorman in the sitcom *The Single Guy.* He still corresponds with some of his old Navy pals, and as an honorary flight leader of the Blue Angels, he often takes the team to dinner when they fly into Naval Air Station Point Mugu, California.

# Frank "Junior" Coghlan

He tried to drop the childish nickname later in his career, when he wanted to be thought of as a grown-up actor, but by that time Junior Coghlan—né Francis E. Coghlan, unbeknownst to him until his enlistment in the U.S. Navy—had already been a child star of the silent screen, his name too easily recognizable, his agents reasoned, to risk changing it. In 1919, when he was just three years old, his parents, intrigued by the continual comments about how cute he was, wondered if they might be able to turn it into cash. It would not even involve a nonexistent travel fund to find out, as the family had recently moved to Los Angeles, near Edendale, the site of several movie studios. His dad, Frank, had immediately started to pick up work as an extra when he was not in his office at the Southern Pacific Railroad, and he had been able to convince his wife, Katherine Coyle, to go down to the studios with him. Soon she was working, too.

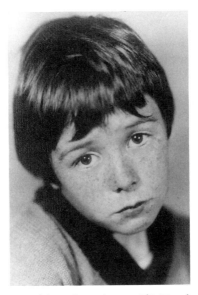

Child film star Junior Coghlan, "homeless waif" (Frank Coghlan collection)

Both Coghlans had completed high school and had been working for the New York, New Haven, and Hartford Railroad when they had met, back in Connecticut. During World War I, Frank spent a year enlisted as a cook and was discharged as a mess sergeant, after which the family came west. There they joined Frank's brother, sister, and mother, who had moved there for the kinder climate. Eventually the Coghlans shared a property, with Frank and his family living in the smaller house behind the yard that separated the two dwellings, the future star's childhood playground.

Katherine was unsure about this business of her baby being in movies, but she took him to one studio, Garson, and registered him anyway. They cast him in *Mid-Channel* (1920, starring Clara Kimball Young), where he was the youngest person on the set. When he was paid three dollars for his first day's work, his mother finally consented to registering him at several studios as well as at the employment agency for actors, Central Casting.

By this time Frank and his brother, Harry, had decided to become trained as chiropractors, and it would be Junior's steady work in movies that funded his dad's schooling. The boy was glad to do it, for he was taking to this new experience like a fish to water. During the following four years he got to play not only on the studios' sets with the other actors but also on location in settings he had never been to before. He especially looked forward to eating the boxed lunches, which he thought of as having a picnic every day.

At age five he began getting full-fledged roles—not that the bit parts he continued to play were such bad work, either. He appeared in three of the early *Our Gang* comedies (1922) and in movies featuring Adolphe Menjou, Pola Negri, Wallace Beery, ZaSu Pitts, and Sally Rand, among many others. He was directed by Charlie Chaplin in *A Woman of Paris* (1923), and until 1943, not a year passed in which Junior Coghlan did not appear in a film. That was when he went into the Navy.

After playing a major role in *Mike* (1926), he was signed to a five-year contract in 1925 with MGM and worked under director Cecil B. de Mille, turning out movies with Carole Lombard, Gloria Swanson, Robert Armstrong, and company. When his contract ended in 1930 he continued to work, and before getting into World War II he had appeared in more than a hundred films, including *Gone with the Wind* (1939; he played a bit part as a Confederate soldier who collapses) and the twelve-episode series *The Adventures of Captain Marvel* (1941). His interpretation of Billy Batson, the lad who said the magic word *Shazam* and was immediately transformed into "the world's mightiest mortal," still gets him invited to comic-book conventions today. By the time he made the transition from silent films to talkies (1930), Junior Coghlan already had more than ten years of experience in the business.

When World War II began officially for Americans, Frank Junior was deferred from the draft, for he was by now the only source of income for Katherine, the two having finally fled his increasingly alcoholic and abusive father. However, as war raged around the world, the twenty-six-year-old Coghlan knew that his deferment could not last. He enlisted in the Navy as a naval aviation cadet, reporting for duty on 7 June 1943. He was shipped first to Dallas and then on to Austin, to the University of Texas. There he received ten weeks of flight preparatory training: intense ground-school study and a rigorous physical-fitness program. He was next sent to Texas Christian University for

As Billy Batson in the *Adventures of Captain Marvel* series (1941), Coghlan turned into "the world's mightiest mortal" whenever he said "Shazam!" (Frank Coghlan collection)

War Training Service, where he received fifty-five hours of flight instruction from civilian pilots. This phase was designed to weed out those deemed unfit for further training by military pilots. Coghlan breezed through the instruction and solo time in a Waco UPF-7 biplane at Singleton Field, just outside Fort Worth.

Ordered to preflight training at the University of Georgia, Coghlan and his fellow cadets were subjected to a rugged physical-fitness program. The Navy believed that a pilot in top physical condition had the best chance of survival if he was shot down and had to make it in the wilderness or the ocean. The officer in charge at the time was a Marine, Col. Bernie Bierman, former coach of the University of Minnesota's Golden Gophers football team (national champions in 1940 and 1941). Among Coghlan's coaches was Angelo Bertelli of Notre Dame fame, a former all-American and Heisman Trophy winner.

Coghlan's Hollywood colleague Lt. Robert Taylor was passing through Georgia at this time, en route to his next assignment as a flight instructor. The brass invited him to act as honorary inspecting officer during the cadets' weekly parade. When he got to Coghlan, Taylor at first began his standard scrutiny of face, shoes, uniform . . . wait a minute . . . face? Snapping his surprised gaze back topside, Taylor recognized his fellow thespian. After requesting permission, he stopped for a brief chat, which of course earned Coghlan even greater visibility than he already had. (Unlike some of his Hollywood associates, however, Coghlan did not suffer much because of his fame.)

Next it was on to Naval Air Station Dallas for primary training. Here the cadets got five periods of instruction in the N2S Stearman, an open-cockpit biplane. Then there was a check flight, after which they could fly solo. Normal procedure was for a cadet to go up with his instructor, who demonstrated certain flight maneuvers; then the cadet would go up again and try it by himself. They learned rolls, loops, stalls, and how to recover from stalls—including the frightening "falling leaf"—and land in tiny fields from absurd positions. Coghlan passed the various check rides, moving on to Pensacola, Florida, the "Annapolis of the Air."

During twenty more hours of training in the Vultee SNV basic trainer, more commonly known in the Navy as the Valiant, Coghlan was almost dropped from the program when an instructor thought he had flown too close to the tree line. Fortunately he was able to redeem himself during the two following check rides. After a few more harrowing events, including a near collision during a nighttime landing, the young cadet was ready for his final phase of training prior to winning his wings.

Coghlan's last unit was Squadron 7, which consisted of OS2U Kingfisher aircraft, his first choice for operational duty. The Kingfisher was a scout observation float plane, single-engine, that was catapulted from fleet cruisers and battleships. (Those who served in such squadrons were often called slingshot aviators.) But before graduating to the Kingfisher, Coghlan had to learn how to fly the two-seat float biplane N3N. This involved a new technique that was more like sailing than flying, as it was critical that the pilots know how to maneuver the machines on the water. Only after they had mastered those skills were they allowed in the air, which meant taking off from the water's surface.

Then, finally, Coghlan got to fly the Kingfisher. He learned to glide-bomb, dive-bomb, search for downed pilots, and take off with 650 pounds of extra weight (depth charges). Upon completion of this final phase of training, Coghlan underwent a final physical and thought he was all set to receive his Navy wings of gold.

But on the day of his commissioning, the medical department sent him notice that he was disqualified to become a naval aviator because he was an eighth of an inch shorter than the minimum requirement of five feet six inches. Astounded, Coghlan read on. A waiver had been granted, it said in the final paragraph, because of the war. Thus he was eligible to be commissioned as an officer. Francis Coghlan received his wings and commission on 12 December 1944. He was now Ensign Coghlan.

After completing his operational training at Squadron 7, the ensign was retained as an instructor. During this duty he had the misfortune to witness a cadet go down, fixated so intently on the practice target he was supposed to hit that he flew directly into it and was lost with his Kingfisher. It was also while Coghlan was an instructor that he married Mary Elizabeth Corrigan, the best friend of a fellow instructor's brand-new bride. They met at the wedding and were wed themselves just two and a half months later, on 22 December 1945, a year after Coghlan got his Navy wings. Betty and Frank stayed together for the next twenty-nine years, until her passing in 1974; they had five children.

After several more months at Pensacola, the newlyweds moved with the rest of Coghlan's unit to Naval Air Station Jacksonville, Florida. There his squadron transferred into new Curtis SC-1 Seahawks, single-engine high-powered float planes. Coghlan was responsible for flying one of them to the new base while Betty motored over in their Ford convertible.

With his squadron due for decommissioning, and with several months to go before he would be eligible for release from active duty, Coghlan was available for other duties. NAS Jacksonville housed the headquarters of the Seventh Naval District and the Naval Air Operational Training Command, and two Waves had written a radio script for use on Armed Forces Day. No one knew how to go about getting it on the air, and Coghlan was asked if he could help out. Calling on his show-business background, he went to visit a radio station in the area and arranged to get airtime. Next he began auditions for musicians, and the result of it all was a fine show using the Waves' script.

Coghlan's success in the venture soon led to his being transferred to the public-relations office of the joint command. One of his assignments there was to interview and write the first press kit for a newly formed Navy flight demonstration team, the Lancers. Flying three F6F Hellcats in a vee formation, they made their public debut in Jacksonville and then moved on to wow New York. While there, they were entertained at a nightclub called the Blue Angel. The pilots liked the name—and others obviously agreed. Coghlan worked with the Blue Angels in these early stages, setting up interviews with the press and on the radio, sometimes serving as announcer during the shows. His boss was so pleased that he suggested Coghlan travel to Washington to investigate the possibilities of getting into the regular Navy. But Coghlan learned that he was too old, by just one month, to be accepted as an ensign. He elected to leave the Navy in May 1947. However, the Navy was not finished making use of Coghlan's valuable services. Not only would he eventually end up a naval aviator; he would remain on active duty in the Navy for twenty-three years, making a career as a naval officer and winding up as the head of the Navy Public Affairs Office in Hollywood.

Returning to Hollywood to resume his acting career, Coghlan soon found that although the major studios had tried to support the war effort through morale-building films glorifying military service, many of the actors who had actually served their country had been replaced by younger new talent. Actors who had been under contract at the time they had gone into the service had work waiting for them afterward, but most others, Junior Coghlan among them, met with tough times. For the first time in his life, and after twenty-four years in the movie industry, the amiable, hardworking, uncomplaining former star could not land a job.

Betty and Frank waited fruitlessly in Hollywood for six months, after which Frank called his friend William P. Lear in Grand Rapids, Michigan. Lear had once promised him a job if he got his Navy wings, and soon the Coghlans were off to Michigan. There Frank worked as a test pilot, helping out as well in sales and advertising. He liked working with Lear, whom he greatly admired, but the work was often less than inspiring, and the company was at an in-between point. It was at that point that the Navy asked him if he would be interested in returning to active duty.

Frank joined the Navy's Continuous Active Duty (CAD) program for reserve officers. He was assigned to the Naval Air Reserve Training Command's public-relations office at his old post, NAS Jacksonville. The Coghlans stayed for four years, during which time their family continued to grow, and Frank had the pleasant experience of working as technical adviser on the movie *Slattery's Hurricane* (1949). He got to visit with his old friend Linda Darnell (costarring with Richard Widmark), which did not prevent him from carrying out his main duty of coordinating sixty Corsairs and Hellcats (thirty each) to fly over the set in formation.

Following that tour, in 1952 Coghlan was given a plum assignment in Washington: head of the Motion Picture Section at ChInfo (Chief of Information). He was to be the lead liaison contact between the Navy and the Hollywood studios. His job consisted of arranging for the use of ships, aircraft, and shore installations in films that the Navy deemed appropriate for cooperation. He also assigned technical advisers to movies, handled the approval of scripts, and produced

As officer in charge of ChInfo's Hollywood office, Coghlan got to renew old friendships and work at the same time. Among the many films for which he served as technical adviser was *A Ticklish Affair* (1963, with, from left, Red Buttons, Carolyn Jones, Shirley Jones, and Gig Young). (Frank Coghlan collection)

public-information documentaries using the huge film library archived at the Naval Photographic Center, Anacostia, District of Columbia. During the next two and a half years, Lieutenant Coghlan oversaw naval cooperation on *The Caine Mutiny* (1954), *The Bridges at Toko-Ri* (1954), and *Mister Roberts* (1955). He also helped his crony Jackie Cooper with his television series *Hennesey* (1959–62).

The Navy people referred to him as Lieutenant Coghlan, but to the numerous members of his old Hollywood family with whom he was once again in contact, he was and always would be Junior. Respected by all, the diligent, trustworthy Lt. Frank "Junior" Coghlan did an outstanding job for both the Navy and Hollywood.

It was while he was holding down this key public-relations job that Coghlan suddenly learned he had lost his status in the CAD program (he was an aviator serving in a nonflying job). If he wanted to continue on active duty, he would have to join an operational squadron. His best option, at age thirty-eight and with a family that he wanted to take with him and keep close by, was transports. He requested and was ordered to VR-7, which flew Lockheed Super Constellations out of Hickham Air Force Base, Oahu, Hawaii. On the way there, Frank took his two sons, now aged four and seven, on a cross-country driving tour whose high points included Boys Town, the Badlands, Mount Rushmore, Old Faithful, Salt Lake City, and Lake Tahoe. They then rejoined Betty, their daughter, and Frank's mother in San Francisco, and from there all the Coghlans shipped off to Hawaii on the former Navy transport ship *General Shanks*.

During the next three years (1954–57) Coghlan worked for the Military Air Transport Service (MATS) and VR-7. Rusty at first, not having flown on a continuous basis for almost ten years, he took on the task with his customary good nature and learned to fly four-engine transports (previously he had flown only single-engine aircraft). He covered the Pacific carrying servicemen and dependents, flying cargo hauls, and making air evacuations (medical emergency flights). His two main routes were to Haneda Airport in Tokyo, with a stopover at Wake Island, and to Clark Air Force Base near Manila, but there were also trips to Vietnam, Thailand, India, and other destinations. Coghlan saw the war's debris scattered throughout the Pacific islands, and he got to know as much about Japan, with its soothing steam baths and artful dining ceremonies, as he had time for during his three-day layovers. He collected shells in the Philippines and toured the Intramuros and Santo Tomas University in Manila, witnessing firsthand the ravages wrought by the combat that had raged there.

Having satisfied his requirement for fleet duty, Coghlan was continued on active duty and promoted to lieutenant commander. The next three years were spent near Chicago with the chief of Naval Air Reserve Training, Naval Air Station Glenview. Coghlan's job was industrial liaison officer, which involved frequent travel to inspect other Air Reserve stations, host yearly public-information seminars at Pensacola, and recruit naval aviation cadets.

Next came a surprise, after he had already been assigned as public-information officer to Naval Air Station Point Arguello, California, where he had already put a down payment on a house and enrolled the children in a Catholic school. He was offered the job of officer in charge of ChInfo's Hollywood office.

So 1960 found the Coghlans back in Junior's home town, with the Navy. For the next five years he renewed old friendships and handled numerous television programs and feature films. He was liaison officer on shows including *Hennesey, Ensign O'Toole, Convoy* (starring ex–Navyman John Gavin), and *The Wackiest Ship in the Army*. His film liaisons included *All Hands on Deck* (1961, with Pat Boone, Barbara Eden, and Buddy Hackett), *PT-109* (1963, with Cliff Robertson playing the late President John F. Kennedy), and *In Harm's Way* (1966, with John Wayne, Patricia Neal, and Kirk Douglas).

Coghlan retired from the naval service in 1965 at age forty-nine. His Hollywood contacts having been reinvigorated during his last tour with the Navy, acting jobs now began coming his way again, after a twenty-three-year hiatus. Among other TV shows, he appeared in *The Beverly Hillbillies, The FBI, 12 O'Clock High, The Outcasts,* and *Here's Lucy.* He played an American businessman in the movie *The Sand Pebbles* (1966), and his other film credits include *Dragnet 66* (1966, with Jack Webb), *Valley of the Dolls* (1967, with Susan Hayward, Patty Duke, and Sharon Tate), *The Love-Ins* (1967, with Richard Todd), and *The Shakiest Gun in the West* (1967, with Don Knotts). He has been featured on *Entertainment Tonight, Wheel of Fortune, The Republic Pictures Story* (a two-hour special on the American

Movie Classics cable television network), and *Shirley Temple: America's Little Darling* (a 1992 PBS special).

Coghlan also held day jobs, one of which was special-events coordinator for the Port of Los Angeles, and he did television commercials for companies such as Champale Malt Liquor, Toyota, Ben Hogan Golf Products, and La Quinta Motor Inns. In 1975 he was selected to become spokesman for Curtis Mathes, a Texas-based television manufacturer for whom he still makes commercials.

In 1974 Betty passed away suddenly in her sleep. Her devastated husband got a job closer to home and the children and kept working, now as the director of public relations at the Los Angeles Zoo. Fourteen months later he married the former Letha Schwarzrock, a divorcée with three sons. Thus Junior Coghlan's family continued to grow, and before long the children began to produce numerous grandchildren.

During his seventy-plus-year career in television and the film industry, Frank "Junior" Coghlan has made more than four hundred on-camera appearances. Add to this a twenty-three-year career as a naval aviator, and it all makes for a rather extraordinary outcome for someone whose silent-screen image was that of a "homeless waif" almost three-quarters of a century ago.

# Jackie Cooper

Hollywood native (1921) Jackie Cooper began working as an extra in movies before age five. Living within walking distance of the studios, his grandmother would walk there in the mornings with the child in tow, to try for a day's work as extras. This netted two dollars and a boxed lunch, and even though there was no extra pay for having a kid with you, it often meant that Jackie's grandmother was picked. Gradually Jackie became a known face and began to get hired for kids' parts, later sometimes also singing. He had been trained by his mother, who earned her living playing the piano and singing in vaudeville (and filling in with secretarial work as necessary). Eventually the round-faced child was brought to the attention of Hal Roach, who selected him for several of the 1929 *Our Gang* comedy shorts. Later, on TV, this would become *The Little Rascals*.

What all this meant to eight-year-old Jackie was work, which was both good—he was now making fifty dollars a week, bringing the family out of poverty—and bad, because of the pressure. The work represented a serious responsibility, and the child was fully aware of this. He had no formal training; they taught him to cry on-screen by telling him things like they were going to have to shoot his dog. Added to the pinching and slapping his grandmother administered when she was less than pleased with his performance on the home scene, and the fact that there was no daddy in sight, only occasional references to some loser who had abandoned them, these factors might have created a very unhappy little boy.

But Jackie Cooper thought acting was fun, and he loved the vaudeville tours he later got to do with his mother. He gave each show his very best. Long days left little or no time for school, which he later regretted. He did learn to play the drums, having become enthralled while watching the drummer during the cruise he finally persuaded his mother to take him on. The congenial musician showed him a few things and later brought a set of drums to the Cooper home. Jackie practiced regularly, and his teenage Sundays became jam sessions. Eventually he became skilled enough to play professionally and sit in with Bunny Berigan's band along with fellow invitees Tommy Dorsey and Benny Goodman.

Jackie grew up working with people such as Wallace Beery, George Raft, and Judy Garland, another child star who became one of his first (fleeting) love interests. Not everybody was nice to him, but he knew he had a job to do. Director Norman Taurog was his uncle by marriage —later, Jackie sometimes suspected, maybe, but probably not, his real father? It was he whom the boy strived to impress. His mother repeatedly instructed him to listen to Uncle Norman, who knew what was best for the boy. Norman and Jackie would eventually part ways, but during Jackie's growing-up years Norman held the professional reins, and the two were, in a way, very close.

In 1929 Jackie appeared in eight *Our Gang* shorts, but there was other work too, and in 1930–31 he was nominated for an Oscar for his work in the film *Skippy* (directed by Uncle Norman). This catapulted him to stardom, and more movies followed, including four with Wallace Beery: *The Champ* (1931), *The Bowery* (1933), *Treasure Island* (1934), and *O'Shaughnessy's Boy* (1935).

After Pearl Harbor, Jackie, now twenty, wanted to get into the fight and help defend the country. His fantasy was to serve in PT boats in the Navy, a desire that was fueled by a chat with Robert Montgomery during a visit to Washington. Jackie was flown there as part of a Hollywood group to wish President Roosevelt a happy birthday, and the uniform-clad Montgomery mentioned that he would probably soon be on a motor torpedo boat. This, as far as the younger actor was concerned, was the apex of accomplishment. But Uncle Norman would not hear of it and arranged for deferment after deferment, along with a few USO tours to in-country bases. Jackie did not give up, though, and finally Norman agreed, provided he went into an officer program. Jackie was satisfied with this compromise and filled out the application his uncle got for him.

Cooper had registered for the draft during a California USO vaudeville tour, and he was in Massachusetts when the time came for him to report to a draft board. He passed the V-12 qualifying tests but was all too aware that he did not have the academic background to get through the program. He had completed only kindergarten, first grade, and one year of high school. The rest of his spotty, regularly interrupted education had come from private tutoring. And the Navy's tough stance did not help convince him that he could do it. He was continually reminded that he was nothing special now; there was no star treatment in the Navy.

In December 1942 he was assigned to Loyola University in Los Angeles, where, as an undergraduate, he did not have to wear a uniform and could have his own apartment. Jackie being a normal American boy, this meant parties and late nights spent not studying, which made it even more difficult for the tutors Uncle Norman hired to help him make the grade. After Loyola the boys were put in uniform, and in November 1943 Jackie was transferred to the V-12 program at Notre Dame University in South Bend, Indiana. Here the training became much more rigid, with early-morning calisthenics, inspections, marching, formations, and bugle calls.

The academic program was difficult, and Cooper had to work hard, often stealing away into the head at night to continue studying. Unfortunately he was repeatedly caught, and demerits began to pile up. On top of all this, there was the usual Navy who-do-you-think-you-are approach, and then widely publicized allegations that Cooper had contributed to the delinquency of a minor. Even though he was subsequently proven innocent—the sixteen-year-old girl had been with someone else, for whom an uninformed Jackie had been asked to make a hotel reservation—the former actor was left with the unwelcome headlines. Finally, because of incomplete grades and too many demerits, he was forced to leave the V-12 program in November 1944. He was transferred into the inductees' Navy, for boot-camp training at the Great Lakes Naval Training Station. After his Notre Dame ordeals, Cooper found boot camp relaxing.

While Cooper was enjoying Great Lakes, bandleader Claude Thornhill, a Navy chief petty officer, was forming a band in Hawaii with the plan of touring outlying bases in the South Pacific. The admiral on whose staff he served had given him free rein to put together the group with any Navy musicians he wanted. Jackie Cooper was by now a recognized drummer and had once sat in for a session with Thornhill himself at the Palladium. Thornhill called Cooper and made him the offer, explaining that he already had a drummer but thought he could use Cooper as well, for entertainment and drum solos. Other entertainers he had gathered included Tommy Riggs, Betty Lou, and Dennis Day (a singer who had been a regular on Jack Benny's radio show)—all known talent. Cooper enthusiastically accepted, Thornhill handled the details, and before long the actor and musician found himself on a troop train headed for the West Coast. His final destination: Hawaii.

In California he had two weeks' leave prior to shipping out, and he took advantage of this lull to marry his girlfriend, June Horne, in a small ceremony at the Beverly Hills Hotel on 11 December 1944. June had stuck by him through his South Bend troubles, writing and visiting regularly, unlike most of his own family. Their intimacy was not to endure the tests of time, but for now June had movies to make and Jackie had a war to get to.

In January 1945 he traveled into the Pacific on a Liberty ship to join the Service Force, U.S. Pacific Fleet. Upon arrival at the Aiea Naval Hospital on Oahu, where Thornhill's band had been given rehearsal space, Cooper was promoted to seaman third class and began to get his act together. He planned to tell Hollywood anecdotes, play a bit of drums, and sing as part of the Thornhill band's quartet. Reveling in their privileged Hawaiian status, with permanent passes and severe warnings of

A drummer since childhood, Jackie Cooper played in the Navy with Claude Thornhill's band. (U.S. Navy photo)

the dire consequences that would ensue should they in any way draw attention to themselves, the company did not let playtime interfere with work, and soon they were ready to take their show on the road.

They toured the Pacific for eight months, first stop Kwajalein, and stayed until they thought every serviceman in the area had seen them perform. Thornhill believed strongly that his group's job was to get to the boys, rather than the other way around, and he made it his personal mission to make sure his band played for everyone, including soldiers stuck in the far reaches of the Pacific islands. His seriousness of purpose spread to the rest of the company, who began calling themselves Thornhill's Raiders.

But differences arose between commissioned ensign Dennis Day and noncommissioned chief petty officer Claude Thornhill, his superior in the band but not in the Navy. Finally, on Tarawa, Thornhill said he was ill and went into sick bay; he never returned to the band. Dennis Day assumed command.

By now all the musicians were fatigued and irritable, and infighting began to develop. Coteries formed, and any serious efforts to reach the outlands ceased. Conditions had never been comfortable, with the war only slightly in front of them and never any mail, but Thornhill's Raiders had felt a sense of purpose. Now it was just getting the job done, a sense of apathy that grew with the passing months. The band's disagreements eventually caused one of the island's shore patrols to order them to surrender their weapons, which, it was reasoned, they did not really need anyway. Craftily, Cooper taped his .45 to the inside of his drum.

One positive change did occur for Cooper, who had always wished he could be the band's permanent drummer and drop the rest of his act. He approached Day, who shared the limelight with him on stage, and put the idea to him, suggesting that the other drummer be moved to the brass section, where he also had abilities. Day agreed, and Cooper from then on was left to play away contentedly on the drums, keeping the beat for the band at the back of the stage.

They frequently played in hospitals and visited with patients after their shows, a duty that brought home the brutal reality of why they were there. They saw action once, while on the island of Ulithi. On 11 March 1945 a Japanese Frances twin-engine bomber hit the carrier USS *Randolph* (CV-15) on the starboard side aft below the flight deck. Twenty-five men were killed and 106 wounded. The following day Cooper went aboard the carrier and witnessed the carnage. It was the first time he had seen the atrocity of war up close, and he was grateful that he had not been caught in it as so many of his compatriots had been.

The war finally ended, while the group was on New Caledonia. With almost half the band out of commission after a jeep accident, one day a bored Cooper wandered over to the Armed Forces Radio Service Station for a chat about possible work. When Sgt. Hy Averback, later to become the famous movie director, was sent to take over Radio Tokyo, Cooper wound up being left in charge of the operation with two others, one of whom was Jack Paar.

The injured band members now healed, the group was next sent on a glorious tour around New Zealand, traveling in their own plane to thirteen cities where they played not only on bases but in concert halls as well. It was a grande finale, after which the band was shipped back to the States in October 1945.

Cooper's final, delightful duty was playing with Sam Donahue's all-service band making "V disks," prefab shows on phonograph records to be sent overseas. Landing talent such as Ella Fitzgerald as guests, the band produced a show called *Jubilee,* with drummer Jackie Cooper keeping time. His honorable discharge came in January 1946, just over three years after he had enlisted.

After the war Cooper's acting career temporarily floundered. Sporadic work was not enough, and finally he decided to give it a go in New York City, after hearing repeatedly that getting onstage could turn things around for him. But June, a native Californian, could not adjust to New York, and eventually this ended the already weak union.

New York did turn things around for Cooper, both professionally and personally, opening new doors for him and introducing him for the first time to a more artistic, intellectual crowd, whose company he enjoyed. He got on the stage, winding up in the role of Ensign Pulver in the road production of *Mister Roberts.* This eventually took him to Broadway, where he starred in 1954 in *King of Hearts.* He also worked on live television.

Finally, having resisted its lure for several years, he turned to the world of TV series and headed back west. Soon he was playing Sock Miller in the sitcom *The People's Choice* (1955–58) and then a Navy doctor in the hit series *Hennesey* (1959–62). By this time he was successfully directing and producing as well, and by 1964 he was the head of Screen Gems. He won Emmys for directing episodes of *M*A*S*H* and *The White Shadow;* he produced *Gidget, I Dream of Jeannie, The Flying Nun,* and others. He also appeared on TV shows and in movies, including *Superman* (1978) and two of its sequels (1980, 1983), in which he appeared as Perry White.

It was the *Hennesey* TV series that brought him back to the Navy. In search of real Navy settings for the show, Cooper went to the Los Angeles public-affairs office to present his request. The PAO at the time turned out to be Claude Jarman, Jr., another former child star (who played in the 1946 movie *The Yearling*). The Navy was impressed with the *Hennesey* series, which respected the service and its traditions while still presenting the comedy of human errors. Soon Cooper was doing recruiting spots for the service, and it was not long before the brass urged him to join the Naval Reserve, which he did in September 1962.

Commissioned as a lieutenant commander, Cooper rose to the rank of captain in 1973. He served the Navy well, making numerous training films and radio and television promotions as well as appearing at official functions. He refused one request: to participate in promoting the Vietnam war effort, of which he disapproved. He did, however, believe in a strong national defense, and he continued working for the Navy. Quite a turnaround from his first Navy experiences.

When Cooper became the head of Screen Gems, frequent flights between New York and Los Angeles became part of his job. He had always been afraid of flying, but at the suggestion of a TWA pilot, he decided to learn how to do it himself. This, the pilot explained, would make him feel in control. Cooper was hooked from his first lesson. By 1970 he had logged some nine hundred hours of flight time and owned several different types of aircraft. When it was time to heed the call of his Naval Reserve responsibilities, he would fly to the bases in a twin-engine Aero Commander.

One day the commanding officer of Naval Air Station Los Alamitos suggested that Navy wings might look nice on his uniform. Cooper was pleased with this possibility, and the request was put in. Approval was granted up the chain of command, and in 1970 Jackie Cooper was made an honorary naval aviator who could wear wings of gold on his uniform. (Others so honored have included aviation artist R. G. Smith, *Grampaw Pettibone* creator Robert Osborn, and entertainer Bob Hope.)

Captain Cooper retired from the Reserves in 1974. In addition to previously being awarded the Distinguished Public Service Medal, upon his departure he was presented with the Legion of Merit with citation.

Jackie Cooper continues to work in television. After his first divorce he married twice more; since 1954 he has been with Barbara Kraus. She had never even heard of Skippy when they met. Cooper has had four children.

# Tony Curtis

A head-turner since earliest childhood, Tony Curtis was born as Bernard Schwartz in New York City in 1925, to Hungarian Jewish immigrants Manuel and Helen Klein Schwartz. Manuel worked long hours as a tailor, and in summers he sometimes took the family to the Catskills for getaways. It was not in mountain lakes that little Bernard learned to swim, though; he developed that skill in Central Park, diving for change with the other boys.

But summer days were not all fun-filled in the city, where frolic was snatched in respites, as circumstances allowed. The youngster also spent quite a bit of time running, hiding, and trying to stay out of trouble's way. Constantly aware of the fact that he was a Jewish kid, he was on permanent alert for tormentors. His startling good looks seemed particularly to irritate his enemies, and Bernie learned to move fast enough to get away from almost anyone. He was conscious of his looks and thankful for this one asset, which he protected fiercely.

The Boy Scouts provided a haven, as did summer camp, when he was able to go. He loved movies and movie theaters, and every chance he got throughout his childhood and young-adult years, Bernie would spend hours in the comforting darkness, lost in the fantasy of someone else's created reality, mesmerized by his hero Errol Flynn in pictures such as *Captain Blood* (1935), *The Charge of the Light Brigade* (1936), and *The Adventures of Robin Hood* (1938). In his later teens Bernie also began to slip into Broadway theaters from time to time, during intermissions.

Home was another refuge for the beautiful little boy, although Helen and Manuel's relationship was not harmonious, with Helen always seeming to be blaming someone for something, often expressing her anger physically. Her spirits would improve considerably after Tony-made-good brought everyone to live in Hollywood.

Manuel had entertained ideas of becoming some sort of performer in America but was never able to bring his dream to fruition. He did play the violin, which brought some joy into his overworked youth and pleasure to those around him. He moved his tailor shop and family several times in search of a better neighborhood; Bernie's favorite was the East Side. That was where the family at one time lived behind the shop, five of them in one room, but these quarters were not as tight as those of others the Schwartzes knew, some of whom lived ten or more to a room.

Around high-school time, Bernie joined a small theater group at the Young Men's Hebrew Association (later known as the Ninety-second Street Y Playhouse). He appeared in a few productions and took to acting far better than he did to school (Seward Park High), where he almost flunked out. Education seemed insignificant, unconnected to anything that was going on around him.

It was 1943, and the war beckoned. Inspired by Tyrone Power in *Crash Dive* (1943; Power was pulled out of Marine boot camp to finish the film) and by Cary Grant in *Destination Tokyo* (1944), Bernie decided to join the Navy, with hopes of becoming a submariner. The Navy suited him well; he appreciated in particular the challenges of boot camp, which he underwent in Buffalo. With the toughness and survival training he had already had on New York City's streets, boot camp to him was fun.

Signalman Schwartz, aboard the sub tender *Proteus* (AS-19) when the Japanese signed the peace treaty in Tokyo Bay, watched the historic event through binoculars. (U.S. Navy photo)

He was ordered next to signal school at Champaign, Illinois. Graduating from the school as a signalman third class, USNR, he applied for submarine training and was shipped off to sub school at New London, Connecticut. From there he was ordered to San Diego and duty aboard the USS *Proteus* (AS-19), a sub tender. In addition to his duties on the *Proteus*, Schwartz was part of a relief crew on the USS *Dragonet* (SS-293) that cleaned up the boat and got her ready for sea. The *Proteus* was one of five new tenders that reported to the Pacific Fleet in 1944; fifteen years later, she would be converted to a Polaris fleet ballistic missile tender.

The future Tony Curtis was then sent to Guam, where he injured his back while cleaning the outside of a sub. During the scrubdown, the scaffolding he was standing on came away from the boat, and he landed with a whack on his back. The injury got him four days in the infirmary, after which he returned to duty. Later, while making movies, he was sometimes bothered by back pain when he did stunts.

When the defeated Japanese signed the peace treaty in Tokyo Bay, Signalman Schwartz was aboard the *Proteus*. As all ships in the bay witnessed the pivotal event with colors flying, Schwartz and his shipmates watched the Japanese and Allied delegations through binoculars.

Guam had been converted to a submarine relief base with rest and recreation facilities. Though secured by the time Schwartz arrived there, many Japanese soldiers still roamed the island, starving. To find food, they often scaled the barbed-wire fences surrounding the U.S. base, and sometimes a Japanese soldier would steal a U.S. sailor's uniform and line up for chow with everybody else. They were spotted quickly and taken into custody. One time during a baseball game Schwartz was playing in, a sailor went over the fence to retrieve a ball and was stabbed to death. Marine patrols became even more alert, and one night a Japanese soldier met a sudden end when a Marine spotted him trying to get in and threw a grenade. Just as Schwartz and a few others arrived on the scene, they saw the Marine pull the Japanese soldier off the fence, minus his head.

When Schwartz was released from the Navy he returned to his parents' home, now in the Bronx. Thanks to the GI Bill he was able to enroll in New York's Dramatic Workshop, adding his name to a list of future stars that included Walter Matthau and Harry Belafonte. Determined to succeed, he left the school after one semester and joined a company that put on plays in the Catskills, after which he did a stint at a Chicago Yiddish theater. In 1947 he went back to the Dramatic Workshop, where he was not considered likely to succeed. But Schwartz had no intention of giving up his chosen profession, and in the spring of 1948, during a performance of *Golden Boy* in the Cherry Lane Theater, an agent noticed him. Before long he was in California with a contract from Universal Studios.

It was in Hollywood that he changed his name to Tony Curtis. Making his film debut with a bit part in *Criss Cross* (1948), he was noticed at once by admiring moviegoers. He worked steadily after that, appearing in scores of films throughout the 1950s, including *City across the River* (1949), *Sierra* (1950), *The Prince Who Was a Thief*

(1951), *Houdini* (1953), and *Six Bridges to Cross* (1955). Then, branching out from Universal, he played different types of roles, achieving critical acclaim in *The Sweet Smell of Success* (1957) and *The Defiant Ones* (1958, for which he was nominated for an Academy Award). Other popular efforts included *The Vikings* (1958) and *Some Like It Hot* (1959). He also played in a few films about the Navy, notably *Operation Petticoat* (1959). In *The Boston Strangler* (1968) he proved his ability to portray a twisted mind, adding new depth to his repertoire.

Success brought money, which in 1950 allowed Curtis to bring his family out to California. He became the chief provider, which at times was burdensome and extremely stressful, but he accepted his role as family caretaker. Still unmarried upon his arrival in Movieland, in 1951 he married actress Janet Leigh. He was married three times more, most recently in 1993 to Lisa Deutsch, in whose company he continues to enjoy his six children and his ongoing work.

★

# Kirk Douglas

At 1100 on 18 November 1943, the U.S. patrol craft 1139 was commissioned at Naval Station Algiers, New Orleans. The 173 foot 260-ton vessel carried a crew of seventy-two enlisted and five officers. Among the latter was Ens. Kirk Douglas, newly assigned ship's communications officer. One thing he would not have to worry about was being accused of expecting special treatment in the Navy: Kirk Douglas would not become a movie star until after the war.

Most of the crew, including Douglas, had never been to sea before. After the commissioning ceremony the commanding officer, Lt. (jg) J. O. McCormick, USNR, attempted to maneuver the ship away from the dock and the other vessels positioned fore and aft of his charge. After ramming into the dock, colliding with another ship and partially sinking her, then tearing a life raft off another, 1139 finally made it to open water.

Among those watching from the dock, trying unsuccessfully to suppress her laughter amid the general embarrassment, was the actor's new bride, Diana Dill, in attendance with the other families for the ceremony bidding their men farewell. Her twenty-seven-year-old husband had recently graduated from the U.S. Naval Reserve Midshipman's School at Notre Dame University, South Bend, Indiana. His college degree had not made the 120-hour course any easier for Douglas, mostly because he was not particularly interested in subjects like navigation, damage control, gunnery, and aircraft identification. But he had toughed it out and made it through the course.

Toughing it out was something Douglas did well, having grown up the only son among the seven children of Herschel and Bryna Sanglel Danielovitch, an impoverished, illiterate Russian Jewish immigrant couple in upstate New York—Amsterdam, on the Mohawk River. Issur Danielovitch (Kirk Douglas's original name) joined the girls in 1916. The family barely managed to scrape by on the money Herschel reluctantly earned as a ragman, along with whatever the others could pick up, and hunger was a familiar visitor to the household.

Issur had a close relationship with the numerous women in his clan, but Herschel rarely displayed much warmth toward him. At night the boy often heard his dad in the tavern with the men, telling stories and laughing. Issur longed to be introduced into this private world of men, and one hot afternoon Herschel did take him into the sanctuary, briefly, when only the bartender was there. It was a moment of joy whose reverberations would last a lifetime for the child sipping quietly on his loganberry.

Sometimes, without warning, Herschel would show such flashes of genuine affection for his family. One Christmas morning, toys, stuffed stockings, and a laughing, storytelling father greeted the children of this Jewish family that did not acknowledge the holiday. But Herschel wanted them to experience Santa Claus, and he told his enraptured brood all about how he had heard the reindeer in the sky the night before, how they had landed on the Danielovitch roof, and how he himself had met the plump, jolly, generous Santa.

Storytelling was Herschel's forte, and no doubt his son inherited his dramatic competence. But the norm for this frustrated and disillusioned man, whose creative abilities had never found their outlet, was a cold distance characterized by absence from the hearth. Bryna struggled on cheerfully despite it all, thrilled to be in America where her little ones—all American-born, as she had planned—would have opportunities she could not have dreamed of in her Ukrainian homeland.

As the children grew and learned how to earn their way, the Danielovitch fortunes gradually improved, and the daughters, by now dating, wanted a better house. Herschel refused to leave Eagle Street, and eventually Bryna left him there, moving with their children to a better neighborhood. Young Issur, torn by conflicting emotions, wrenched himself away from the father he wished would ask him to stay.

His future began to take shape in high school, where his English teacher took a special interest in the boy and carefully nurtured his curiosity about literature and drama, encouraging him to set his sights on a college education despite his financial constraints. Eventually she got him there. In 1935 he was accepted at St. Lawrence University, Canton, New York, with the help of a college loan and a job as a janitor.

Money was very scarce, and hunger continued to haunt Izzy, as he now called himself, through college. He devised various ways of scrounging for food, taking nightly visiting walks through the dorms in hopes that he would be offered some of the treats that more comfortable families had sent for their boys' snacks. He also stole food, on occasion, and snuck into the school cafeteria until he was caught and informed in no uncertain terms that he had not purchased the meal plan.

But the resolute Izzy toughed it all out and prevailed, becoming president of the Mummers (a dramatic group), of the German Club, and finally of the student body, much to the disgust of the university's lively and vocal anti-Semite faction. Such problems were not new to him, though; since childhood he had been keenly aware of the fact that he was Jewish, and that many people hated Jews. He also became a star wrestler, winning an intercollegiate championship. And, perhaps most distressing to the school's racists, he seemed to appeal to a significant portion of the female student body. In fact, Izzy may have been a little girl-crazy. Loved 'em, could not resist the attentions of a beautiful woman—a predicament that would plague him for many years to come.

After earning his B.A. in 1939, Izzy went to New York City and enrolled at the American Academy of Dramatic Arts, where he remained for two years. It was here that he officially adopted the name Kirk

Douglas. He supported himself by working as a dramatics coach and as a waiter at Schrafft's, and during summers he acted in theater productions in New York State and Pennsylvania.

He read about the war and about Hitler's speeches; he saw and heard the Jewish refugees at Schrafft's. He was aware of what was happening in Europe, but it seemed remote to the young actor, who was completely focused on securing his future. By 1941, having graduated from the academy, he was beginning to get minor parts on the Broadway stage.

And then the Japanese bombed Pearl Harbor, and Kirk Douglas, like so many other young Americans, decided to do something about both that and the situation in Europe. He was rejected by the Air Force as being too old, and he continued to work on the two plays he was involved in: *Three Sisters* (with Ruth Gordon) and *Spring Again*. As usual, Kirk Douglas was driving himself hard.

Enlisting in the U.S. Naval Reserve on 10 December 1942, he took the qualifying tests and before long was on his way to Notre Dame Midshipman School in South Bend, Indiana, to be trained as a naval officer. Surprised by the difficulty of the courses, Douglas quickly got to work, drawing on all his powers of concentration just to keep up. After commissioning, he was ordered to attend antisubmarine training at the Submarine Chaser Training Center, Miami. After satisfactorily completing that course, the ensign was ordered to Naval Station Algiers for additional training. On 2 November 1943 he and model Diana Dill, a former classmate from the Academy of Dramatic Arts, were married on the base. Later that month Ens. Kirk Douglas was off to the 1139 to serve as one of her original crew members.

Finally clearing the dock, the 1139 made her way down the Mississippi en route to Miami to pick up electronic gear. It was not long before Douglas, who was instructing his small crew on how he intended to run his shop, found himself feeling nauseous. Before the 1139 had reached the Gulf of Mexico, he was hanging over the side, seasick. The rest of the trip to Miami was more of the same, only worse. The seas were rough, and Douglas continually had to fight off seasickness, as did most of the crew. He felt more comfortable while standing deck watches, when he was distracted by the responsibility of having command of the ship.

During World War II, Ens. Kirk Douglas served on board the accident-prone patrol craft 1139 (sister ship of PC-1138, above), which was harassed en route to Manzanilla by U.S. patrolling aircraft that mistook her for the enemy. Frantic signaling from PC-1139 saved her from attack. (U.S. Naval Historical Center)

One day while serving as officer of the deck he decided, on his own initiative, to call the crew to general quarters. He had seen such exciting drills in the movies and really did not consider his action anything out of the ordinary. His commanding officer, of course, thought otherwise. After McCormick raced to the bridge to take command of the situation and discovered what had happened, Douglas never made the mistake again.

Diana was waiting for him in Miami, having rented an apartment in Miami Beach for what was to be their two-week reunion. But the Douglases' Floridian adventure lasted almost a month and a half, courtesy of the 1139. Each time the patrol craft tried to get back out to sea, some mishap would occur. The ship finally went to sea in mid-January. As they headed for the city of Cristobal, at the eastern entrance to the Panama Canal, the rough seas had a predictable effect on Douglas, who was almost constantly seasick. Nevertheless, his duties as communications officer demanded his decoding of messages, and he somehow managed to keep up with his work.

There were other problems, too. One night while Douglas had the watch, two sailors got into a fight. The actor drew his sidearm and ordered them to stop, but one of the sailors taunted him, daring him to go ahead and shoot. Ensign Douglas was forced to back off, feeling extremely foolish. But the incident taught him a lesson he was able to use later in his performances: whenever he played a tough character who drew a gun, that character was prepared to use it.

Once through the canal and in Pacific waters, PC-1139 conducted antisubmarine exercises with a U.S. sub off the Galapagos Islands. Douglas liked such war-gaming even though he had sighting problems; he was the last one to spot a periscope during such maneuvers, and frequently it had to be pointed out to him.

Finally the ship was ordered to join the Pacific Fleet and conduct operations against enemy submarines. Before proceeding westward, the 1139 was directed to escort two ships, the U.S. tug *Cubits Gap* and the AFD 17, a floating dry dock, to Hawaii. But Douglas's small warship lacked sufficient fuel to make the long passage to Hawaii, and she suffered the indignity of having to be towed by the ships she was to convoy. The journey across the Pacific was nonetheless enjoyable for the crew, with the weather pleasant and the seas much calmer than in the Atlantic. Douglas often stood the 0400–0800 watch, serene in the moonlit nights and clear dawns. Once the ships reached a position from which the 1139 could make her own way with sufficient fuel to reach the destination, the towline was released and the ship took up her escort duties. Those standing watch on the bridge could hear the pings of the QCS-1 sonar system in the sound room as it searched for a prowling enemy below.

Late in the afternoon of 7 February, the echo of the sound waves signaled a return, suddenly changing to ping-*ping*. Immediately the crew went to general quarters, positive that they had located a Japanese submarine. Once the contact's position was fixed, the ship fired six rocket explosive projectiles from its mousetrap launcher in the direction of the sub. These small charges went off only when they made contact with an underwater object, and the crew was jubilant when an explosion sounded below. Douglas's post was the gunnery officer astern. The skipper slowly eased the ship toward the position of the explosion and ordered the release of a dye marker as they passed over

Most of PC-1139's crew, including Douglas, had never been to sea before. Douglas is second from the left in the front row. (John Balzer collection)

the site. Douglas relayed the order to a nearby crewman, and within seconds the ship was rocked by an eruption that sent crewmen sprawling to the deck. Douglas was smashed up against the side of the iron carrier for the depth charges and suffered severe stomach bruises.

In the confusion following the sudden blast, all had assumed that the ship had been torpedoed. However, it was soon discovered that instead of dropping a dye marker, the sailor had released a Mark IX depth charge set at 250 feet. The ship had nearly been destroyed by her own charge. The steering gear, badly damaged, had to be repaired as quickly as possible so that the craft could continue her escort duties. Luckily, no further contact was made with the underwater object, and the ship forwarded an action report citing the particulars of the incident and the accidental dropping of the depth charge. Ship's repairs were hurriedly made, and the convoy continued on its way.

A few days later a sailor was diagnosed with an acute case of appendicitis, and the 1139 was ordered to Manzanilla, Mexico, to deliver the man to a local hospital for medical attention. Far from feeling unprotected, the convoy was happy to let the clearly accident-prone 1139 go off to find her own destiny, whatever that might be.

And at first the future indeed did not look bright for the small patrol craft. En route to Manzanilla, she was harassed by U.S. patrolling aircraft who mistook her for an enemy ship or submarine. During night hours Douglas and the crew frequently heard the engines of an aircraft change in intensity as it began its dive on the 1139. More than once, frantic light-signaling by the ship's crew saved them from being sunk by friendly fire.

After dropping the sailor off in Manzanilla, the patrol craft proceeded as ordered to San Diego. By this time Ensign Douglas's body bruises were causing him continuous pain, and he was gradually becoming ill. After a few days at San Diego, suffering severe cramps and a fever of 104 degrees, he was taken to the naval hospital. As his shipmates in the 1139 went on to the war without him, tests revealed that, in addition to internal injuries, Douglas had amoebic dysentery.

On 24 February 1944, Ens. Kirk Douglas was detached from the ship with the following log entry:

> 1620—Moored as before. 1625—pursuant to BUPERS Dispatch Orders of 210857, H. F. Tingley, Ens., D-V(s), USNR, 275454, reported on board for duty. 1900—Ens. James aboard. 1925—Ens. James Ashore. Pursuant to BUPERS Dispatch Orders of 210857, K. Douglas, Ens., D-V(G), USNR, 228042 detached.
>
> Hugh Lewis, Ens. USNR

While recovering in the U.S. Naval Hospital in San Diego, the injured ensign received months of back mail. Shocked, he read the news from his wife that he was to be a father (of Michael Douglas), news that precipitated a phone call to New Jersey, and before long the family was reunited.

Finally the Navy determined that Kirk's amoebic dysentery could be recurring and could affect his performance of further duty, and he was honorably discharged from the Navy in July 1944. The Douglases moved back to the New York area, where Kirk dressed daily in his white uniform and took the train into the city, making the rounds of casting offices and radio programs. He knew he would have to tough this out too until something clicked.

It happened after he tried out for *Kiss and Tell,* a comedy in which Richard Widmark had been playing the part of an Army lieutenant. Widmark was leaving the play to begin another, and Kirk Douglas became his replacement, to his delighted amazement.

Several plays later, Hollywood producer Hal Wallis, who had heard about Douglas from his former classmate and friend Lauren Bacall, offered Douglas the opportunity to work in movies. At first unintrigued, in September 1945 the actor finally decided to give it a go, and soon he made his screen debut in *The Strange Love of Martha Ivers* (1946).

Truly an American success story, Kirk Douglas never left California after that. He still lives there with his second wife, German-born film public-relations assistant Anne Buydens (he and Diana were divorced amicably in 1949). Anne had fled a tumultuous home life and the Nazi regime in 1940, at age fifteen, moving to Belgium and becoming a nationalized citizen. She and Kirk met in Paris, where he was making *Act of Love* (1953). At the time he was engaged to marry actress Pier Angeli, but Pier was dodging him, and he was slowly realizing that this might be a better plan anyway.

Kirk Douglas has four sons, all involved in the movie business. Among the myriad movies their father has to his credit are *Twenty Thousand Leagues under the Sea* (1954), *Gunfight at the O.K. Corral* (1957), and *The Man from Snowy River* (1982). He has been nominated three times for an Academy Award: for *Champion* (1949), *The Bad and the Beautiful* (1952), and *Lust for Life* (1956).

He has kept himself busy outside of Hollywood as well, serving as ambassador of goodwill throughout the globe, representing the United States for the State Department and the U.S. Information Agency. In recognition of his assistance, in 1981 Kirk Douglas was awarded the Presidential Medal of Freedom. Other countries, including France and Germany, have also honored him, and in 1988 the American National Board of Review presented him with a career achievement award. All in all, not too bad for the ragman's son.

★

# Buddy Ebsen

Most TV viewers know Buddy Ebsen as Jed Clampett of *The Beverly Hillbillies,* or as George Russel of Disney's *Davy Crockett* programs, or more recently as Barnaby Jones. It is perhaps less widely known that Ebsen made his debut on the stage, singing and dancing, in 1928. In the midst of a lifetime of show business, Ebsen served his country during World War II as a Coast Guard officer, after trying repeatedly to obtain a Navy commission. He saw no action, but he spent his war years in hostile Pacific waters. Monotonous duty for the men, their contribution was nonetheless indisputable.

Christian Rudolph Ebsen, Jr., was surrounded by fancy footwork from the beginning (1908, Belleville, Illinois), in his father's dancing school. When Buddy was ten years old the family moved to Orlando, Florida, where the sprouting adolescent was more attracted to activities like sailing than to dancing, but his father finally convinced him to learn. Graduating from Orlando High School, he enrolled as a premedical student at the University of Florida, Gainesville, but by this time the Depression had hit Florida and the Ebsen family. Buddy had to leave Gainesville but was able to continue college, at Rollins, just a short distance from home. It was there that he became interested in drama.

But difficult years took their toll on the family, and by 1928 the Ebsens could no longer afford Buddy's college education. At this point the enterprising young man decided to take advantage of his dad's training, and that summer he moved to New York City to seek his dancing destiny.

At first Buddy was lucky; he got a chorus-line job in the Broadway musical *Present Arms*. But he was let go almost right away, having been ruled out as too tall. Intrepid, he continued to audition for musicals while working as a soda jerk. Finally he landed another chorus-line job in what became the Broadway hit of the season, *Whoopee,* starring Eddie Cantor. Buddy convinced the casting director to hire as well his kid sister, Vilma, and at the close of the show in 1929 the two Ebsens put together their own vaudeville act for nightclubs. They appeared in Broadway productions during the early 1930s, including Billie Burke's *Ziegfeld Follies* in 1934. In 1935 the siblings went to Hollywood, where Buddy's comic style became quite popular. They made one movie, MGM's *Broadway Melody of 1936* (1935), after which Buddy was on his own; Vilma had decided to dance only with her new husband.

Buddy did well solo, though, appearing in numerous roles throughout the 1930s. His musical abilities were featured in movies such as *Captain January* (1936, with Shirley Temple), *Born to Dance* (1936), *Banjo on My Knee* (1936), and *The Girl of the Golden West* (1938), but he also played more serious parts, as in *Yellow Jack* (1939).

He was cast in *The Wizard of Oz* (1939) as the Tin Man, but tin itself prevented him from finishing the job. Although not exactly comfortable, the makeup and costumes for the Scarecrow (Ray Bolger) and Cowardly Lion (Bert Lahr) were at least workable; the actors could move fairly easily. But the Tin Man getup was punishing. Ebsen had initially been enveloped in metal, but the director needed him to be able to achieve quite a bit of movement, and in the end they settled for cardboard.

It was the makeup that was almost the end of Buddy Ebsen. After applying an undercoat of grease paint over his head and neck, they powdered him all over with aluminum dust, and before each film take they diligently repowdered him. Several days passed, and then Ebsen began to feel some cramping and to have difficulty breathing. Next his chest started to hurt. He was rushed to the emergency room, where it was determined, not surprisingly, that the aluminum had gotten into his system. Six weeks later he was ready to get back to work, but he had been replaced. Jack Haley was now the Tin Man—with modifications to the makeup. (Ebsen was not the only casualty in the filming of this timeless favorite. Margaret Hamilton, the Wicked Witch, was repeatedly burned by the exploding powder that accompanied her appearances and disappearances, and stunt woman Betty Danko was smashed against the ceiling during a scene in which the witch flies through the air on her broomstick.)

By the time the United States entered World War II, Buddy Ebsen had already been aloft as one of MGM's premier stars, and then fallen. He and MGM studio chief Louis B. Mayer had had a falling out at contract-negotiation time. Like other Hollywood magnates, Mayer was known for ruthlessness; he also had a paternalistic attitude that did not always go over well with actors and employees. After their disagreement—Ebsen refused to be "owned" by MGM—movies did not come the performer's way nearly so easily. In fact, thirty-year-old Buddy Ebsen had almost no work, apart from a few RKO Radio productions such as *Sing Your Worries Away* (1941). So he talked to Vilma, and the two went back temporarily onto nightclub stages.

The seventh of December 1941 found Buddy in his sailboat, racing (and winning) in Santa Monica Bay. As he and his friend David Baird triumphantly prepared to get the *Moira* back onto her trailer, Ebsen noticed a Coast Guard officer calling out to the shore boatman, with specific instructions not to take any more Japanese out to fishing boats. Perplexed, he spoke with the boatman and learned about Pearl Harbor. He would later hear that, consistent with the paranoia of the times, some local Japanese were suspected of being in contact with submarines from their homeland.

Next morning he and Baird went down to the U.S. Naval Armory in Chavez Ravine to offer their services as operators of an offshore patrol boat. Ebsen had extensive experience in boat handling, and Baird had secured the use of a sixty-five-foot schooner. With the addition of machine guns and depth-charge racks, they proposed to conduct antisubmarine patrols off the West Coast, which appeared to be vulnerable to enemy attack.

The Navy turned them down, reassuring them that such operations were already being handled. The naive entertainer was not convinced. Pearl Harbor had just been surprise-attacked; did the Navy think they had been "handling" things there, too? But later Ebsen and Baird would discover the technical truth that their craft was completely unsuitable for such work anyway. The boat was too slow for dropping depth charges, and had the zealous friends succeeded in reconfiguring her, they would have blown up.

Meanwhile, Buddy had begun to get more acting work, and in 1941 he costarred with Skeets Gallagher in Cyrus Wood's version of the popular farce *Good Night, Ladies*. Cleverly, Buddy had by contract secured a share of the profits of this play, which did not do well on critics' pages but did very well at the box office. Buddy Ebsen's financial fortunes were improving.

His first marriage, though (to Ruth Cambridge, mother of his first two children), was beyond repair, and the emotional trauma made the war seem straightforward and uncomplicated by comparison. His desire to help beat his country's enemies was further fueled by all the uniforms he saw in the audience night after night. He should be among them, he thought.

He decided that with two years of college he had a shot at a commission in the Navy. A Navy commander advised him to learn celestial navigation and gain experience with twin-engine boats, so he enrolled in and aced a course in navigation at the Chicago Great Lakes Cruising Club. Then, through a personal favor, he was put in charge of a friend's forty-foot twin-engine cruiser, which had been offered to the Navy League for training the "ninety-day wonders" (selected personnel who underwent short training courses leading to a commission) stationed at Abbott Hall. Buddy spent many early-morning hours taking the aspiring admirals out on Lake Michigan for seamanship and boat-handling training. But despite all his preparation, his request for a commission was denied.

About ready to give up on a service tour and focus instead on making money and having fun, Buddy ran into a well-known agent friend one evening at the stage door of the theater. There stood Walter Kane in a handsome blue U.S. Coast Guard uniform, greeting the beautiful actresses as they left for the evening. Buddy wanted one of those uniforms, too. Kane offered to take him to a bar next door to meet Jim Kimberly, a lieutenant commander in the Coast Guard Reserve who shared Buddy's avid interest in sailing, and who would become a lifelong friend. That first meeting quickly turned into a rowdy night on the town, during which Buddy evidently agreed that the Coast Guard was for him and signed some papers.

Within weeks he received official notice that he was a lieutenant (jg) in the U.S. Coast Guard. His orders were to report to St. Augustine, Florida, for four months of general indoctrination followed by two months of training in antisubmarine warfare. Next he was ordered to report to the newly commissioned patrol frigate USS *Pocatello*. Following their shakedown cruise, which ended in April 1944, they were run through an operational-readiness inspection and found to be among the top antisubmarine ships in the fleet. The crew members, ecstatic over their performance, were ready for action.

But the high morale plummeted when the skipper informed the ships' officers that the *Pocatello* had been designated as a weather ship. Her orders were to assume Station Able, a two-hundred-mile circle in the Pacific Ocean fifteen hundred miles due west of Seattle. There the ship was to send up weather balloons, relaying the findings about the atmosphere back to the Navy's navigational data network. The *Pocatello* began her first tour on Station Able in July 1944. Designated PF-9, Ebsen's patrol frigate displaced 2,415 tons and carried a complement of 180 men. She carried three 3-inch and four 40mm guns. The *Pocatello*'s patrols consisted of thirty days at sea followed by ten in port at Seattle. The ship alternated on station with the Coast Guard cutter *Haida*, and by the end of the war she had completed a dozen patrols.

On board the *Pocatello*, Ebsen initially was assigned as damage-control officer and stood regular deck watches. Within a short while after reaching their station for their first patrol, boredom and a sense of futility set in à la *Mister Roberts*, providing Buddy with excellent

Coast Guard weather ship *Pocatello* (PF-9). (U.S. Coast Guard photo)

experience for his onstage role as the leading character later, in 1947. For the time being, in the middle of the Pacific Ocean in World War II, Buddy concluded that some entertainment would improve the men's spirits. He gathered what talent he had aboard ship and produced several shows, writing the material himself and directing. Rehearsals were fun, and a spark of life returned to the crew. Nevertheless, the facts were undeniable: they were in danger of never seeing any action during the entire war, which by 1945 was definitely turning in the Allies' favor.

Buddy decided to give it one final shot; maybe he could get to Europe with the USO. Taking a thirty-day leave, he went to New York and tried to persuade his friends in the organization to let him assemble a company to entertain the troops, thereby using his best talents for the war effort. The USO thought it a fine idea, as did the Coast Guard. But the Navy Personnel Office rejected it on the grounds that Ebsen was a qualified seagoing naval officer who could not be spared. Though somewhat gratified to hear himself described in this way, Ebsen found bitter irony in the Navy's decreeing him an essential presence when it had twice rejected his application for a commission.

Regardless, it was back to the *Pocatello,* which was in even greater disarray than before. The skipper had departed, and the former gunnery officer was in command. Buddy was now the executive officer of a disheartened ship. Things got so bad that one night, in a stormy sea, covered with spilled milk and food after having lost his balance in the wardroom, Ebsen was motivated to turn the experience into music. Full of the obscenities one might imagine, it was named by its creator "The Loving Sea." He sang it at his next performance—the crew had requested that Buddy continue to produce shows—and it was a smash hit. The song was mimeographed and began selling for ten cents a copy. The *Pocatello*'s morale began to revive.

The remaining patrols were completed with little difficulty, and crew members came to accept the comforting reality that the war was almost over and they had survived. At length the *Pocatello* was ordered home, and on 16 October 1945 Buddy Ebsen transferred to the District Coast Guard Office in Seattle, before being honorably discharged in January 1946.

Soon he was back on Broadway, singing and dancing in a revival of *Show Boat* (1946), which proved a success. While in the service he had been divorced and had married Nancy Wolcott (whom he met in the Coast Guard and with whom he has had five more children). He may have achieved personal happiness, but Ebsen also now had alimony payments and no Hollywood work after a 1947 tour with *The Male Animal*.

But Walt Disney came to the rescue. He decided that the performer's loose dancing style was just what he needed for an animated puppet he was designing in 1947, the precursor of Disneyland's audio-animatronic figures. Nothing further came of the connection, though, at least not for the time being. Seven years of little or no work followed, punctuated by two of appearing in Rex Allen Westerns, then a few TV shows, and finally a season in New York playing in *The Male Animal* again. As the years passed, the actor seriously considered leaving his chosen profession and going into construction.

But something made him stick it out, and in 1954 his break finally came, again in the form of Walt Disney. Ebsen was hired to play George Russel, the laid-back partner of Davy Crockett (Fess Parker) in the television episodes. The series was an immediate success that brought fame to its costars and led to a movie, *Davy Crockett, King of the Wild Frontier* (1955). That year Disney offered Ebsen a long-term contract as a singer, dancer, and actor. Numerous roles followed, not only in Disney productions but in other movies and TV shows. Ebsen brought Jed Clampett to life in CBS's *The Beverly Hillbillies* (1962–71), which was a runaway success, much to the dismay of the critics. His *Barnaby Jones* appeared in 1973 and ran until 1980, and the extraordinary Buddy Ebsen continues to be available for work.

# Tom Ewell

Lanky, witty, red-haired, with an impish, friendly way about him, Tom Ewell had already worked long and hard in the industry by the time he appeared in the comedy *The Seven-Year Itch* (1955), playing Richard Sherman, the man standing near Marilyn Monroe on a subway grating at the moment her undies are suddenly exposed as the hot air rises. Actually, Ewell had appeared first in the Broadway play, taking time out to make the movie version with Marilyn. He played the lead on Broadway from its opening in 1952 until 1955, to the delight of reviewers. That was one of the highest points of his acting career, upon which he had been focusing since 1931, when he quit law school.

Yewell Tompkins's native town was Owensboro, Kentucky (1909). He decided to become an actor at age six, after being awed by a musical production on an Ohio River showboat. At Owensboro Senior

Lt. (jg) Tom Ewell was in charge of an armed guard unit that sailed aboard merchant ships, offering protection against German U-boat attacks. (U.S. Navy photo)

High School he joined the drama club, the Rose Curtain Players, and won a scholarship to attend the University of Wisconsin in Madison. There, temporarily swayed by parental preference, he initially planned to become a lawyer, as both of his grandfathers had done. He got as far as finishing up three years of liberal-arts studies and one of law school.

Ewell achieved considerable success in his chosen profession despite repeated down times; no doubt the pleasure he took in everyday activities such as spending time with family and friends, storytelling, and golfing helped him through the dry spells. Before enlisting in the U.S. Naval Reserve in February 1942 (he was called to active duty in March),

## The Naval Armed Guard

Often thought of as the forgotten stepchild of the Navy, the Naval Armed Guard contributed almost 145,000 men to the war effort. Their job was to protect merchant ships and their cargo along sea lanes around the world, acting as gunners, radio operators, signalmen, and medics aboard some six thousand ships. During the course of World War II they amassed a memorable record. Armed Guard personnel were honored with five Navy Crosses, two Legion of Merit awards, seventy-five Silver Stars, twenty-four Navy and Marine Corps Medals, fifty-four Bronze Stars, more than fifty-eight thousand combat and engagement stars, and over eight thousand individual citations.

One destroyer, five destroyer escorts, and one transport ship were named after Armed Guard officers for conspicuous gallantry, all posthumously. They were:

DE-790, Lt. (jg) John R. Borum
DE-13, Ens. John J. Brennan
DE-178, Lt. (jg) William R. Herzog
DE-602, Ens. Hunter Marshall
DD-878, Ens. Kay K. Vesole
APD-111, Lt. (jg) Patrick Walsh
DE-354, Ens. Kenneth M. Willett

The ships carried an array of weapons to fend off attacks from both air and sea. Early in the war, a gunnery officer might direct a ten-man crew, a 4-inch gun, and a couple of .50-caliber machine guns; later, heavier weaponry placed aboard included two dual-purpose 3-inch guns, or a 4- or 5-inch gun aft and a 3-inch gun forward, and eight 20mms with explosive shells. In seas often dominated by U-boats, some eighteen hundred men lost their lives to enemy action while carrying out their charge: "You will engage the enemy until your guns can no longer be fired; until the decks are awash and the guns are going under."

he had appeared in more than fifteen plays, including several on Broadway (the first in 1934), and traveled around the world on a freighter, during which time he wrote a couple of plays himself. He received his Navy precommissioning instruction at Cornell University. After that he was sent on to the Princeton (New Jersey) Naval Training School, followed by the Naval Armed Guard's Local Defense Training School in Boston.

Young Tom Ewell became a gunnery officer. Armed Guard contingents served on board merchant ships sailing in Atlantic, Pacific, and Mediterranean convoys. Their mission was to protect the ships and their cargo along sea lanes that were regularly infested with German submarines. It was a highly dangerous assignment that would cost almost eighteen hundred American lives before the end of the war.

But Ewell survived, and in January 1945 he was detached from Armed Guard duty and assigned to the Navy Liaison Unit, Entertainment Branch, New York City. This was definitely more fun, as his chief responsibility was organizing and approving shows. Representing the Army and Navy, Lt. (jg) Ewell evaluated the USO Camp Shows, Inc., overseas entertainment units, which required official approval before they could leave the country. He had to travel several times a week, with little or no notice, to military bases up to two hundred miles away from New York City. His fitness report of 20 August 1945 reads, with typical military gusto, "Lt. Ewell has performed all his duties with dispatch and initiative. His thorough knowledge of entertainment has been instrumental in the establishment of the entertainment program of this activity."

Released from active duty on 31 October 1945, Lieutenant Ewell was authorized to wear the American Campaign and European–Africa–Middle Eastern Campaign medals and the World War II Victory Medal. He stayed on in the Naval Reserve until 6 November 1953, when he was honorably discharged.

After his wartime service he got back to the real entertainment business, playing on both coasts until his performance in the play *John Loves Mary* (1947–48) won him critical plaudits and film-industry attention. His first movie was the rollicking *Adam's Rib* (1949), which again attracted favorable commentary and led to roles in, among others, *Up Front* (1951), *The Seven-Year Itch* (1955), *The Lieutenant Wore Skirts* (1955), and *The Great American Pastime* (1956). For a while he had his own television show, *The Tom Ewell Show* (1960–61), and later he costarred with Robert Blake in the series *Baretta* (1975–78). He was sought after chiefly for his comic flair.

But Ewell also showed his sensitivity to the tragicomedy of the human experience off the stage and screen. When prominent Broadway photographer Tommy Vandamm, né George Robert Thomas, passed away in April 1944, he had conveyed to his wife (and fellow photographer and business partner) his wishes to be buried at sea. Florence Vandamm called Ewell, who had recently returned from a convoy, and asked if he could do her this service; her husband's body had already been cremated. The obliging Ewell readily agreed, but he was staying in a questionable hotel at the time and did not trust the maid, believing that her curiosity about the package on his dresser might get the better of her. Accordingly, he took Vandamm's ashes to the well-known and respected Sardi's restaurant, his home away from home, where he placed the package in the safekeeping of Renée, the hat-check girl. On his next convoy out, London-bound, the ashes traveled with him. After reading the burial-at-sea service from a prayer book, Tom Ewell and his gunnery group dropped his friend's ashes into the sea at sunset.

Ewell was married twice, first to Judith Ann Abbott, in 1946; they were divorced shortly thereafter. In 1948 he married advertising copywriter Marjorie Gwynne Sanborn, with whom he had one child. Tom Ewell died in 1994.

★

# Pat Hingle

Born Martin Patterson Hingle in Denver, Colorado, in 1924, veteran character actor Pat Hingle did not gravitate toward the acting business until after World War II. The son of Clarence Martin and Marvin Louise Patterson Hingle, who were divorced before he had a chance to know his father, Pat was used to changes. After his parents had gone their separate ways, his mother—who could not make ends meet on her teacher's salary—relocated, Pat in tow, whenever she thought she could make a little more money. Each move meant another fight for the brawny, square-jawed boy in the tattered clothes, who was challenged every time and had to prove himself to the new school's rowdies. By the time he got to Westlaco High School, Texas, he was involved in football, baseball, journalism, speech, and the band. All these activities may have helped him win his scholarship to the University of Texas, where he played tuba in the Longhorn band.

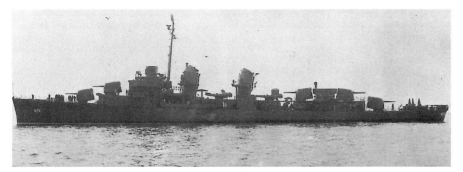

After Hingle's nomadic childhood, the destroyer *Marshall* (DD-676) seemed like his first real home. Hingle was a fireman first class when his ship participated in most of the key battles of the Pacific. (U.S. Navy photo)

When his country went to war, Pat Hingle joined the Navy through the V-6 program, on 4 November 1942. (This was an enlisted Naval Reserve program that trained the men for general service work.) Hingle spent much of his wartime service on board the destroyer USS *Marshall* (DD-676), to which he reported at Lido Beach, New York, on 16 October 1943 as a fireman first class. It was a job he performed with a strong sense of belonging, a new feeling in the young Hingle's previously nomadic life. The *Marshall* participated in most of the key battles of the Pacific, including Saipan, Guam, the Marianas, Leyte, Luzon, Iwo Jima, and Okinawa. Hingle was transferred from the *Marshall* as a water tender second class on 28 November 1944, to the Water Tender Class Center Receiving Station in San Diego.

He returned to the university after being discharged on 7 January 1946. He majored in radio broadcasting, which doubtless helped hone his well-known deep, powerful voice. While completing his B.A., he joined the school's dramatic society and appeared in numerous plays. It was during this time that he made two decisions that would alter the course of his life: he would pursue the acting profession, and he would marry the cute, feisty stage manager.

Alice Faye Dorsey and Pat Hingle were wed in 1947 and moved to New York after his 1949 graduation. There they worked at whatever jobs they could find, mostly behind counters, while Pat tried to get acting roles. And he had succeeded in appearing in several productions

## The USS *Marshall* (DD-676)

The *Marshall,* operating with Task Force 58, participated in the battles of the Philippine Sea and Leyte Gulf, as well as the amphibious operations on Hollandia, Saipan, Luzon, Iwo Jima, and Okinawa. The destroyer supported the landings at Palau, where forty-four Japanese prisoners were taken who had made their way to the islands after surviving the sinking of the 5,700-ton light cruiser *Natori* by the American submarine *Hardhead* (SS-365) in August 1944.

On 19 March 1945, during an air strike on Kyushu Island in Japan, a single Japanese plane made a low-level run on the aircraft carrier *Franklin* (CV-13) and made two direct hits with semi-armor-piercing bombs. Fires and explosions gutted the ship, which was all but sinking. The *Marshall,* ordered to stand by the flattop, rescued a total of 212 while steaming back and forth under unrelenting Japanese attacks from the air. After the crew of the *Franklin* had managed to bring the fires under control, the *Marshall* screened her to safety, transferring all survivors.

In June 1945 she steamed home, after fourteen months of combat duty. The ship had been involved in thirty engagements and eight "star" campaigns, had rescued twenty-one airmen, and had helped bring down five enemy planes. Deactivated after the war, the *Marshall* was recommissioned in 1951 and joined Task Force 77 for action against the enemy during the Korean War.

She resumed her old job in the Sea of Japan: screening carriers as they launched air strikes against shore installations, this time in Korea. She was sent next to the Formosa Straits patrol, supporting U.S. efforts to protect Chinese Nationalists from invasion. In November 1951 the *Marshall* reentered Korean waters, now with the United Nations Blockade and Escort Force. Her mission: to pound the shore relentlessly and destroy enemy supplies, shelters, and ammunition depots. In carrying out this duty, the destroyer sent out more than seven thousand shells and inflicted an estimated six hundred casualties. Next she screened carriers in Korea's Yellow Sea, regularly bombarding the enemy shoreline.

In March 1952 the *Marshall* was ordered back to San Diego for overhaul, the first complete one she had had in her eight and a half years of service. Following her yard period, she returned to waters off Korea and acted as a screening unit for carriers, performed antisubmarine duties, and participated in the bombardment of Wonson in December 1952. She was next ordered to patrol the Formosan Straits, after which she returned to San Diego in May 1953.

During the early 1960s she served as a Naval Reserve training ship. The *Marshall* was decommissioned on 19 July 1969 and scrapped. For her services in World War II and the Korean War, she received twelve battle stars (eight for World War II and four for Korea).

and live-TV programs by the time the Korean War broke out and the Navy recalled him.

From May 1951 to September 1952 he served again, this time as a boiler technician first class on board the escort destroyer USS *Damato* (DDE-871). During Hingle's tour the ship operated in Atlantic and Mediterranean waters conducting antisubmarine operations. He left the service with the Good Conduct, World War II Victory, Navy Occupation Service, American Campaign, and Asiatic-Pacific Campaign medals.

Returning to Alice and New York, Hingle joined the recently formed (in 1947) Actors' Studio. There the Method system of acting, developed by Russian actor, director, and producer Konstantin Stanislavski, would strongly influence many other students as well, including Marilyn Monroe and James Dean. Hingle appeared in the studio's production of *End as a Man* (1953–54), which earned him critical attention. Accolades were to follow for performances in plays including *Cat on a Hot Tin Roof* (1955), *The Dark at the Top of the Stairs* (1957–58), and *J.B.* (1958–59). His first film was, propitiously, *On the Waterfront* (1954).

Alternating between the stage and movies, cast frequently as a heavyweight, Hingle enjoyed successes such as *Splendor in the Grass* (1961, with Warren Beatty), *Hang 'em High* (1968, with Clint Eastwood), *Norma Rae* (1979), and *Batman* (1989; also the 1992 sequel). He has made more than a hundred television appearances over the years, in shows including *Bonanza* (1969), *Gunsmoke* (six episodes in 1971), and *Hawaii Five-O* (several times from 1975 to 1977). He played J. Edgar Hoover in the 1992 TV movie *Citizen Cohn* and Chief Justice Earl Warren in another, *Simple Justice* (1993).

Pat and Alice Hingle have had three children. Often assumed to be outgoing, probably thanks to the characters he portrays, in real life Hingle seeks quieter relaxation, and when not working he might be found playing a bit of guitar or softball.

★

# Rock Hudson

R oy Harold Fitzgerald had wanted to be an actor ever since he had first thought about wanting to be anything, but the verbalized desire got him only a crack from his stepfather, Wally Fitzgerald. An unmanly, impossible dream—best to nip it in the bud, Wally must have thought. But the child simply learned not to talk about his fantasy. He nourished it in silence, catching every movie he could, imagining himself diving into the ocean and swimming to the rescue of a heroine in Tahiti.

Roy was born in 1925 in Winnetka, Illinois. By 1931 he and his parents, Roy and Katherine Wood Scherer, were living with his grandparents, James and Mary Ellen Wood, in a one-bedroom, one-bathroom house along with his mother's brother, his wife, and their four children. To the kids, the crowded conditions were fun. There was no shortage of food, and Grandma and Grandpa ran a lively household with big dinners every evening, after which the grownups played cards and the kids frolicked outside or listened to radio shows. But Roy Scherer was not content, and in 1932 he took off for California, abandoning his shocked seven-year-old son. Roy Junior did not ask about it, though, nor did anyone explain to the other children that Uncle Roy was gone forever. Such things were not discussed. His wife apparently had been expecting the development, though, because soon thereafter she began dating and married another man: Wally Fitzgerald, who shoveled coal at the power plant. The adopted Roy, now with a new last name, continued to grow up.

Not particularly studious, and unathletic, skinny, and shy, Roy did not distinguish himself in high school. Wally, who had apparently decided that the boy needed toughening up, beat him regularly. Finally he began hitting Kay as well, and she divorced him only to marry him again, for a while. By the time Roy was sixteen, Wally was out of their lives. Roy and Kay remained close throughout it all, best friends, the two of them facing the world together. They played piano together, sang songs, danced, and laughed.

Roy loved to have fun, and his laughter spread like wind among his cousins when they got together for some music, him playing piano and everyone else jitterbugging. In 1943, at age eighteen, he enlisted in the Navy, probably imagining that this would get him out of the workaday life that faced him otherwise.

Fresh-caught out of New Trier High School, he was sent to the Great Lakes Naval Training Station for boot training, followed by orders to report to Aviation Repair and Overhaul Unit 2 (AROU 2), located at the naval air base on the island of Samar in the Philippines. The young seaman was shipped to his duty station on board the Liberty ship SS *Lew Wallace*. As the ship passed under the Golden Gate bridge, Fitzgerald and his shipmates listened to "Sentimental Journey" as interpreted by the popular vocalist Doris Day. (Years later Day would become one of his favorite people to work with. The two always had a ball on the set, as did most of the others who acted with the fun-loving Hudson. He and Day costarred in a series of comedy hits such as 1959's *Pillow Talk*.)

Hudson spent the bulk of his Navy service as an aircraft mechanic with AROU 2 on Samar. He worked on all types of planes—fighters,

Fresh-caught out of high school, Fitzgerald was sent after boot training to Aviation Repair and Overhaul Unit 2 on Samar, the Philippines. There he worked on planes from the carriers in the western Pacific. Fitz's sense of humor made him a popular shipmate. (U.S. Navy photos)

torpedo bombers, dive bombers, and others that were brought in for repair from the U.S. aircraft carriers amassed in the western Pacific. Known to his shipmates as Fitz, the future superstar was just one of the guys in the Navy, generally very well liked, doubtless largely because of his frolicsome pranks.

Fitz returned to the States in 1946 on board an aircraft carrier, passing again under the Golden Gate Bridge in a festive spirit that was celebrated with Cokes all around. He was discharged that year.

He returned to Winnetka and worked at various odd jobs while pondering his next move. Aside from his desire to get into the acting field somehow, he had always nourished a desire to be with his dad again, and finally he decided to join him in Southern California. But living with his father's new family was not everything the son had hoped for, and after trying unsuccessfully to sell vacuum cleaners for his father, he moved into a boardinghouse and got a job as a truck driver.

He also regularly stood outside movie-studio gates thinking that some producer might notice him, discover him. But it would take more effort than that, and it was many mailings of head shots and introductions at parties later that he was finally offered the opportunity to take screen tests. Despite the evening acting classes he had been taking, his performances were so bad that his test at Twentieth Century–Fox is still shown to beginning classes as an example of what not to do—and as a lesson about the critical importance of perseverance. Roy Fitzgerald, now Rock Hudson, continued to pursue his dream.

Finally his looks landed him a combination bit part/screen test, in the movie *Fighter Squadron* (1948). He played an Air Corps officer, with the job of delivering just three lines; but he botched one of them each and every time he tried. In the end, so that he could get the scene shot, the frustrated director changed the line.

Hudson was picked up by Universal after *Fighter Squadron,* and the studio executives—impressed, like everyone else who met him, by his handsomeness and powerful, sensual presence—methodically set about creating a star. He was brought along slowly. They gave him lessons in acting, fencing, riding, and singing. They enhanced his radiant smile by capping all of his teeth. Rock Hudson's picture in various poses and locales appeared in fan magazines well before he made his first picture for the studio, *Undertow* (1949).

The following few years were spent playing minor roles in almost thirty movies. Then, in 1953, Hudson was cast opposite Jane Wyman in *Magnificent Obsession* (1954). The movie was a smash. Rock Hudson became a star overnight and remained one for the next twenty years. The lessons had paid off, and among the movies in which he gave fine performances were *All That Heaven Allows* (1955), *Giant* (1956), and *The Tarnished Angels* (1957). He worked as well in theater and television, starring in *McMillan and Wife* and then *McMillan* from 1971 to 1977. But by the time he guest-starred on *Dynasty* (1984–85), he had been diagnosed with AIDS, for the first time focusing widespread media attention on the killer disease.

Although the virus can be contracted in a variety of ways, it is likely that Hudson was exposed to it during one of his homosexual liaisons. Only his intimate friends knew this secret, which for professional reasons he guarded carefully, and successfully, for his entire career, until he knew and had accepted the fact that his life was coming to an end. At that point his main interest centered on telling the truth.

He had been married once—to his agent's secretary, the charming and entertaining Phyllis Gates, from 1955 to 1958—and did have occasional dalliances with women, especially in his younger years, but Hudson had actively pursued his homosexual preference since the 1940s, possibly earlier. When he moved to the Los Angeles area he found the gay community there within a year and became part of this subculture for life. A gay friend threw parties to introduce him to people in the industry, and his first agent was gay. Many of his closest lifelong friends were gay, but Rock Hudson had good friends across the sexual spectrum.

He was universally loved for his childlike sense of play and generosity of spirit. He hosted gala holiday dinners in his cherished Beverly Hills Spanish-style home, known as the Castle, where he also held legendary Hollywood parties. Hudson spent more than twenty years gradually remodeling his home and enjoying it, often outside where he could pursue his favorite recreations, barbecuing and gardening.

Fun aside, Hudson could also be downright heroic, as in 1965, during the Watts riots, when he struck out in the middle of the night with his housekeeper and her son to rescue her best friend from the battle-torn neighborhood. He drove his station wagon right into the fray, through barricades and roadblocks, his German shepherd on the alert in the back of the car. The friend secured, all returned to Beverly Hills and ingested several nerve-calming cocktails.

Hudson empathized with neither the demonstrations against the Vietnam War nor the insistence of the gay community to be openly accepted. He was not affiliated with any political party, though he generally voted Republican, nor did he engage in political discussions or activities. On a personal level, he believed that preferences need not be made public in order to be valid; and he knew well that public knowledge of his sexual orientation, socially taboo for most of his career, would have meant no more work.

Rock Hudson had a splendid career, receiving numerous national and international awards and being nominated for an Oscar for his performance in *Giant*. He died in 1985.

# Gene Kelly

Few movie scenes have become as well known as Gene Kelly's dancing and singing down a rain-drenched street in the *Singin' in the Rain* (1952; he also co-directed the film). A dancer since his childhood in Pittsburgh, Pennsylvania, the exuberant, congenial, incessantly working and internationally beloved Eugene Curran Kelly was born in 1912, number three in an Irish Catholic family of five children. The family was reasonably comfortable, with Dad (Patrick) working as a sales executive for Columbia Gramophone and Mom (Harriet Curran) an actress with a Pittsburgh stock company.

Harriet, who ran a dance school, forced her eight-year-old son to take dancing lessons. He resisted the idea without success but would later be grateful for his mother's firm stance on the issue. He stuck out the humiliation of it for a year, in what would become the early foundations of his future career. After that he talked Harriet into letting him replace dancing with the more popular sphere of sports. In high school he became involved in several, including hockey and football, and he became the editor of the school paper as well as the chairman of his class. He even auditioned for plays and began dancing again. Graduating at age sixteen, he began taking classes at Pennsylvania State University, then left to help out with improving the family's financial picture during the worst part of the Depression. He worked in construction, at a gas station, and as a gym teacher.

It was when he went back to college, this time at the University of Pittsburgh, that Kelly became involved on an ongoing basis with theater productions. He directed the annual Cap and Gown presentation in his senior year, and he and one of his brothers worked up their own act, singing and dancing locally—and successfully—in nightclubs and amateur contests. Kelly started his own dance studio after receiving his B.S. in economics from the University of Pittsburgh in 1933. His business did so well that by 1938 the young hoofer felt ready to take on New York City. Broadway welcomed him with several bit parts in musical comedies.

When he was cast to play the lead character in the 1940 Broadway production of the musical *Pal Joey*, Gene Kelly's star began to rise. After he appeared in *For Me and My Gal* (1942), MGM signed him to a contract. The next few years brought work in movies such as *Thousands Cheer* (1943), *Cover Girl* (1944; Kelly got rave reviews for his portrayal of a nightclub entertainer), and *Anchors Aweigh* (1945, with Frank Sinatra), which earned him an Academy nod.

It was at this moment in his star-studded career that MGM gave him a leave of absence to join the military service. Eugene Kelly enlisted in the U.S. Naval Reserve on 27 November 1944 and was sent to boot camp in San Diego. He was older than most of the other "men," who were really still kids with whom the thirty-two-year-old performer shared little common ground. But what disturbed him more was the program's brutal treatment of those in training, and the way his fellow enlistees simply accepted it. He abhorred the rigorousness of the services in general and felt as if he were living under some repressive regime. He was despondent for the entire thirteen-week duration.

When ordered to Washington at the end of his training to make a film, he was utterly disgusted. He had thought that at least the hellish training had qualified him to fight his country's enemies in the Pacific. Had he known that his military service would consist of making movies, he would have stayed in Hollywood and made them for a lot more money.

However, he changed his tune when it became clear that this was going to be a film about battle fatigue, a subject of critical importance and one to which Kelly responded immediately. In order to gain first-hand knowledge about it, he spent two weeks in a rehabilitation hospital near Philadelphia, closely observing the men in the wards. The film he produced proved to be a significant contribution to the understanding and treatment of the syndrome, and shortly after its completion, on 26 April 1945, Kelly was commissioned a lieutenant (jg). He never did experience combat action during the war, but he made a notable contribution to the war effort.

He was ordered next to the Naval Photographic Science Laboratory Branch, Photographic Division of the Bureau of Aeronautics in Washington. His first task was to film the results of a new fire-dousing foam that would snuff out the devastation inflicted on U.S. ships by Japanese Baka bombs (manned flying bombs). Using as props two dozen gasoline-splattered aircraft filled with explosives, Kelly's crew of thirteen camera operators filmed the exploding aircraft as charges were ignited. They captured the action of the firefighters, who moved into the fiery scene swiftly, extinguishing the flames with the experimental foam. Once Fleet Admiral Ernest J. King had reviewed the film and witnessed the success of the foam, he ordered that tons of the substance be sent immediately to the Pacific.

Kelly by now fully understood and accepted the importance of his job. His next assignment was to create a photographic study of the cruiser *Fall River* (CA-131), docked at the Philadelphia Navy Yard. He was to be particularly attentive to the radar equipment, since the survey results were to be reviewed by high-ranking naval personnel in Washington. (The *Fall River* was later assigned to Joint Task Force 1, organized to conduct Operation Crossroads, atomic-weapons tests in the Marshall Islands in the summer of 1946.) Kelly knew little about combatants and their equipment, but the commanding officer of the ship turned out to be an old friend from college days. With this invaluable assistance, Kelly managed to collect all the footage he needed. He sailed with the *Fall River* to Cuba while filming the ship, and upon arrival he flew back to Washington, assignment successfully completed.

In the end Gene Kelly even made it to the Pacific, his original goal upon joining the Navy. He was ordered with a crew of eleven to head toward Japan, but when the first atomic bomb was dropped on Hiroshima, they were stopped at Hawaii. Sent back to San Francisco, they had to wait for a few days in uncertainty, something Kelly did not do well. He managed it anyway, and when the second bomb was dropped and Japan surrendered, he was ordered back to his Washington base.

Even though the war was over, Kelly was assured that there was still a need for his talents and he should not look to leaving the service just yet. His next detail was to be with the Silent Service. He was to make an indoctrination film about bold wartime U.S. submarine raids off the coast of Japan. Kelly had great anxiety about this assignment, fearful of being trapped underwater with no air, enclosed in a small space. Nevertheless, he was able to put his claustrophobia aside, and once he got below, a sense of great tranquillity came over him. He produced an inspired film that would prove to be a valuable recruiting vehicle for young men considering the submarine service. For Kelly, who finished the film at little cost and with a resourceful cast and crew, it was to prove invaluable directing experience.

Soon he was sent off to direct another Navy film, the story of the aircraft carrier *Franklin* (CV-13), which was hit and nearly sunk by an enemy semi-armor-piercing bomb off the coast of Japan. In the incident, 724 men were killed and 265 wounded, and the ship was saved by a gallant crew who sailed her back to the States. They arrived in New York Harbor on 28 April 1945. Kelly and his film crew spent a week aboard the ship at the Brooklyn Naval Yard, filming and interviewing the survivors of the attack.

He was then ordered to Washington again, where he edited seemingly endless footage of film, mostly U.S. Navy, but also a bit that had been captured from the Japanese. Occasionally he came across a riveting battle, but for the most part this was not exciting duty. However, it did add to his steadily growing repertoire of filming skills, as this

One Navy film that Kelly directed told the story of the *Franklin* (CV-13), which was nearly sunk by an enemy semi-armor-piercing bomb off the coast of Japan. The ship was saved by her crew, but 724 men were killed and 265 wounded. Kelly and his film crew spent a week aboard the *Franklin* at the Brooklyn Naval Yard, filming and interviewing the survivors of the attack. (U.S. Navy photo)

was the first time he had worked with the editing technology. Finally he was given responsibility for the Navy section of the weekly *Army-Navy* screen magazine, produced in New York. This was a collection of the best and latest footage, which Kelly was to select and comment upon for the edification of the fleet—more experience that would prove useful in his future work.

He was discharged on 13 May 1946, receiving the World War II Victory Medal and the American Area Campaign Medal. Kelly returned posthaste to his wife—actress Betsy Blair—and their baby in the new Beverly Hills home Betsy had found for them. Upon his return to Hollywood, he was recognized not only as an actor but also as a director and producer. There followed a string of hits, including *Ziegfeld Follies* (1946), *The Pirate* (1948), *Take Me out to the Ballgame* (1949),

*On the Town* (1950; he was co-director as well), *Summer Stock* (1950), and *An American in Paris* (1951, which won him an honorary Academy Award for his extraordinary versatility). The following year he co-directed and appeared in *Singin' in the Rain*.

Gene Kelly continued to perform during the late 1950s and the 1960s, directing, dancing in, and choreographing *Invitation to the Dance* (1956), which earned him the West Berlin Film Festival's highest honor in 1958 and the attention of the Paris Opéra. He then choreographed a ballet for that company, with a superb pas de deux accompanied by George Gershwin's Concerto in F at the 1960 premiere. To express its appreciation, the French government made Gene Kelly a Knight of the Legion of Honor.

With the heyday of lavish musicals passing, Kelly now began to appear in more dramatic roles and to turn an increasing amount of his creative effort to directing. Notably, he directed the extremely entertaining movie *A Guide for the Married Man* (1967) as well as *Hello, Dolly!* (1969, starring Barbra Streisand). Still athletic and never one to stop dancing, Kelly co-hosted and appeared in *That's Entertainment* (1974) and its sequel (1976), and he was featured again in 1994's *That's Entertainment III*.

He and Betsy Blair, married in 1941, were divorced in 1957. In 1960 he married Jeanne Coyne, with whom he stayed until her passing in 1973. Gene Kelly died in 1996. He had three children.

★

# Jack Lemmon

His full name is John Uhler Lemmon III, and his first home (as of 1925) was Boston. His father, general sales manager and vice president of the Doughnut Corporation of America, sang barbershop tunes and danced the softshoe in his spare time. It was with him that the four-year-old Jack saw his first theater production, deciding there and then to become an actor and musician. His mother, Mildred LaRue Noel Lemmon, was an independent Boston socialite, slightly on the eccentric side, who would later adjust easily to the wilder Hollywood atmosphere in which she joined her son. The parental union was not to last, but the Lemmons remained on good terms for life, never officially divorcing, and both remained on very close terms with their only son. John and Jack would go on a month-long trip to Europe together, John would play a bit part in one of Jack's movies (*The Notorious Landlady*, 1962), and Millie would become an integral part of Jack's daily life in Southern California.

A product of the prestigious Phillips Academy in Andover, John Lemmon III went on to Harvard and the Navy's V-12 Reserve Officers Training Program in 1943. His major field of study, war-services sciences, was as far as possible from being to his liking, and he spent most of his academic life on probation. A couple of his unimpressed professors went so far as to offer him their considered opinion that he would never amount to anything much. He managed anyway to receive a commission in the Navy in 1945, at which time the captain congratulated him for his achievement of the lowest marks of any ROTC officer, ever.

But Lemmon did distinguish himself in the school's theater that same year. He was elected president of the dramatic society's Hasty Pudding Club and vice president of the Dramatic and Delphic Clubs, and was one of Harvard's standout actors. A gifted pianist, he became a main attraction at parties. Lemmon was known by all as a genuinely nice guy, a designation that has stayed with him throughout the years for genuinely good reasons. Working with Anne Bancroft on the set of *The Prisoner of Second Avenue* (1975), he cut himself to avoid injuring her with his prop (a shovel); Walter Matthau wrote an ode to his niceness after getting to know him when they worked together in *The Odd Couple* (1968); even his divorce from Cynthia Stone, to whom he was married from 1950 to 1956, went smoothly, with no animosity.

He was also to become known as a devoted, thoroughly professional, and extremely talented actor, but first he had to make it through the U.S. Navy. He had entered the V-12 program during World War II, in which he never did participate, and the year after his commissioning he was ordered to the *Lake Champlain* (CV-39) before completing his studies, such as they were. The aircraft carrier's deck log for the 1600–2000 watch on 12 February 1946 reads, "1835: Ens. John Uhler Lemmon, III, (DL) 477240, USNR reported aboard for duty from the Commandant Third Naval District."

It had taken him two tries to board the ship successfully. The first time he had climbed the after gangplank, where a petty officer informed him that the officer's gangplank was forward. Picking up his gear, Lemmon went back down, climbed the forward gangplank, approached

Ens. John Uhler Lemmon III. (Joe Baltake collection)

the ship's quarterdeck, and reported to the ship's officer of the day. The ODD asked where he was reporting from. When he heard the word *Harvard*, the officer assumed that Lemmon must be the ship's new communications officer, since that school housed a well-known communications program. Lemmon knew nothing about that particular subject, but things were moving quickly, and before he knew it he had been assigned to the communications department as K1 division officer.

The ship was being deactivated, as it turned out, and was being stripped of everything that was not a part of the superstructure. Suddenly Ensign Lemmon saw a way out of his predicament: get rid of everything that was a part of the communications department. Then, how could he do the job? They would have to send him someplace else, maybe back to school. Everything went—decoding machines, lights, flags, the works. Lemmon accomplished all this on his own, since the communications petty officer was on leave. What the green ensign did not know was that the ship was due to take one last short voyage to Newport News, Virginia, and that basic communications gear would be needed to make the journey.

Commissioned in June of 1945, the *Lake Champlain* had just completed "Magic Carpet" duty, bringing home American troops from the European theater. (She was recommissioned in 1952 and served as flagship for Carrier Task Force 77 during the Korean War.) On 20 April 1946 the carrier was to move from Berth No. 42, Norfolk Naval Shipyard, Portsmouth, to Pier No. 8, Newport News Shipbuilding Company. The chief petty officer returned from leave in time for the short cruise and discovered what Lemmon had wrought, but none of his yelling—without regard for the ensign's rank—could change the facts. The hour-plus voyage would take them through a narrow channel crowded with ships, and they had nothing with which to signal other vessels of their movement.

As the ship departed, the unhappy twosome took up positions below the captain's bridge. Within minutes the ship's executive officer bounded down from the bridge bellowing something about an underway ensign. Of course Lemmon did not know what he was talking about, and the chief petty officer froze. Knowing full well that all the flags were ashore, Lemmon nonetheless went through the charade of running to the flag locker, opening it, and looking in.

Knowing nothing about communications, Lemmon was somehow assigned to the communications department of the *Lake Champlain* (CV-39) and courted disaster during most of the hour he spent at sea. (U.S. Navy photo)

Much to his surprise, a single flag lay partially hidden in a corner of the locker. Lemmon grabbed it, having no idea what it was for, and turned triumphantly to the XO, who nodded and returned to the bridge. Lemmon had the ensign run up—and it was actually the right flag.

Jack Lemmon's proverbial good luck would last him throughout most of the years to come, starting with the very next potential disaster he faced. As the carrier proceeded around a turn in the channel, a tanker was heading straight at them. The ship was obviously in trouble, since she was yawing badly, her crew scurrying across the decks, flags flying, horns and sirens blaring, lights going crazy.

As the ship closed, Capt. Logan C. Ramsey, USN, commanding officer of the *Champlain* (and father of actor Logan Ramsey; see the chapter on him), yelled down to Lemmon. What was wrong with that ship, he demanded, and which flags were they flying? A glance at the chief petty officer told Ensign Lemmon he was in this alone. Quick-thinking as always (and completely winging it), and knowing with certainty that the tanker really was in trouble, Lemmon yelled back that the vessel had lost her right screw and they were out of control: they had the right of way. Ramsey immediately ordered the carrier up against the bank of the channel into the mud, and the tanker passed by, almost hitting the *Champlain* below the flight deck. One of her crew shouted their thanks: they had lost their right screw and were having trouble controlling their steerage.

Within minutes a surprised Lemmon was summoned to the bridge. Ramsey complimented him on his swiftness and promised him a 4.0 rating on his fitness report. This perfect score got him his next duty, after he had completed his short tour on board the *Champlain* (on 30 April 1946).

In Washington, Lemmon was assigned to a message-decoding department until, having requested a transfer to Boston, he was ordered there to run a motor pool. By that summer he had enough points for discharge and left the Navy, after a seven-month tour that had consisted of about one hour and a half at sea and two short-term shore-duty assignments.

He returned to Harvard, completing both a B.A. and a B.S. in 1947. Next it was on to New York, his father having loaned him three hundred dollars and given his approval. John would have preferred to pass his business-world savvy on to his son, but he knew that nothing was more important than following one's inner direction, a basic tenet to which both parents held steadfastly.

For more than a year the younger Lemmon barely scraped by on jobs playing the piano (he appeared regularly at the Old Knickerbocker Music Hall, which would provide valuable performing experience), devouring the hors d'oeuvres that were served. His father, sensing that New York had not showered his son with money and success, arranged to be temporarily relocated to the city. Jack wound up moving in with him, much to John's relief, and kept the apartment with his friends after John had left to carry out duties elsewhere.

Things began to take a new turn when Jack auditioned for and won the lead role in the off-Broadway production of *The Power of Darkness*, by Leo Tolstoi. His costar was his wife-to-be, Cynthia Stone. Loneliness and anonymity were relegated to the past, although overnight stardom hardly resulted from Lemmon's talented rendition in the Russian drama.

It did lead, however, to more work, such as the Hayloft Theater's summer stock and a radio soap opera. During the next few years Lemmon appeared in hundreds of radio and live television shows, including *Studio One* (in 1949) and *Robert Montgomery Presents* (in 1953), and in several plays. Spotted by a talent scout in 1953 and with a seven-year Columbia Pictures contract all but guaranteed, Jack and Cynthia moved to the West Coast.

In 1954 Lemmon appeared in his first film, *It Should Happen to You,* opposite actress Judy Holliday. A year later he was cast as Ensign Pulver in *Mister Roberts* (1955), for which he won the year's Academy Award for best supporting actor. He later received nominations for *Some Like It Hot* (1959), *The Apartment* (1960), *Days of Wine and Roses* (1962), *The China Syndrome* (1979), *Tribute* (1980), and *Missing* (1982). He won his second Oscar in 1973 for *Save the Tiger,* and his outstanding performances include *That's Life* (1986), *Glengarry Glen Ross* (1992), and the *Grumpy Old Men* movies (1993, 1995).

Divorced from Cynthia in 1956, Jack Lemmon was married in 1962 to actress Felicia Farr, with whom he continues to spar cheerfully. He has produced two children and a brilliant career.

# Guy Madison

With no idea of becoming an actor, Robert Ozell Moseley—
TV's future Wild Bill Hickock—just happened to be in Southern California at the time *Since You Went Away* (1944) was
being filmed. He was serving as a Navy lifeguard (one of the few who
had previous experience in the job) as part of his duties while assigned
to the Welfare and Recreation Division at Naval Air Station North
Island, San Diego. The base published a periodical, in an issue of which
Moseley's photo appeared. Somehow the magazine made its way to the
attention of screenwriter and producer David O. Selznick, who envisioned on-screen possibilities for this young man's robust comeliness.

It would be the beginning of a career that produced more than
eighty-five movies, well over a hundred television appearances, and
hundreds of radio programs. Upon his honorable discharge from the

Navy in October 1945 (as a seaman first class), his new name settled upon, Guy Madison signed a contract with Selznick.

The California native (1922) came from Bakersfield, where his parents, Ben and Mary Jane Moseley, raised their five children on a ten-acre ranch. The family's spread made it through the Depression thanks to Ben's being able to work for the railroad, a job he held down for more than thirty years.

Chores left the young Moseleys little time for fun off their land, but Robert's love of working the soil would last throughout his lifetime. He also managed to pursue his talent for gymnastics, at which he excelled both in high school and during his two years of college. When he enlisted in the Naval Reserve, he had been working as a telephone-company lineman. On 23 October 1942 at Los Angeles, Robert Moseley became an apprentice seaman.

During his three-year stint, he was assigned to the U.S. Naval Reserve Station in Los Angeles and then to Roosevelt Base, Terminal Island, before moving on to Transition Training Squadron, Pacific Fleet, San Diego. He was next ordered to Headquarters Squadron Fleet Air Wing 14, located on North Island. The wing was tasked with over-water patrol, convoy coverage, and special missions. Flying PB4Y Privateer and PBM Mariner patrol bombers, Fleet Air Wing 14 trained units attached to its command, maintained training and instruction for pilots and crews, and equipped new squadrons, at the same time serving as the San Diego control station for flights to Hawaii.

Moseley was later assigned to Carrier Aviation Support Unit 5, also based on North Island. It may have been while he was serving with CASU 5 that he somehow injured his back and had to be transferred to the Navy hospital in San Diego and then the U.S. Naval Special Hospital at Banning, California, from which he was discharged.

Following his years in the Navy, Guy Madison went right into his new profession in movies and TV, playing the lead in *Wild Bill Hickock* for eight years (1951–59). In 1960 he began making pictures in Italy, where, working almost nonstop, in twelve years he starred in forty-four films. Madison was married twice and had four children, passing on to them his knowledge of and appreciation for the wilderness and for manual labor, especially gardening and furniture making. He died in 1996.

Robert Ozell Moseley—shown here with actress Alexis Smith—would later become Guy Madison, television's Wild Bill Hickock. Moseley served as a Navy lifeguard at North Island, San Diego. After his photo appeared in the base's magazine, David O. Selznick envisioned an on-screen future for the robust young man. (Bridget Madison collection)

# Victor Mature

Victor Mature, a screen idol by the early 1940s admired for his dark, muscular appearance, enlisted in the U.S. Coast Guard in Los Angeles. Soon he was put on a train bound for Boston, where he joined his ship, the Coast Guard auxiliary icebreaker *Storis* (WMEC-38) on 28 November 1942.

Hoping to be accepted as just another citizen who wanted to join the fight against his country's enemies, Mature met with some resistance, but many of the officers had sympathetic smiles for him. It was not always easy, they knew, being a movie star in the U.S. military, even one who had volunteered his services.

The actor was the son of Austrian immigrant M. G. Mature, whose hard work eventually propelled him from scissors-grinder to business executive, and Clara, who was of Swiss descent. They gave birth to

Victor Mature enlisted in the U.S. Coast Guard and served fourteen months aboard the icebreaker *Storis* (WMEC-38), reaching the rate of chief boatswain's mate. (U.S. Coast Guard photo)

him in Louisville, Kentucky (1916) and educated him in parochial schools, the Kentucky Military Institute, and the Spenserian Business School. After trying his hand at a variety of jobs, Victor finally earned enough money selling candy to go into the restaurant business. But California beckoned, and in the end the young entrepreneur packed up what was left of his candy stock and pointed his car westward, armed with his parents' good wishes.

In Los Angeles, after selling some goods and renting a garage for living space, Victor enrolled in the Pasadena Community Playhouse. Just over a year later, in 1936, he appeared onstage in *Paths of Glory.* But fame did not follow immediately, and Victor had to live on odd jobs, scrimping to feed himself and pay his tuition, even moving into a tent for a while, before he was offered a fellowship in 1937. More than fifty plays later he got his first lead role, and in 1938 he was offered a part in a movie, *The Housekeeper's Daughter* (1939). His brief on-screen appearance was enough to attract fans' notice, and his

Mature stands lookout watch aboard the *Storis*. (From the book *Movie Lot to Beachhead* [1945] by the editors of *Look* magazine)

next movie, *One Million B.C.* (1940), placed him prominently, guaranteeing his future as a star.

After making many more movies and relegating both the tent and the garage to prehistory, Mature joined the Coast Guard in July 1942. He spent fourteen months aboard the *Storis* on operations in the North Atlantic, making all of his rates at sea and eventually reaching the rate of chief boatswain's mate.

The *Storis* was home-ported at Boston for the duration of the war. After the icebreaker's commissioning in September 1942, she began making wartime Greenland patrols, in command of a fleet of 125-foot patrol vessels whose assignment was to stop the Germans from setting up weather stations on the island's east coast. Still a working, commissioned ship today, the *Storis,* known as the Galloping Ghost of the Alaskan Coast, now enforces international fishing treaties and regulations.

Victor Mature may have devoted his best maritime efforts to the Coast Guard, but originally he had been more drawn to the Navy. He attempted to enlist after completing the filming of *My Gal Sal* (1942, with Rita Hayworth), but the U.S. Navy rejected him due to color-blindness. Resolute, the actor in turn rejected these test results, pointing out that he had no trouble distinguishing red, white, and blue. He marched across the hall to the Coast Guard recruiting office and took the same test, flunking again.

Now the normally affable Mature was peeved. His voice level going up a few octaves between swears, he kept insisting that he was *not* color-blind. Among those who overheard the disturbance was a chief boatswain's mate who emerged from an office with a patient offer of assistance and no sign of recognizing the famous, irate, potential enlistee. After listening to the problem, the chief calmly suggested that Mature take a test that was used more rarely, the Williams Lantern test. He had to go back over to the Navy office to accomplish this, since the Coast Guard did not have the more complex testing equipment. Mature passed with flying colors, and the Coast Guard accepted him.

Following his tour, in 1944 he got shore duty as a featured player in the all–Coast Guard stage show *Tars and Spars*. A morale show doubling as a recruiting campaign that also benefited the Coast Guard emergency relief fund, this musical revue opened in Miami in April 1944. The group traveled throughout the States, appearing in film and vaudeville theaters during the next year.

Periodically Mature was also called upon to join bond drives in support of the war effort, a duty that also involved traveling around the country, visiting shipyards and defense plants. One such trip took him to New Orleans, where his friend Errol Flynn was making the same rounds. Neither could find a way to get around town—until they noticed the used-car lot across the street from their hotel. A taxicab was advertised there for six hundred dollars. The actors divided the price by two and bought the car, scrounging a cab driver's hat somewhere, which Flynn donned as he drove them from appointment to appointment, incognito. One day as they were cruising around the city, a man jumped into the back seat at a red light and gave an address. Flynn took off, not having the slightest idea where he was going, and after a few minutes the passenger suspected something was amiss. In the end, the Hollywood residents drove the man home to his family and stayed for dinner.

With the European war just ended, on 15 May 1945 Mature was transferred to the USS *Admiral H. T. Mayo* (AP-125). This troop transport

Chief Boatswain's Mate Mature undergoes discharge process in November 1945. (U.S. Coast Guard photo)

ferried soldiers from France directly into the Pacific action via the Panama Canal. Mature remained with the *Mayo* until 28 September, when he was ordered to report to the District Coast Guard Officer, Twelfth Naval District.

Honorably discharged in November 1945, Victor Mature returned forthwith to the waiting Twentieth Century–Fox, by now his professional home. Director John Ford cast him as the troubled Doc Holliday in the Western *My Darling Clementine* (1946, with Henry Fonda as Wyatt Earp). The movie was a critical and financial success, boosting Mature to a new level of professional achievement.

Mature was an adaptable and capable actor, even though he was typecast as the not-so-bad guy. Among the diverse characters he played were a society Englishman in *Moss Rose* (1947), a gangster-gone-good in *Kiss of Death* (1947), a friendly policeman in *Cry of the City* (1948), the biblical strongman charmed by Hedy Lamarr in *Samson and Delilah* (1949; in 1984 he appeared in a TV version as the strongman's father), a racketeer in *Gambling House* (1951), and the Roman gladiator Demetrius in *The Robe* (1953, also featuring film newcomer Richard Burton).

He was an active player as well in the romantic field for some time; alleged liaisons included Betty Grable in the early 1940s. Mature was married and divorced five times and has three children. He lives in retirement in Rancho Sante Fe, California.

# Paul Newman

He has been nominated six times for best-actor Oscars (*Cat on a Hot Tin Roof*, 1958; *The Hustler*, 1961; *Hud*, 1963; *Cool Hand Luke*, 1967; *Absence of Malice*, 1981; and *The Verdict*, 1982), and he won the actor-of-the-year award at the 1958 Cannes Film Festival for *The Long Hot Summer*, with Joanne Woodward. This down-to-earth, Budweiser-drinking (counteracted by daily workouts), regular-guy superstar has made a career of turning in memorable performances. Delighting his audiences time after time in films including *Butch Cassidy and the Sundance Kid* (1969), *The Sting* (1973), and *The Life and Times of Judge Roy Bean* (1972), Paul Newman was finally recognized with an Academy Award for his portrayal of *The Hustler*'s Fast Eddie Felson, now middle-aged, in *The Color of Money* (1986).

He has directed several outstanding films as well, for instance *Rachel, Rachel* (1968, starring wife Joanne Woodward), which was nominated as one of the year's best pictures. Both Newman and Woodward work only when a script moves them. Their personal integrity and dedication are well known; Newman was commended for them, and for his contributions to his field, in 1985, with an honorary Academy Award. Also well known are their political awareness and commitment to causes such as civil rights and environmental protection. Newman's only son, Scott (by his first marriage, to Jackie Witte), died in 1978 of a drug and alcohol overdose, after which he established the Scott Newman Foundation, an organization that works to promote awareness in schools of the realities of drug abuse. Widely known as well is the fact that all profits from the sales of his salad dressing, spaghetti sauce, popcorn, cookbooks, and other products go to charities and to social-welfare programs such as the Scott Newman Foundation.

His blue eyes have been written about so much that he probably wishes they could be copyrighted. Perhaps less widely known is that Paul Leonard Newman enlisted in the U.S. Navy on 22 January 1943, after his graduation from Shaker Heights High School in Cleveland, Ohio. The second son of a thriving sporting-goods storekeeper (Arthur, his brother, eventually became a film production manager), Paul (born 1925) had acted in a few school productions but had never considered making a profession of show business. He attended Ohio University in Athens while he waited to hear from the Navy, and during his months there he had time to perform in another school production, *The Milky Way,* in which he played a boxer.

Newman was sent to the Navy V-12 program at Yale, with hopes of being accepted for pilot training. But this plan was foiled when a flight physical revealed him to be color-blind. So he was sent instead to boot camp and then on to further training as a radioman and gunner.

Qualifying as a rear-seat radioman and gunner in torpedo bombers, in 1944 Aviation Radioman Third Class Newman was sent to Barber's Point, Hawaii, and subsequently assigned to Pacific-based replacement torpedo squadrons (VT-98, VT-99, and VT-100). These torpedo squadrons were responsible primarily for training replacement pilots and combat aircrewmen, placing particular importance on carrier landings.

During his two years in the Pacific the Newman luck held, especially on one occasion when his pilot fell ill and their aircraft was grounded. The rest of the squadron was transferred to an aircraft carrier operating

TBM-3E "Avenger" torpedo bombers in formation over Mt. Fugi, Japan, during the final weeks of World War II. (U.S. Naval Historical Center)

off the coast of Japan, where a kamikaze hit the carrier, inflicting heavy casualties on the men and aircraft of Newman's squadron.

While he was with VT-99, training personnel in TBM-1Cs, TBM-3s, and TBF-1Cs, the squadron moved to Eniwetok, then to Guam, and in January 1945 on to Saipan. This remained its base of operations until its decommissioning nine months later. A VT-99 contingent including Newman was aboard the aircraft carrier *Hollandia* (CVE-97), which was operating about five hundred miles off Japan when the *Enola Gay* dropped its atomic bomb on Hiroshima.

Finally, Paul Newman served with Carrier Aircraft Service Unit 7, one of many shore-based carrier air-group support units. CASUs operated the facilities, serviced and rearmed, made repairs, and handled routine upkeep and administrative duties. Newman's CASU was based in Seattle, conveniently located for his discharge at Bremerton, Washington State, on 21 January 1946. He was decorated with the American Area Campaign Medal, the Good Conduct Medal, and the World War II Victory Medal.

Paul Newman (smiling broadly at back, left, under the model airplane) and his shipmates onboard the *Hollandia* (CVE-97) in the Pacific have just received word of the Japanese surrender. (U.S. Navy photo)

Courtesy of the GI Bill, his next undertaking was to pursue his education at Kenyon College in Gambier, Ohio. His studies did not interest him, though, as much as his other activities, including football, acting in school productions, and general all-American-boy hell-raising. He managed to receive his B.A. nevertheless, in 1949, after which he took off almost immediately for Wisconsin, where he was scheduled to perform in summer stock. Next it was on to Woodstock, Illinois, where he appeared in numerous plays until 1950, when his father passed away and he was asked to come home and run the family business.

This was definitely not the second son's dream, and he was grateful to be released from it a year later, when the store was sold. He promptly enrolled in the Yale Drama School, New Haven, Connecticut, and one year later, backed by his teachers, he took on New York City. There he began working in television without further ado. Soon Paul Newman was also appearing on the stage, and during the early 1950s he worked on improving his skills through studies at the Actors' Studio.

By the late 1950s a long-term contract with Warner Brothers had taken him to Hollywood, and he was firmly ensconced in the world of moviemaking, where he has been ever since—that is, when he has not been racing cars or making spaghetti sauce or working for his causes or taking his wife out to dinner on golf courses by the sea. Paul and Joanne have been together since 1958, and they have made their home in an eighteenth-century farmhouse in Connecticut, maintaining also an apartment in New York City and a house in Malibu. Paul Newman has five daughters.

# Logan Ramsey

Ens. Jack Lemmon's captain during his brief tour on board the aircraft carrier *Champlain* was Logan C. Ramsey, who saved the ship from colliding with a tanker. Ramsey rewarded his quick-thinking communications officer with a 4.0 fitness-report rating, for correctly advising him about the onrushing tanker's problem. This was the same Logan Ramsey who (then commander) on 7 December 1941, while serving as chief of staff and operations officer with Commander Patrol Wing 2, had sent out the message informing U.S. forces of the attack on Pearl Harbor, and who had immediately set the Naval Base Air Defense Force into motion. With a track record that included the Legion of Merit with Gold Star for his "brilliant initiative and effective resourcefulness in handling all Army, Navy, and Marine aircraft" at Midway, where he was war plans officer; the Bronze

Star for his "skilled and fearless" antisubmarine leadership while in command of the *Block Island* (CVE-106) in the Atlantic during 1944; and a Letter of Commendation with Ribbon for his 1944 antisubmarine work as chief of staff and aide to the Commander Fleet Air, Norfolk, U.S. Naval Academy graduate Ramsey retired with the rank of rear admiral in 1949.

During his command of the *Champlain*, Ramsey's son, Ens. Logan Carlisle Ramsey, Jr., was ordered to the carrier as his previous ship, the *Block Island,* was about to join the mothball fleet. It was to be the junior Ramsey's last month in the Navy, after which he planned to get back to the pursuit of his passion—acting.

The first of two children of the senior Ramsey and his wife, Harriet Lillian Kilmartin, Logan Junior arrived on the scene in 1921 in Long Beach, California. Born into a Navy family, he watched his dad struggle with the adversities and setbacks—as well as savor the rewards and accomplishments—of building a military career while at the same time taking the risk of incurring someone's wrath with his earnest ideas and suggestions, published in forums such as the U.S. Naval Institute's *Proceedings.* Moving around a lot was part of Navy life then as it is now, and the beginning of U.S. involvement in World War II found the family in Philadelphia. There Ramsey Junior attended St. Joseph's College, where he became active in the theater. He also worked in the Hedgerow Theatre Repertory Company, under director Jasper Deeter. Ramsey was on a headlong course to Broadway when World War II took him out of action for a while.

Logan Ramsey, Jr., enlisted in the Navy's V-12 officer-training program in June 1942 and was commissioned upon his graduation, twenty-four months later, from Northwestern University. He had orders to the newly commissioned *Block Island.*

This aircraft carrier had been launched on 10 June 1944 by the Todd-Pacific Shipyards in Tacoma, Washington, sponsored by Mrs. E. J. Hallenbeck, who was Marine ace Maj. Gregory ("Pappy") Boyington's mother. At the time, Boyington was missing in action after having shot down twenty-eight Japanese planes. Held as a prisoner of war in Japan for twenty months, Boyington was awarded the Congressional Medal of Honor at the end of the war.

The *Block Island* was the second ship to bear that name; the first (CVE-21) had been sunk by a German U-boat. Ramsey's father had

Capt. Logan C. Ramsey, USN, CO of the *Lake Champlain,* and son, Ens. Logan C. Ramsey, Jr., USNR. (U.S. Navy photo)

commanded her during her first year of operation in the Atlantic, but just two months after Capt. Massie Hughes had assumed command, on 29 May 1944 the U-549 sank the carrier. The *Block Island,* with her air group and surface escorts, was credited with sinking six U-boats before she was lost.

Captain Hughes then was put in command of the second *Block Island,* which was commissioned on 30 December 1944. He brought with him his surviving crew, and among his new officers was Logan Ramsey, Jr. Hughes had promised Ramsey's father he would keep an eye on the fledgling ensign (who went by his nickname, Skee), who was assigned as the 3d Division gunnery officer.

At North Island, San Diego, the ship took on stores for her upcoming Pacific tour of action. She was the first Navy carrier to carry a full Marine carrier air group on board, Marine Air Group 1. Marine Fighting Squadron 511, with its eight F6F-5N Hellcat night fighters and eight F4U-1 day Corsairs, was hoisted aboard. A few days later, while operating off San Diego, the *Block Island* added Marine Torpedo Bombing Squadron 233, which counted among its inventory eighteen TBM-3 aircraft. Finally, two F6F-5P (photo) aircraft were added to the Marine complement.

Ordered to waters off Okinawa via Ulithi, the air group began operations as soon as it reached Ulithi. In late April 1945 it was ordered to join Task Force 52.1, then operating southeast of Okinawa. From 10 May to 16 June, the carrier attacked enemy installations on the southwest islands of Okinawa, Nasei Shoto. The *Block Island* never came under enemy fire during these sorties, but several aircraft and their crews were lost to ground fire.

With new orders having sent her on to Leyte Gulf in June, the *Block Island,* along with the *Suwannee* (CVE-27) and *Gilbert Islands* (CVE-107), screened by six destroyers, sortied from Leyte Gulf on 25 June to rendezvous with units that were to participate in the last major amphibious landing of the war—the oil center at Balikpapan, Borneo. Designated Task Force 78, this group included the USS *Phoenix* (CL-46), which carried Gen. Douglas MacArthur.

On 30 June 1945, task force fighters and bombers began three days of strafing and bombing enemy installations. On 3 July a lone Japanese Jake floatplane flew out to meet the force but was quickly dispatched by a *Block Island* Hellcat.

After Balikpapan, the carrier saw no more combat. Anchored at Guam and later at Leyte Gulf, she was ordered to join other ships in clearing minefields from the approaches to Jinsen Harbor in the Keijo area of Korea, which was soon to become occupied. But the ship was diverted from that mission to transport Allied prisoners of war from camps on Formosa in early September.

Logan Ramsey and the rest of the ship's company were deeply disturbed by the plight of the prisoners they saw as they were brought on board. The *Block Island* took 474 ex-POWs and provided them with every comfort available—they were just skeletons and "ate themselves into nausea," wrote Ramsey to his mother. But "you have never seen such smiles in your time, and I'll never see any brighter. . . . Mother, if you could have seen their bodies, you would have wept." Among the American, British, Australian, and Dutch men were fifty survivors of the Bataan death march, and among the British troops were some who had escaped at Dunkirk only to be captured later, when Singapore fell in February 1942. The *Block Island,* along with other rescue ships, reached Manila Bay on 8 September 1945, and the survivors were taken to hospitals for further treatment.

Her mission of mercy completed, the *Block Island,* like many other Pacific combatants, headed for the States, and Ramsey and his shipmates learned that their ship was to be mothballed upon her arrival at Norfolk. On reaching their destination, the ship's officers were ordered to a receiving ship, the *Lake Champlain.*

Assigned as deck officer, Ramsey got no special handling from his dad, who once admonished him with a note sent through an orderly: "Mr. Ramsey, aboard my ship when we are on watch we do not wear our gun and holster as if we were a cowboy." But the old man did occasionally soften, as the time he called Junior and said, "Mr. Ramsey, I got a letter from your mother that I would like you to hear." The ensign reminded the captain that he had already read him the letter, to which Senior replied, "Oh, get your butt up here, I'm lonely."

In Junior's final fitness report, when he was about to be discharged from the Navy, his father concluded by adding, "I really would encourage that this young man go on with a naval career." But this young man already had his sights set on the stage, and later his father would become his most enthusiastic supporter.

Discharged in 1946, Ramsey picked up where he had left off—working his way toward Broadway. Three years of sparse living followed, carrying tea bags around to drop in the free cup of hot water provided by Horn and Hardart, which sold a twenty-five-cent lunch to go with it—five vegetables or a meat pie. These were also the days of the five-cent subway, which carried aspiring actors around for their weekly round of rejections.

But Ramsey would not give up, and in 1950 he was cast in George Bernard Shaw's classic, *The Devil's Disciple.* This was the role that took his career forward.

Next came *The High Ground,* which won him 1951's Clarence Derwent Award for best supporting actor. Ramsey stayed in New York until 1966, appearing in plays such as *Sweet Bird of Youth* (with Paul Newman and Geraldine Page) and the Actors' Studio production of *Marathon 33,* the story of young marathon dancer June Havoc, played by Julie Harris. Ramsey was one of the many who enthusiastically took advantage of the local opportunity offered by the Actors' Studio to work on developing and honing his craft.

Hollywood enticed him westward in 1966, and since then he has appeared in more than thirty films, including *The Sporting Club* (1971), *Walking Tall* (1973), *Any Which Way You Can* (1980, with Clint Eastwood), and *Fat Man and Little Boy* (1989). A character actor specializing in villains and dialects, Ramsey has also displayed his talents on television, in, among many other movies and mini-series, *Roots: The Next Generation* (1979), *Blind Ambition* (1979, as J. Edgar Hoover), *The Winds of War* (1983), and *The Law* (1974). He guest-starred on *Murder, She Wrote* in 1991, and his numerous TV appearances include episodes of *The Rockford Files, Star Trek, Knight Rider, Hawaii Five-O,* and *The Hallmark Hall of Fame.* Among his awards he counts the 1980 Los Angeles Drama Critics Award for his supporting role in the play *Luther,* and two Drama-Logue Awards for *A Life in the Theater* (South Coast Repertory Company) and *Best Little Whorehouse in Texas* (Wilshire Theatre; he played the governor).

While playing in summer stock in Peekskill, New York, in the early 1950s, Ramsey met actress Anne Mobley, whom he married in 1954. She too was a character actor, and the Ramsey team often was able to work together, for instance in *Any Which Way You Can, The Law,* and *Scrooged* (1988, with Bill Murray). In 1987 the American Academy of Family Films acknowledged their work with a Career Achievement Award, and in 1988 Anne Ramsey was nominated for an Academy Award for best supporting actress in *Throw Momma from the Train* (1987, with Danny DeVito and Billy Crystal; she played Momma). It was to be her greatest recognition; not long thereafter she passed away.

Her husband lives in Van Nuys, California, and continues to work, still liking the theater best of all. In his spare time he likes to help out younger actors, offering his guidance and the benefit of his substantial, and lengthy, experience.

# Aldo Ray

On-screen super-tough guy Aldo Ray (born DaRe, 1926, in Pen Argyl, Pennsylvania), who starred in such macho films as *Men in War* (1957) and *Terror on Alcatraz* (1986), really was tough. Trained during World War II as a member of Underwater Demolition Team 17, Seaman First Class DaRe was among the frogmen who reconned the shores of Okinawa before the main landings.

UDT 17 was organized in late 1944 and after a punishing training program at Maui was loaded aboard the USS *Crosley* (APD-87). The ship left for the western Pacific on 14 February 1945. Stopping in Leyte, she arrived off Okinawa with a convoy of escorts, part of the Western Islands Attack Force, in late March.

Assigned to the Green Beaches, northernmost of the Hagushi Beaches, Team 17 got a look at the area of operations on 27 March, when the

*Crosley* made a run five thousand yards off Okinawa's western shore. Early the next morning they got a look at the enemy when the ship was able to dodge a kamikaze at the last minute, watching it dive into the sea just thirty feet astern.

Things got moving on the morning of 29 March. At 0900 the *Crosley* was in place six thousand yards offshore, and at 0930 DaRe and his teammates were on their way to the beaches in their boats. The ships pounded the shore with artillery, covering for the frogmen. Dropped five hundred yards offshore, they swam across the reef to the shore, took soundings, studied the reef's floor, and observed everything they could on the shore. With no casualties, the team returned and was picked up, and the operation was over by 1115. About thirty yards from the shore they had seen two hundred or so wooden posts sticking out of the reef. Next morning they destroyed these, still with no casualties, although some of the frogmen reported sniper and machine-gun fire coming from the beach. Now all known obstacles to the landings had been taken care of.

DaRe and his teammates acted as wave guides and assisted the beachmasters during the landings, on 11 April; enemy resistance was almost nonexistent. UDT 17's next task, carried out during the following two days, was to blast ramps and channels into the edge of the reef for follow-on troops who would be coming ashore. Then it was back to the ship. The *Crosley* had been assigned to screening duty and to fending off kamikazes, which by now infested the air. UDT 17 team members manned .50-caliber machine guns, passed the ammunition, fought fires, and rescued the wounded.

On 14 April the team was ordered to recon two beaches on the northern tip of the island, the site planned for the unloading of equipment for a radar station. This mission came off without a hitch, and the team was finished with its work at Okinawa. On 20 April the *Crosley* steamed for Ulithi.

For the next three months UDT 17 was held in readiness and underwent training at Ulithi and Guam, but on 6 July they were ordered back to Pearl, a cheery development for the team. Things got even better when they were ordered back to the States, where they were to remain until 11 August.

Before he became Aldo Ray the actor, Seaman First Class Aldo DaRe (lower left) was among the frogmen of Underwater Demolition Team 17 who reconned the shores of Okinawa before the main landings. (UDT-Seal Museum)

With the war almost over, UDT 17 had one last job to do. Boarding the USS *Blessman* (APD-48), they were off to the western Pacific again, this time headed for Japan. Their task: to conduct hydrographic and photographic surveys of the Wakayama beaches south of Osaka while UDT 3 looked into the docking facilities of the Kino River. It was all part of the planned landing of the Sixth Army occupational troops, which took place on 25 September. Mission accomplished, the team sailed for San Diego in early October 1945 and was decommissioned at the end of that month.

Seaman First Class Aldo DaRe was honorably discharged from the Navy in 1946. With no interest in becoming an actor, he enrolled in the University of California at Berkeley and played football. The family had relocated to Crockett, California, when Ray was two years old, and after college he decided to run for sheriff's office in Crockett (he won). During the elections, his brother took him along to the auditions for a movie in San Francisco, *Saturday's Hero* (1951). The husky veteran—blond, blue-eyed, and six feet tall—was offered a bit part, attracting instant attention with his gritty voice and an air about him that somehow marked him as the genuine article.

After making the film he decided in favor of the job in Crockett, only to give in to the enticement of the screen a year later when he was offered another part, in *The Marrying Kind* (1952). The movie went over well with the critics, assuring Aldo Ray more work in Hollywood. Cast mainly in tough-guy parts, he also showed himself to be capable of deeper performances, such as the one he gave in his first movie and in *Battle Cry* (1955). Other work included *Pat and Mike* (1952, with Spencer Tracy and Katharine Hepburn), *Miss Sadie Thompson* (1953), *The Naked and the Dead* (1958), and *We're No Angels* (1955, with Humphrey Bogart and Peter Ustinov).

By the 1960s personal problems, including the deterioration of his third marriage, had taken their toll, reflected in a lack of steady work. But later in the decade Ray had a comeback, appearing in such films as *What Did You Do in the War, Daddy* (1966), *Riot on Sunset Strip* (1967), and *The Green Berets* (1968). Financially strapped by the late 1970s, he was still getting parts, although most of them were far from plum.

Unfortunately the picture did not get much better for World War II veteran Aldo Ray, and during the 1980s, while fighting cancer, he appeared in low-budget films and tried to save money for his three children. He died in 1991, doubtless comforted by the knowledge that one of his two sons (Eric DaRe) had achieved a solid foothold in the acting field with his performance as Leo Johnson in the popular TV series *Twin Peaks* (1990–91).

# Buddy Rogers

In 1937 "America's Boyfriend," Buddy Rogers, married "America's Sweetheart," Mary Pickford. He had met the famous Toronto-born actress and former wife of Douglas Fairbanks ten years earlier, when they had costarred in *My Best Girl* (1927). Unbeknownst to the actress at the time, Rogers would turn out to be "the man of my girlhood vision," she enthused in her autobiography, *Sunshine and Shadow*. With his "blue-black hair . . . that lay in thick waves on his beautifully shaped head," his dark "eyes that look out upon the world completely without guile," Rogers captivated her.

He too was spellbound, and he would remain so until his wife's passing in 1979. They lived together at Pickfair in Beverly Hills, originally a hunting lodge, called by some a mansion and by others a charming cottage (very), which the actress and Douglas Fairbanks had bought during their 1920–35 marriage. Fairbanks and Pickford remained on peaceful terms after the dissolution of their unhappy union, she retaining the magnificent "cottage," which boasted exquisite antique furnishings, expansive lawns, spreading trees, and a pool. There Pickford and Rogers raised the two much-loved children whom they adopted.

The neighborly atmosphere in which Charles "Buddy" Rogers was reared may have had something to do with his guileless manner and trusting nature. Born (1904) and bred in Olathe, Kansas, he was the son of Maude Moll Rogers and her husband, Probate Judge B. H. Rogers, who knew everyone in the county by name. In school the boy took to music, playing several instruments and forming small groups. He continued to develop his talent at the University of Kansas, where he was majoring in journalism and had a band going in his fraternity when, in 1925, the Paramount Studios School of Acting in Astoria, New York, sent out a call to colleges across the country for ten guys and ten gals to be sent to the school. Buddy was not interested, but his father was, and, urged by the judge, he put in an application.

Paramount signed him in 1926 and began the grooming process. By the following year a busy and popular leading man, Rogers worked through the transition period from silent movies to talkies, appearing in, among others, *So's Your Old Man* (1926, with W. C. Fields) and *Get Your Man* (1927). *Wings* (1927), in which he played an Army Air Corps World War I pilot, won the distinction of being the first movie to receive the Academy Award. Buddy had to learn how to fly for the film; his U.S. Army flight instructor was Hoyt S. Vandenberg, who later became a general and commanded the Ninth Army Air Force during World War II.

Rogers went on to star in more than forty musicals and comedies, including *Close Harmony* (1929), *Young Eagles* (1930), *The Road to Reno* (1931), and *Let's Make a Night of It* (1938). He also formed a dance band, in which he enchanted his audiences by leaping from instrument to instrument, seemingly a master of them all.

As the actor held a private pilots's license in 1941, when his country got into World War II, he opted for the Navy and naval aviation. He joined up in June 1942, completed the Navy's flight-training program at Pensacola, and won his wings of gold. Since he was considered somewhat old (thirty-four) for combat duty, Rogers and other Navy pilots of his vintage were assigned as ferry pilots in Air Ferry Squadron 3 (VRF-3), stationed at the Naval Operating Base, Terminal Island, in San Pedro, California. Rogers flew new aircraft from manufacturers' plants in the West to modification centers, aircraft commissioning units, and fleet operational squadrons.

He logged hundreds of hours, mostly in fighter aircraft. VRF-3 was distinct from other Navy ferry squadrons in that it serviced every naval activity in the western half of the United States. VRF-3 pilots flew all types of aircraft—F6Fs, SB2Cs, TBMs, PV-1s and 2s, PB4Y-2s, and others. During its first year in operation, the squadron logged twelve million miles delivering more than nine thousand aircraft. The comely Rogers, acutely aware of the jealousy that could be provoked by his success and his appearance, dreaded being seen as expecting any special treatment. But no one thought he expected that—clearly dedicated to the naval service and to his flight duties, the hardworking former actor was well liked.

There was also some appreciated and needed relaxation time involved with this duty, and Rogers spent as much of it as possible with Mary. At other times there were outings from bases, one of which occurred in May 1943 at Avenger Field, Sweetwater, Texas. Women Airforce Service Pilots, the first of their kind ever allowed to fly U.S. military aircraft, were undergoing training at Avenger. Like Rogers and company, the WASPs also ferried planes from factories to airfields, carried out test flying, and performed other duties that until then had been assigned only to men. Avenger was generally closed to transient pilots, but the commanding officer permitted Buddy Rogers, curious about his female counterparts, to land there because the CO himself was curious about Buddy Rogers.

All this curiosity resulted in a pleasant visit, including breakfast and a tour of the facilities, with bowling and drinks in town. Buddy and his fellow male aviator, another naval lieutenant (jg), were thus able to learn more about these unusual (and, many of them, beautiful) trainees. One of them, Marion Stegeman, described the visitors, in a letter to her mother, as "the best-looking men ever to grace Avenger."

But Mary had nothing to be jealous of: her husband's heart remained at Pickfair, where Mary was doing her bit for the war effort by hosting

USO events on the property. Buddy attended whenever he could, making a special effort when the wounded were brought in from local military hospitals. Many of the veterans, including the blind, limbless, and lame, were invited back to Pickfair for the annual lawn party, for swimming and relaxation under the trees, with entertainment provided by the likes of Dinah Shore. They came as well at Christmas.

Honorably discharged in 1946, Rogers remained in the Naval Reserve until 1949, reaching the rank of lieutenant commander. He could then devote himself more fully to his family and to his philanthropic activities, in both of which fields he has remained involved since that time. He played supporting roles in just two more films, *An Innocent Affair* (1948, with Madeleine Carroll and Fred MacMurray) and *The Parson and the Outlaw* (1957). After Mary's death, Buddy sold Pickfair and built a house on its former grounds, nearby. There he continued to work, mostly in radio and television.

In 1981 he married Beverly Ricono, with whom he continues to live in the house on Pickfair grounds and pursue his many interests. The 1986 Academy Awards included the presentation to Buddy Rogers of the Jean Hersholt Humanitarian Award, and in 1987 the University of Kansas awarded him its Distinguished Service Citation. The Palm Springs Air Museum dedicated the Buddy Rogers Wing in his honor in 1996.

# Cesar Romero

T he dashing grandson of nineteenth-century Cuban hero José Martí, Cesar Romero arrived on the Hollywood scene in the early 1930s. A professional dancer, he was a resourceful actor as well and was kept steadily busy in either movies or TV from then on. Tapped mostly for villain parts, to his mild disappointment but willing cooperation, the six-foot-three Latin never did achieve major-star status. Even so, by 1942 he was one of Hollywood's most successful and sought-after actors. He would also remain the perennial desirable bachelor.

Cesar Julio Romero, Jr., was born in New York City in 1907. Cesar Senior was an export-business executive, married to the Cuban concert singer Maria Mantilla Romero. Junior was schooled in New York and Connecticut, and his intention was to go into banking; to start off his career, he therefore got a job with the New York City Bank as a messenger.

Then, during the mid-1920s, he met Lisbeth Higgins, who became his professional dancing partner. The two worked in hotel showrooms, in supper clubs, and at parties, Romero keeping his day job as well. In 1933 he moved on to Broadway, appearing in *Dinner at Eight* and *Spring and Autumn.* Next he went on tour with Bert Lytell's *Ten-Minute Alibi,* and from there it was on to Hollywood.

He quickly found work, appearing over the years in dozens of films, including *The Thin Man* (1934, as one of the suspects), *The Devil Is a Woman* (1935, with Marlene Dietrich), *Show Them No Mercy* (1935), and *Wee Willie Winkie* (1937, with Shirley Temple). He played the title role in the Cisco Kid series (1939–40), which gave him immediate recognition among young moviegoers, and he was a regular in Twentieth Century–Fox musicals during the 1940s, dancing with Betty Grable in *Springtime in the Rockies* (1941).

When the nation went to war, Cesar Romero enlisted in the Coast Guard at Long Beach, California, in October 1942. He spent his service years on board a Coast Guard–manned attack transport, the USS *Cavalier* (APA-37). Before joining the transport ship, he went through boot camp at the Coast Guard Training Center at Alameda, California, followed by three months at a San Francisco receiving station. He went aboard the *Cavalier* in November 1943, shortly before she was commissioned.

Romero never suffered from antistar prejudice. His shipmates, both officers and crew, considered him one of the guys, boasting that he never expected to be treated differently from anyone else. Romero never tried to obtain an officer's commission, preferring to serve with the enlisted men. He took great pride in his work as a boatswain's mate, eventually working his way up through the ranks to chief boatswain's mate.

His ship cleared Davisville, Rhode Island, on 17 February 1944, with the men and gear of two construction battalions that disembarked a month later at Honolulu. After amphibious training in the Hawaiian Islands, the *Cavalier* sailed for the invasion beaches of Saipan in the Joint Expeditionary Force Reserve. American forces met with unyielding Japanese resistance on D-Day, 15 June, after which Romero's group was called upon to unload reinforcements. The

Chief Boatswain's Mate Cesar Romero spent his service years on board a Coast Guard–manned attack transport, the USS *Cavalier* (APA-37). When he was not serving as first powderman on a 5-inch gun, he spent much of his time loading and unloading landing craft. (U.S. Coast Guard photo)

landings began at dusk the next day, at maximum speed because of a fast-approaching Japanese fleet. The *Cavalier* landed her troops but was ordered to retreat before having time to unload artillery. Many of the ship's boats had to be left behind, to be used for future shuttle duty.

The *Cavalier* moved to the east as the Battle of the Philippine Sea raged. Romero and company came back to the beachhead on 25 June, completing their offloading of artillery and then taking on casualties. The next day they went on to Eniwetok to put the wounded ashore and load cargo, including thirty-seven tons of dynamite for underwater demolition.

Romero's regular job was with the deck force, which meant that he was at work by 0530 at the latest, sweeping down, emptying trash, making sure all was shipshape. Next it was to the winches, where he spent the rest of the day, sometimes working into the night. Here he loaded or unloaded cargo and maneuvered the landing barges back and forth over the ship's side.

When battle stations were called, he moved posthaste from the winches to a heavy 5-inch gun, serving as first powderman. He had had to beat out the competition to win that position, sought by men at least ten years younger. An unpretentious hard worker, Romero did not waste time complaining. He had known the service was going to be difficult.

Back at Saipan for unloading on 13 July, the *Cavalier* took the 2d Marines and their vehicles to Tinian, arriving off the island designated White landing beaches on 24 July. A few days later the ship sailed to Pearl Harbor with a load of casualties.

After completing assault training in preparation for the battle for Leyte Gulf and suffering both air and surface attacks en route to Lingayen Gulf, the *Cavalier* was the first ship to make radar contact with the Japanese escort destroyer *Hinoki*, on 7 January. The enemy warship was subsequently sunk by the U.S. destroyers *Charles Ausburne* (DD-570), *Shaw* (DD-373), *Braine* (DD-630), and *Russell* (DD-414), during action that would be the last surface engagement between warring naval forces in the Pacific.

Two days later, while unloading on White landing beaches in Lingayen Gulf, the *Cavalier*'s barges took Japanese mortar fire, and six men were wounded. One more was killed that evening and three injured during a kamikaze attack. On 10 January, while withdrawing from the gulf, Romero's ship's gunners shot at another kamikaze but then had to watch as it exploded into the *Dupage* (AP-41). With 35 killed, 136 wounded, severe damage to the ship, and fires that were fought throughout the night, the *Dupage* nevertheless continued as guide ship, arriving in Leyte three days later.

At the end of the month the *Cavalier* participated in the Philippine campaign, and on 30 January a brutal underwater explosion rocked the ship, probably caused by a torpedo from the Japanese submarine RO-115 —which was sunk the next day by the U.S. destroyers *Bell* (DD-587), *O'Bannon* (DD-450), and *Jenkins* (DD-447), and the destroyer escort *Ulvert M. Moore* (DE-240). The *Cavalier* was hit port side aft, resulting in fifty men injured as well as flooding and buckled decks. The engines stopped and steerageway was lost. The crew was able to bring the damage under control, but the propeller was hopelessly jammed.

The *Cavalier* was towed on to Leyte for temporary repairs, after which she was ordered to Pearl Harbor for more permanent mending. Following the end of the war, Romero's ship embarked military passengers from various Pacific islands, bringing them home. Years later the *Cavalier* also saw action during the Korean War. The Coast Guard transport ship was eventually honored with five battle stars for World War II service and four for Korean War service.

After leaving the ship, Romero was sent on cross-country speaking and bond-selling tours. His mission was to bolster the morale of those working in defense plants and other war-related industries, telling the workers of his war experiences at Saipan and Tinian and stressing how important their work was in supporting their country's effort. The United States was winning the war, he said, and they were essential for victory.

Romero was mobbed for autographs and pictures, and, always the gentleman, he complied graciously with the workers' wishes. He did not particularly like this duty, finding it tiring and unproductive, but he followed his orders and remained on tour until discharged from the Coast Guard. He corresponded with his 1st Division shipmates still aboard the *Cavalier*—who did not envy him this new duty—and he stayed in touch with them throughout his life, attending reunions and continuing to take great pride in his Coast Guard war service.

Returning to Hollywood, Cesar Romero got one of the best parts of his career, as the Spanish conqueror Cortés in *Captain from Castile* (1947). He continued over the following decades to find work in many movies, such as *Around the World in Eighty Days* (1956), *The Specter of Edgar Allan Poe* (1972), and *Lust in the Dust* (1984). After 1950 his appearances were increasingly on television rather than the big screen. One of his better-known characters was the Joker in the *Batman* TV series (1966–67; he also appeared in the 1966 movie). In 1985, at age seventy-eight, he played the object of Jane Wyman's desire on *Falcon Crest,* remaining with the show for the next two seasons.

Romero continued to work, crediting his youthful appearance to his constant activity. An outspoken advocate of protecting children from unnecessary depictions of violence and sex on the screen and stage, he was highly esteemed, known for being loyal and professional, a true gentleman. He threw himself into his pursuits with excitement; his surprise at his success and his wonder of Hollywood never seemed to fade.

Cesar Romero died in January 1994. He has three nieces and one nephew. His brother, Eduardo Romero, is a former Marine who survived the invasion and battle of Okinawa.

# Robert Stack

Robert Stack, since 1987 host of the TV series *Unsolved Mysteries,* had quite a bit of previous experience fighting on-screen crime. As the incorruptible Prohibition-era G-man Eliot Ness in *The Untouchables* (1959–63), he won an Emmy award in the series' first year of production. Off-screen, though, Stack has enjoyed a genteel life, one filled with music, culture, and time in Europe. He has pursued vigorous athletic activities and relaxed in a serene atmosphere at home.

His many years of sport shooting served his country well during World War II, when the Navy was able to put his considerable skill to practical use: Stack served as a gunnery instructor. This handiness also provided him with guaranteed respect in a wartime Navy in which actors were often heckled about their previously privileged station.

Handsome, sophisticated, and an accomplished athlete, Robert (born 1919) and his brother grew up in Hollywood when Spencer Tracy and Jean Harlow were already grownups, and partying filled the air. The young Stack—curious, intelligent, with a tremendous love of adventure and zest for life—had a blast. His family was far from hurting financially, and Robert became acquainted with people like Clark Gable and Howard Hughes at the shooting club long before crossing paths with them on the stage and screen.

His mother, Elizabeth Modini Wood, was a stunning dark-haired, bright-eyed Southern California socialite and Renaissance woman. She sang, wrote, carved, sculpted, gardened, and studied botany. She took voice lessons in Paris and hosted small theater and musical productions in her home, where her large family and numerous friends and acquaintances were welcome. Musicians, artists, dancers, and the aristocracy mingled regularly there.

When little Robert was a year old, Elizabeth and James Langford Stack were divorced; James Senior's immoderate alcohol intake, though not unusual for the 1920s, may have been a problem. Two years later Elizabeth moved to Paris with her youngest son, leaving James Junior with his dad. She took Robert everywhere with her, to the opera as well as to Italy for summers. When they came back to the States six years later, Robert, who spoke only French and Italian and had never been told he was American, had to learn his native culture as if he were an immigrant, albeit a comfortable one. Meanwhile Elizabeth and James Senior were reconciling, and in 1928 they were remarried. James L. Stack was a witty, industrious, handsome self-made businessman of Irish descent who loved polo, hunting, and success. He was generous and hardheaded, an honorary police chief and fire marshal. His advertising agency spawned famous beer-selling slogans, and his summer home at Lake Tahoe became a gathering place for celebrities such as Hedda Hopper and Carole Lombard. He counted among his close friends Will Rogers and Jack Dempsey.

It was no wonder that, growing to manhood in this fairy-tale world, Robert Stack was looked upon as a playboy, excelling in sports such as skeet shooting, polo, and speedboat and car racing while fending off the advances of the beautiful women who crowded Hollywood. He graduated from Los Angeles High School and went on to the

University of Southern California and the El Capitan College of the Theater, where he made his stage debut playing Captain Denny in *Pride and Prejudice.*

Before too long he was self-consciously making his film debut alongside America's darling, Deanna Durbin, in *First Love* (1940). His job was to give the young singing beauty her first movie kiss. As a result, Robert Stack became instant hot property with the ladies—and in the fan magazines. Universal Studios offered him a contract after that well-publicized kiss, and by the time the nation went to war in 1941, Stack had been featured in several movies, including the satire *To Be or Not to Be* (1942, with Carole Lombard and Jack Benny).

But, as with most young American men of the time, his career was interrupted by the war. Robert Stack's first duty was to serve his country, he felt, and he chose the Navy. There were a few Navy people in the family tree: his cousin was Rear Adm. William R. Monroe, USN, aide to President Roosevelt, and his uncle Perry Wood had been a World War I naval aviator. But more than anything else, it was the numerous flying roles Stack had played in movies that made him want to become a real U.S. Navy pilot. Besides, they had the snazziest uniforms.

This aspiration did not last long, though. Enlisting in 1942, he could not pass the depth-perception test, critical for carrier landing operations. His failure may have been due to his many years of skeet shooting, which had produced a dominant right eye. But all was not lost; he had also been an all-American with a shotgun, and the Navy was able to use his talents as a gunnery officer.

Ordered to Pensacola for training, Stack broke the Navy machine-gun record. With this recognized skill, he was sent to Naval Air Station Alameda, California, and then to Barber's Point, Hawaii, assigned to teach air-to-air gunnery and train dive-bomber and torpedo rear-seat gunners. This extremely dangerous duty involved shooting a .30-caliber machine gun out the back of a plane at heavily armed enemy fighters coming right at the young sailors. The mortality rate for gunners being high, there was a chronic shortage.

The Navy's solution was to have gunnery training officers like Stack make recruiting tours with decorated veteran gunners. Now twenty-one, the former actor was given the job of escorting five veterans fresh from the Pacific war around the country's naval stations in search of volunteer gunners. The five ex-gunners considered the trip a celebration of their survival and converted their bus into a bar and the hub of an ongoing party, during which they wreaked havoc on society wherever they went. Somehow all escaped being brought to task, much to their nervous supervisor's relief.

One of Stack's least favorite assignments was giving refresher training to Navy PB4Y2 bomber crews, which included waist gunners who shot at sleeves towed by passing training planes. He was not at all comfortable in the Flying Coffins, as they were called, since there was just one way out in case of trouble: through the bomb bay. Worse, while Stack was training the gunners in the after station, a student pilot would be undergoing training in the front cockpit. Crowding his way up front when landings were under way, he anxiously watched students sweat their way through touchdown and landing.

While aloft, PB4Y2 waist gunners could be a scary lot. The gunners might take their .50-caliber machine guns out of the gun stops, which were designed to prevent them from shooting up their own planes, and freewheel their shooting—this meant randomly shooting in all directions. On one particularly unpleasant occasion, the bomber Stack was riding did a high-side maneuver while the gunners were firing at a passing towed sleeve. The starboard gunner shot right through the wing of the bomber, nearly hitting the main wing spar. In PB4Y2s such a hit could cause a wing to fold. This time Stack gave both the gunners and the pilot what-for and demanded that the bomber be brought down immediately.

In at least somewhat more relaxing duty, Stack also served on board various aircraft carriers, which included the *Hancock* (CV-19) and *Sitkoh Bay* (CVE-86). There he provided rocket training for dive-bomber pilots and instructed ship's gunners in the use of "quad fifties" (quadruple .50-caliber antiaircraft guns).

There was also some genuine relaxation. As a "brown shoe"—Navy air officers wore brown shoes; shipboard officers wore black—Stack was "adopted" in 1943 by Ma Chung, a Chinese woman who opened her San Francisco home to military air officers as a haven for rest and recreation. Ranks and titles were ignored, and all members were identified only by a "bastard" number, Ma Chung's personal tribute to the

One of Stack's least favorite duties was giving refresher training to the bomber crews of Navy PB4Y2s, or Flying Coffins. (U.S. Naval Historical Center)

Flying Tigers who had fought for her country and in whose honor she had originally founded this informal, if admiral-studded, club. Stack was Bastard No. 644.

Ma Chung had been a friend of Gen. Claire Chennault, who formed the Flying Tigers. Starting in December 1941, this group of American pilots supported the Nationalist Chinese Air Force against invading Japanese forces. Flying P-40 pursuit planes with tiger teeth painted on their nose sections, the group proved to be fierce combat pilots and became world-famous. They were something of an unauthorized force at the time, so Ma Chung called them her beloved bastard sons, welcoming them into her home when she got to the States. Thus began the Bastard Club, which grew to include hundreds of airmen during the war.

After the hair-raising—and, for Stack, hair-losing—PB4Y2 training, which lasted a few months, the former actor found himself in the Pacific on V-J Day, which he celebrated with his buddies, mixing up horrid concoctions of every kind of alcohol imaginable. World

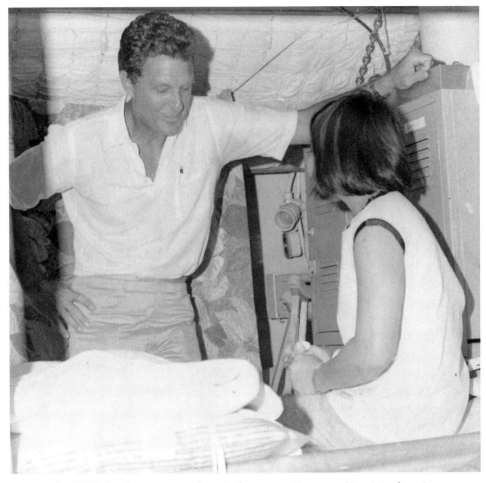

In 1968 Stack went on a hospital tour to Vietnam. He visited patients on board ships that included the *Repose* (AH-16) and was helicoptered to places like Khe Sanh, Pleiku, and Cua Viet. (U.S. Naval Historical Center)

War II was over, and Lieutenant Stack, after finishing out his Navy service, received an honorable discharge in 1945. Then it was back to Hollywood, which welcomed him even though he had some difficulty reestablishing himself in the industry.

Returning from the wars, the twenty-seven-year-old actor naturally thought of himself as a man. The silver screen, though, still wanted him for boy's parts, a predicament he found frustrating even though it meant being cast opposite a teenaged Elizabeth Taylor in *A Date with Judy* (1948, also with Carmen Miranda). But with typical self-effacing good humor and gentlemanly patience, Stack eventually prevailed and became a grown-up man on the screen. He moved back to the stage for a while, notably in 1949's *Girl of the Golden West,* a revival at the prestigious Westport (Connecticut) summer playhouse, and in 1950 a quality film role came his way: *The Bullfighter and the Lady* (1951). Shot in Mexico, it featured plenty of real bullfighting and real danger. Soon thereafter he was offered a role in a new medium: three-dimensional film. So began his experience with making *Bwana Devil* (1952), a horror movie that became a box-office hit. *The High and the Mighty* (1954) won him plaudits and a contract with Twentieth Century–Fox; *Written on the Wind* (1956) brought the Academy's best-supporting-actor nomination. Things were looking up in his personal life as well, and in 1957 he married actress Rosemarie Bowe. It was a lifelong union that would produce two children.

Although he did not believe that the United States should have become involved in the Vietnam conflict, Robert Stack was all too aware of what the U.S. servicemen there were going through, and in 1968 he went on a hospital tour. He was helicoptered to places like Khe Sanh, Pleiku, and Cua Viet, surprising those who were dug in there. He settled arguments about various movies' endings, visited, and told the men he was proud of them.

# Rod Steiger

Rodney Steven Steiger enlisted in the Navy on 11 May 1942 at age seventeen, having left Newark, New Jersey's, West Side High School before graduating. Severe problems with alcoholism in his home had driven him to seek a safe haven from family turmoil, and he loved being in the Navy.

His parents, Frederick and Lorraine Driver Steiger, had worked together in vaudeville but were divorced before their only son's first birthday (14 April 1925). Lorraine moved away from their home in Westhampton, Long Island, taking Rod to New Jersey. There he grew up, known as the Rock for his remarkable strength and bulk. He liked to act in school plays, a pastime he took up again after his Navy service. While working for the Office of Dependents and Beneficiaries of the Veterans Administration, he became involved with the Civil

Service Little Theater group, where an acting coach recognized his talent and encouraged him to develop it. He took this advice to New York City, with the help of the GI Bill. At the New York Theatre Wing, the Dramatic Workshop, and later the Actors' Studio, Steiger honed his craft, landing the lead in a television production of *Marty* (the role that would later bring an Oscar to Ernest Borgnine).

But in 1942, no glamour yet glinted on Rod Steiger's horizon. After schooling at the U.S. Naval Training Station in Newport, Rhode Island, and tours of duty with various naval units, Steiger joined the newly commissioned destroyer USS *Taussig* (DD-746) on 20 May 1944. Serving as a torpedoman's mate third class, he saw action in Pacific battle campaigns. Pounding the beaches at Iwo Jima is today a hellish memory for him, highlighted by the worry that some Americans may have been hit during the barrage. Later, while operating off the coast of Japan as part of fast carrier Task Force 58.1, the *Taussig* was forced to sink any sampans she encountered, because any one of them could harbor a radio with which to report the presence of American naval forces close to the Japanese mainland. There were women and children on board the small craft, and Steiger has been tormented by the memory ever since the war.

The closest he came to being seriously injured during the tour was during a vicious typhoon that hit the *Taussig* and other ships of Task Force 38. The storm, which roiled the seas with hundred-knot winds and eighty-foot waves, ripped through the group on 17 December 1944 as it was operating in waters north of Luzon, the Philippines. Three U.S. destroyers were lost in the typhoon: the *Hull* (DD-350; sixty-two survived), *Monaghan* (DD-354; with six survivors), and *Spence* (DD-512; twenty-four survived).

In an effort to secure a depth charge that had broken loose, Steiger tied a rope to himself and went out onto the deck as the destroyer rolled in the churning sea. As he turned to move down the deck toward the wayward depth charge, he looked up and saw a nightmare: a towering wave was about to engulf the ship. He flattened himself on the deck as the water crashed over him, and he was dragged down the deck, almost going overboard. Suddenly he was stopped, entangled in the guide wires that ran along the deck. Then the ship rolled down onto her side, and he found himself under several feet of water. As the

Rod Steiger joined the newly commissioned destroyer USS *Taussig* (DD-746) and served as a torpedoman's mate third class. He saw action in Pacific battle campaigns, including Iwo Jima. (U.S. Navy photo)

vessel rolled onto her other side, Steiger caught his breath, waiting for his chance to untangle himself and reach safety. At last, several waves later and during a brief lull in the storm, he was able to crawl back inside the ship.

On 11 March 1945 he was transferred to the USS *Admiral Coontz* (AP-122) for transport to the Advanced Torpedo Training School in San Diego. Because of an acute skin disease, he received a medical discharge from the Navy on 15 August 1945 in San Diego, missing by just two weeks the official Japanese surrender on board the USS *Missouri* (BB-63) on 2 September. He returned to Newark and took the Veterans Administration civil-service job, then moved on to New York.

In 1947 Rod Steiger got his Equity card and began getting small parts in live television and on the stage. By the early 1950s he was on Broadway, recognized by critics as a talented actor. This led him eventually to Hollywood, and he won his first Academy Award nomination for his performance as Marlon Brando's bad brother in *On the Waterfront* (1954). A second nod came eleven years later, when he appeared as a concentration-camp survivor in *The Pawnbroker* (1965). He won the Academy's 1967 best-actor award for his portrayal of *In the Heat of the Night*'s redneck Southern sheriff.

Plagued by periodic bouts of severe depression, the actor has not only persevered, he has prevailed, turning out numerous notable films such as *Oklahoma* (1955), *Al Capone* (1959), *The Longest Day* (1962), *Doctor Zhivago* (1965), *No Way to Treat a Lady* (1968), and *The Specialist* (1994). His multifaceted skills and intense renditions on stage, screen, and television have won him accolades time after time, and Steiger continues to contribute exceptional work to his field. Married four times, he has one daughter. Steiger is a passionate collector of art and books.

# Robert Taylor

The "Heartthrob of America" was sworn into the Naval Reserve in February 1943 as Spangler Arlington Brugh, his given name. Several months later, despite his extraordinary good looks, only the commanding officer recognized Lieutenant (jg) Brugh when he reported for duty. The CO had advance notice of the movie star's arrival, without which even he might not have taken particular notice of the unfamiliar name and familiar buzz cut. The actor had been deferred until August in order to complete filming *Song of Russia* (1943).

Spangler was born in Filley, Nebraska, in 1911, the son of a doctor. With a love of and talent for playing music, he was trained as a cellist and continued his musical studies at Pomona College in Claremont, California, receiving his B.A. in 1933. It was at college that Spangler was drawn to acting, and he began working in the school's productions.

With sharp features accentuated by a pronounced widow's peak and enhanced by his powers of verbal delivery—he had won the 1929 Nebraska State Oratorical Championship in high school—the handsome young man was a noticeable presence on the stage, where an MGM talent scout picked him out.

He appeared in *Handy Andy* (1934) with a new screen name, and MGM signed Robert Taylor to a long-term contract in 1934. He got on-screen grooming in a few mediocre movies before *The Magnificent Obsession* (1935) catapulted him to fame. The studio then used Taylor as the good-looking male lead for many of its beautiful stars— Greta Garbo, Jean Harlow, Loretta Young—in movies such as *His Brother's Wife* (1936) and *This Is My Affair* (1937). By the time he made *Yank at Oxford* (1938) and *Waterloo Bridge* (1940), his skills as an actor were honed, and *Bataan* (1943) still stands as a premier war movie.

It had taken some talking to get Taylor to make *Song of Russia*. A confirmed anticommunist, he was one of the first actors to declare his sentiments, doing so well before the postwar frenzy on the subject. So strong were his feelings that he refused to have anything to do with what he thought was a procommunist movie. He also suspected the studio of trying to delay his naval service. Eventually MGM convinced him that the movie was not pro-Red but pro-USA, and that the government favored it. (After the war, the government revisited the issue with Taylor.)

His request for overseas duty had been turned down because he was thirty-two, too old for combat. Since he held a current civilian pilot's license, he was appointed lieutenant (jg) USNR, and assigned to the Navy's Aviation Volunteer Transport Division. His basic training took place at Naval Air Station Dallas, Texas, after which he was ordered to NAS New Orleans, where he received three months of instructor training. He finished fifth in his class and was designated a naval aviator on 11 January 1944.

Next ordered to NAS Livermore, California, Taylor made numerous training films in 1944 for naval-aviation trainees. His combination of knowledge about both acting and aviation made him an ideal instructor on film, and his Navy training films—seventeen in all—were some of the best produced during the war.

Lieutenant Taylor and Lieutenant Hall inspect aircraft at NAS Glynco, Georgia, 5 April 1945. (U.S. Navy photo)

After nine months at Livermore he was transferred in October 1944 to NAS Glenview, Illinois, as aircraft operations officer. During this tour he was assigned temporary duty in connection with the Navy film *The Fighting Lady*, which covered fourteen months of the wartime service of a battle-scarred aircraft carrier. It won the 1944 Academy Award for best documentary, the highest film honor the actor would ever receive.

Taylor felt that his wife (since 1939), actress Barbara Stanwyck, and boss, Louis B. Mayer, were just humoring him, letting the little boy have his playtime. But Taylor loved being in the Navy and took his military service seriously. A perfectionist, he devoted his best efforts to all of his undertakings, but serving his country may have filled him with a particular sense of pride and duty. He repeatedly requested overseas duty but was turned down each time. During his time at

Livermore and Glenview, he complained of being used simply for his acting background. And he was right: the Navy brass thought he was most valuable as an instructor and narrator in morale-building films. Finally, though, he succeeded in moving from cameras to airplanes, as an instructor. He returned to NAS New Orleans in February 1945 to realize his dream of active flying.

Since he had not been in the air for some time, he was given refresher training with another instructor, Tom Purvis. During their first flight together, Taylor did a perfect right slow roll only to lose his three-hundred-dollar cigarette lighter out of his pocket. It fell right into the Mississippi River, far below. This was no ordinary loss: Barbara had given it to him. One of the highest-paid actresses in Hollywood—she made over three hundred thousand dollars in 1943—Stanwyck had given her husband a gold Zippo, embossed with the seal of his graduating naval station and engraved with the year he was sworn into the Naval Reserve, 1943. Now it had vanished. He dreaded telling her. However, two good things came out of the incident: Barbara gave him another expensive lighter without griping, and Taylor and Purvis began a lasting friendship. Tom Purvis and "Bob" Taylor would become inseparable pals. Purvis, over six feet tall and weighing in at around 240 pounds, was often mistaken for Taylor's bodyguard when they were seen in public.

As for being seen in public with Barbara, Taylor avoided it. When they got together, he did his best to ensure that their visits were publicity-free, not only because the couple wanted to be left alone for a while, but also because of his strong sense of responsibility toward the Navy. He was not interested in being seen as a Hollywood curiosity, and he resented publicity when he was in uniform.

Being a star did not always sit well with Taylor, who once told Mayer he would rather be called Lieutenant than Heartthrob of the Nation. During one well-publicized incident, he and Purvis were in a hotel lobby where Taylor was patiently signing a few autographs. Suddenly a young woman whipped out a pair of scissors, snipped off his Navy tie, and made off with it. Taylor saw no humor in this at all. He was still angry the next day, and he stayed that way until he and Purvis got back into the air and put some perspective on the matter.

But it took him a little longer to put perspective on another incident that occurred during his naval service. Scheduled to serve as master of ceremonies at a celebration in Ottumwa, Iowa, he flew into the city's airfield in a twin-engine Beechcraft. Crowds of people were awaiting him that wintry day, waving as he landed. A band stood smartly at attention, along with an admiral, other naval personnel, and civilians, all anxious to welcome him to the city. Recent rain had turned to ice, and patches of the parking tarmac were slick. After the aircraft stopped on the icy pavement, the band began to play "Stars and Stripes Forever" just as Taylor jumped from the rear door and suddenly found himself flat on his back. He tried several times to get up, but each time he would slide down again. His hat had rolled away, beyond his slippery reach. Finally he made it to a steady upright position, and someone got his hat. By the time Taylor at last was able to salute the admiral, the band was on its third chorus of "Stars and Stripes Forever." The admiral was waiting patiently, albeit possibly with twitching face.

Interested only in doing his best for the Navy, Taylor was pleased that none of his trainees washed out or seemed to make a big deal about who he was. Naturally, though, at least a few of them could not help but notice. Personable and down-to-earth, Taylor often conversed and joked with "regular people," with whom he was doubtless more comfortable than when he was surrounded by adoring fans. He also took naturally to the role of teacher. He was commended as one of the Navy's best flight instructors, remaining in that capacity until late 1945. That December he was relieved from active duty and discharged from the Navy as a full lieutenant; he had been promoted a year earlier. Taylor continued to look back on his service days with pride. In interviews he often talked about Navy pilots, who had clearly impressed him with their courage, their skill, and especially their eagerness to serve (and fly).

Following his discharge, back in Hollywood, Robert Taylor found that a fresh crop of rising stars, such as Peter Lawford, Van Johnson, and Frank Sinatra, had made their mark and were getting most of the best parts. But Taylor was not broke; he had his contract with MGM, guaranteeing him a retainer income. After the war the studio threw in a new twin-engine Beechcraft, which he rented back to them as needed and for which all parts were replaced as needed, rather than repaired. Eventually Taylor got back into the swing of things and made about forty more movies, including *Undercurrent* (1946), *The Bribe* (1949), *Ambush* (1950), *Quo Vadis* (1951), and *Ivanhoe* (1952).

Robert Taylor retired from the movie industry in the early 1950s, in part to devote more time to one of his favorite hobbies, breeding prizewinning field dogs and horses. But he kept his hand in the acting business as well, starring from 1959 to 1962 in the TV series *The Detectives*. He hosted *Death Valley Days* from 1966 to 1968, sometimes appearing in the shows.

In 1947 he willingly appeared before the House Committee on Un-American Activities, charging once again that *Song of Russia* had been a procommunist movie and hoping by his testimony to help eradicate communist influences in Hollywood.

Taylor and Barbara Stanwyck were divorced in 1951, and three years later he married actress Ursula Thiess. He had two children. Robert Taylor died in 1969.

★

## PART 4

# The Korean War and Afterward

Within a few years after the Allied World War II victory, the United States became embroiled in another conflict. Bloody and vicious, it was an undeclared war that the U.S. Congress had not voted on. It was in fact a United Nations war, prompting President Harry Truman to call it a "police action."

*1950*

25 June    North Korean premier Kim Il Sung sends seven divisions and five brigades of soldiers across the thirty-eighth parallel, supported by 150 Soviet T-34 tanks and a small force of combat aircraft. Reeling under the surprise onslaught, the outnumbered South Korean ground troops retreat to the south.

President Harry Truman promises American military support to South Korea. North Korean forces ignore a United Nations call for a cease-fire. The United Kingdom, Canada, Australia, New Zealand, Turkey, France, the Netherlands, Greece, Belgium, the Philippines, Thailand, and Colombia pledge troops to fight the invaders.

28 June    Seoul, the capital of South Korea, falls. The North Koreans continue their push to the southern tip of the peninsula at the port city of Pusan. There, American and South Korean troops make their stand. American and British aircraft carriers launch air strikes against bridges, oil depots, railroad yards, and roads, causing severe damage to the enemy and destroying his air force.

Sept.     Gen. Douglas MacArthur sweeps up the western sea coast of South Korea and lands an American and British force at the port of Inchon. His brilliant plan is to drive across the peninsula behind the North Korean forces and cut them off from supplies, eventually catching and destroying them between his force driving south and General Walton Walker's force, which holds Pusan. More than one hundred thousand enemy prisoners are taken during the engagement.

27 Sept.   The U.S. Joint Chiefs of Staff authorize MacArthur to drive into North Korea. Soon thereafter the U.S. Eighth Army enters and captures the North Korean capital of Pyongyang. Allied forces continue their push toward the Yalu River, which separates China from North Korea.

25 Nov.    The Chinese hurl a 180,000-man force across the Yalu and into the gap separating Walker from General Almond's X Corps. The Allies are driven back across the thirty-eighth parallel. The 1st Marine Division fights its way out of the Chosin Reservoir entrapment in one of the most courageous military feats in history.


*1951*

11 April   MacArthur, having threatened the Chinese with his own independent ultimatum, has refused to comply with the peace-seeking directives of the Joint Chiefs and Truman and is relieved. Gen. Matthew B. Ridgeway assumes command. UN forces turn

the tide of the battle and push the enemy back to the thirty-eighth parallel.

May     A two-year negotiation for a cease-fire begins at Panmunjom. More soldiers and civilians die in the process. North Koreans keep holding out for more territorial gains during tedious and often hostile negotiation talks.

*1953*

July     An armistice is signed, in which the boundary line agreed upon is more defensible for opposing armies.

In all, approximately two million soldiers and an equal number of civilians were lost during the war. Of the 131 Medals of Honor awarded to Americans, 93 were posthumous.

# Bill Cosby

Superstar, comedian, athlete, and jazz musician William Henry Cosby, Jr., served in the U.S. Navy from 1956 to 1961, trained as a hospital corpsman and working mostly with veterans of the Korean War. He also ran track on the Navy's team, as well as playing basketball and football, and completed his high-school diploma. It was in the Navy that he came to accept the fact of his above-average intelligence and concluded that not to do something with it would be a "mental sin." On the strength of his naval experience, in 1961 Cosby won a scholarship to Temple University, Philadelphia.

However, it was also during his Navy years that Cosby experienced for the first time the insult of being refused in a restaurant along with the rest of the guys. His travels with the U.S. Navy track team took him into the Deep South, where he was forced to enter restaurants through the back door and eat in the kitchen. This outrageous practice persisted in the South at least through the 1960s, and even though the kitchen offered better service, better food, and more of it, for a man born and raised in the North, it was particularly appalling. Fortunately he never had to ride a bus and face the insolence of being told to sit at the back of it.

Fortunately as well, Bill Cosby (born 1937) had a naturally good image of himself, one that had been carefully instilled by his mother, Anna Pearl Cosby, a domestic worker who read Mark Twain and the Bible to her three sons at night. It was she who inculcated in them the certainty that a better life was available than what surrounded them in their impoverished neighborhood of Germantown, North Philadelphia.

The boys grew up in the projects, but their parents programmed them from an early age to expect, and to work for, more. Their father, William Henry Cosby, was a mess steward in the Navy; his tours of duty took him away from home for months at a time. To his parents' dismay, Bill could not wait to start working himself: he quit high school in the tenth grade and got a job fixing shoes.

This did not satisfy the bright lad, who moved on to fixing auto mufflers, but that did not do it, either. Finally, at a loss for how to improve his future, he decided to follow his father's example and join the Navy. At least there, if he could stick it out for twenty years he would be guaranteed a decent income for life.

At the U.S. Marine Corps base at Quantico, Virginia, his high IQ scores earned him training as a physical therapist, followed by assignment to the Bethesda Naval Hospital, Maryland. There he worked as a corpsman, helping to rehabilitate mostly Korean War veterans, a duty that he liked and at which he excelled. He was also sent briefly on board ship, from Newfoundland to Guantánamo Bay. Finally he was assigned to the Philadelphia Naval Hospital.

With the track team, he traveled around the country and improved his skills, getting his time in the hundred-yard-dash down to 10.2 seconds; clearing six feet, five inches in the high jump; and reaching forty-six feet, eight inches in the hop-step jump. He also had a more-than-passing interest in three other sports (football, basketball, and baseball), playing with the Quantico Marine football team in 1956 and playing guard and forward on the National Naval Medical Center varsity basketball team. In 1954 he had tried out for the Baltimore Orioles. During his Navy years, the popular, jocular Cosby made a lot of friends, meeting people who were working hard to better their prospects through the courses offered in the service. Realizing that many of them were applying themselves more than he had ever done—it had never taken much effort for him to do minimally well, thanks to his mental prowess—Cosby came to appreciate the gift he had been born with and resolved to put it to work. He began by earning his high-school diploma while still in the Navy.

After being honorably discharged in 1961, he was determined to continue his studies, and Temple University provided the way. With a track-and-field scholarship, he majored in physical education, running track, playing football, and throwing the discus and javelin. He also worked part-time jobs, which is how his show-business career got started.

Shortly after he started school, someone offered him a few bucks to fill in at a coffeehouse, tending bar and telling jokes. This led to a job at a Philadelphia nightclub, where he told some more jokes and earned a few more bucks. From there he made his way to New York City's Gaslight Cafe, where another of the comedians was Woody Allen. Cosby's own popularity was growing, and it was time to make a decision. He could not pursue both school and all the entertainment jobs that were now coming his way.

Ever the worker, Bill Cosby took the jobs. By 1963 he was being interviewed by *Newsweek,* and in 1965 an appearance on Johnny Carson's *Tonight Show* led to a screen test for the television series *I Spy* (1965–68). Cosby won the part. His future—and that of his family—was now assured. Aside from his bountiful television work, featuring *The Bill Cosby Show* (1969–71), *The New Bill Cosby Show* (1972–73), *The Cosby Show* (1984–92), and *Cosby,* which premiered in the fall of 1996, he has appeared in several movies, including *Hickey and Boggs* (1972), *Uptown Saturday Night* (1974), *California Suite* (1978), and *The Devil and Max Devlin* (1981). *The Cosby Show* was the top-rated TV series of the late 1980s and one of the most successful ever, turning its creator into one of the richest entertainers in the country. The show has had a lasting positive effect across the racial spectrum.

Cosby has also made numerous records and has remained active in community work. He is the author of several books. He has played the drums since childhood and loves to listen to Miles Davis, Thelonious Monk, and other jazz classics. Since 1964 he has been married to Camille Hanks Cosby, who, like her husband, has a Ph.D. in education. Their son, Ennis, met an untimely and violent death while changing a tire on the Los Angeles freeway in January 1997. The Cosbys have four daughters to help them cope with this devastating loss; their ongoing work no doubt also helps.

# Glenn Ford

Canadian native (Quebec, 1916) Gwyllyn Samuel Newton Ford, naturalized as an American citizen with the name Glenn Ford, enlisted in the U.S. Marine Corps Reserve on 13 December 1942. By that time he was already an established Hollywood actor, if not yet a famous one.

Of Welsh descent, Ford was the only child of business executive Newton Ford and his wife, Hannah. He was brought up in the town of Glenford (his future screen name), Quebec, where the family's paper mill was located, and then in Santa Monica, California, where the Fords relocated. When he was five years old they dressed him up and put him on the stage in a production of *Tom Thumb's Wedding*, in a role that necessitated his eating a big bowl of chocolate ice cream. That job showed him the path to his future.

Gwyllyn's fantasy of becoming an actor grew closer to reality in high school, where he excelled in both English and sports and spent his evenings involved with small theater groups. He graduated in 1934, having also learned manual labor at the insistence of his father, and having held down a weekend job working the lights at the Wilshire Theater in Los Angeles. Eventually he became the stage manager.

This led to his move onto the stage in 1935, when he was cast in a walk-on role in *The Children's Hour*. More small parts followed, and some touring, all supplemented by his earnings from construction work. By 1939 Glen Ford was in the movies, in *Heaven with a Barbed Wire Fence*. Columbia Pictures then offered him a contract, starring him in several B movies such as *Texas* (1941) and *The Desperadoes* (1943).

World War II and the Marines interrupted his screen career, but Ford would remember his military service with a great sense of pride and accomplishment. Enlisting in Los Angeles as a photographic specialist at the rank of sergeant, he was assigned in March 1943 to active duty at the Marine Corps Base in San Diego. He was sent to Marine Corps Schools Detachment (Photographic Section) in Quantico, Virginia, that June, with orders as a motion-picture production technician. Sergeant Ford returned to the San Diego base in February 1944 and was assigned next to the radio section of the Public Relations Office, Headquarters Company, Base Headquarters Battalion. There he staged and broadcast the radio program *Halls of Montezuma*.

Glenn Ford was honorably discharged from the Corps on 7 December 1944 and returned to Movieland, where he was still under contract with Columbia Pictures. Among the many noteworthy films that followed were *Gilda* (1946, opposite Rita Hayworth), *A Stolen Life* (1946, with Bette Davis), *Framed* (1947), and *The Big Heat* (1953). He worked for other studios as well, and his superb portrayal of a dauntless teacher in a trouble-ridden city school in *Blackboard Jungle* (1955) drew critical cheers. By this time a top star, Ford distinguished himself with subsequent fine work that included performances in *Ransom* (1955), *The Teahouse of the August Moon* (1956), *Don't Go Near the Water* (1957), and *Experiment in Terror* (1962).

In 1958 Glenn Ford joined the U.S. Naval Reserve and was commissioned a lieutenant commander with a 1655 designator (public-affairs officer). During his annual active-duty tours he promoted the

During World War II Glenn Ford was a sergeant in the Marines, serving as a photographic specialist and broadcasting the radio show *Halls of Montezuma*. During the Vietnam War he served again (above), this time in the Naval Reserve as a public affairs officer, and he spent a month in Vietnam in 1967. (U.S. Navy photo)

Navy through radio and television broadcasts, personal appearances, and documentary films. He was promoted to commander in 1963 and captain in 1968.

Ford went to Vietnam in 1967 for a month's tour of duty as a location scout for combat scenes in a training film, *Global Marine,* later used in a recruit-training program. He traveled with a Corps camera crew from the demilitarized zone (the seventeenth parallel) south to the Mekong Delta, joining the Marines there who were engaged in Operation Deckhouse Five.

This joint U.S.-Vietnamese amphibious operation, the first of its kind, was a carefully planned assault against the Viet Cong, ending on 15 January 1967. Debarking from LSTs (landing ships, tank) and LSM(R)s (landing ships, medium, rocket) in the shallow channels of the Co Chien and Ham Luong rivers, American and Vietnamese Marines took control of the area without too much trouble, most of the enemy having already departed.

Making sporadic forays into U.S. Army domains to capture on film the overall effect of the American military effort in Vietnam, the unpretentious Ford got along with U.S. and Vietnamese personnel alike. He was looked upon and dealt with as just another competent military man carrying out his assignment. He came under sniper fire once during his tour of the delta, dropping posthaste to the ground along with everybody else.

Glenn Ford was awarded the Navy Commendation Medal for his exemplary service during his Vietnam tour. South Vietnamese premier Nguyen Cao Ky awarded him as well the Republic of Vietnam Legion of Merit, First Class. Ford counts among his other military decorations the Marine Corps Reserve Medal, the World War II Victory Medal, and the Rifle Marksmanship Badge.

Back in Hollywood, he returned to making movies, such as *Midway* (1976) and *Superman* (1978). Even in lesser films, Ford's own performances, for which he studiously prepares, have been noted for their consistent quality. His television work has included the series *Cade's County* (1971–72) and *The Family Holvak* (1975).

This multifaceted man has occupied much of his free time with organic gardening (he even wrote a book about it, *Glenn Ford, R.F.D. Beverly*

Whether under fire or traveling undisturbed around the Mekong Delta with his camera crew, the unpretentious Ford got along well with both U.S. and Vietnamese personnel. He counts among his awards the Navy Commendation Medal and the Republic of Vietnam Legion of Merit, First Class. (U.S. Navy photo)

*Hills*), as well as fishing, cooking, traveling, swimming, horseback riding (on his own horses), and hunting, especially for deer. He has held to the tenet of hunting only for meat he would eat. At eighty-plus, Ford operates from his spacious Beverly Hills home, which he designed in 1962. He has been married four times; the first union (1943–59, to dancer Eleanor Powell) produced his only child, Peter, who in turn has produced three Fords.

★

# John Gavin

John Gavin was one of the few movie stars to serve in the U.S. Navy during the Korean War. Originally named John Anthony Golenor (arrival date 8 April 1931, in Los Angeles), he became John Gavin when his mother married Ray Gavin, who adopted him. The future actor and diplomat attended St. John's Military Academy of Los Angeles and Villanova Preparatory School at Ojai, California, before entering the Naval Reserve Officers Training Corps program at Stanford University. He was in the Holloway Plan, which financed NROTC students, and upon his graduation in 1951 he was sworn into the operational Navy for a four-year stint. He had graduated with a degree in economics and Latin American affairs and was fluent in Spanish, a proficiency that would play a significant role in his future.

Gavin's first tour of duty was on board the aircraft carrier USS *Princeton* (CV-37/CVA-37), a World War II ship that was reactivated at the outbreak of hostilities in Korea and operated off Korea until the end of the war in the summer of 1953. The *Princeton* was the ship of Lt. (jg) John K. Koelsch, USNR, who in 1955 was awarded a posthumous Medal of Honor for the heroism of his attempt four years earlier to rescue a downed Corsair pilot, an ordeal that eventually led to his death in a North Korean prisoner-of-war camp. Koelsch's staunch insistence that prisoners be treated according to the Geneva Convention, his unfailing willingness to share what little food he got, and his refusal to divulge information set the standards for the U.S. military's Code of Conduct, adopted in 1955.

Gavin shipped out on a troop carrier with Air Force and Army personnel to Yokohama. He then flew out to the *Princeton* on board a COD (carrier onboard delivery) aircraft from the U.S. Air Force Base at Fukuoka, Japan. Shortly after reporting aboard, he found himself waiting to see the executive officer for assignment. The ship's operations officer, a commander, happened by and asked him who he was and what he was waiting for. Upon learning of Gavin's educational

John Gavin spent his first tour on board the *Princeton* (CV-37/CVA-37), a reactivated World War II ship that operated off Korea until the end of the war in 1953. (U.S. Navy photo)

background, the ops officer went in to see the XO and had Gavin assigned to the operations department as assistant air intelligence officer. It was to be on-the-job training all the way, a feature, the actor later noted, that characterized much of his professional life—not only his time in the Navy, but also his years in the film and business worlds.

When the ship returned to the States after her first Korean deployment, Gavin was sent to Air Intelligence School at Naval Air Station Alameda, California. There he learned for the first time the art of public speaking and giving presentations, training that would prove to be invaluable when he began his acting career, and also later, in his business and diplomatic ventures.

Gavin went back to Korea on the *Princeton* when the carrier rejoined Task Force 77 in February 1953. He received orders, before the end of that tour, to report to Adm. Milton E. Miles, commandant of the Fifteenth Naval District, Panama. The staff there needed a flag lieutenant and aide who was fluent in both Spanish and Portuguese; Gavin was tailor-made for the job. He was reluctant at first—away from the operational Navy, a "horse-holding" position like this one would not necessarily be career-enhancing—but soon he established a close relationship with the admiral. This may have been due in part to Admiral Miles's loss of a son in an auto accident; his son had graduated from the Naval Academy the same month Gavin had received his commission.

Adm. "Mary" Miles (nicknamed after a popular World War I actress, Mary Miles Minter) was himself an Annapolis graduate, class of '22. He spent most of his career in the Pacific, serving aboard various ships and staffs until ordered to head up the U.S. Naval Group, China, in 1942. The group's mission was to set up weather stations in China in preparation for U.S. landings on the mainland. But then Allied strategy for the Pacific changed, and China was bypassed as Allied forces moved northward toward Japan by island conquests. Mary Miles and Chinese general Tai Li nevertheless formed the Sino-American Cooperative Organization, which would become a highly effective guerrilla warfare operation. SACO, known as the Rice Paddy Navy, set up intelligence units, sabotage groups, guerrilla bands, and communication facilities, tormenting Japanese occupying forces until the end of the war.

Gavin left Miles's staff at the end of his four-year commitment. He remained in the Reserves and eventually was designated as a 1635, reserve intelligence officer. His active-duty tours were often spent at the Pentagon, where he worked on Latin American affairs for Adm. Samuel B. Frankel, deputy director of Naval Intelligence. Later he changed his designator from intelligence to public affairs.

Released from the Navy in 1955, Gavin offered his services as a technical adviser on a film about the Navy. The producer, a family friend, thought that Gavin would be able to get into the movies and suggested that he take a screen test. He turned to his father, expecting him to confirm his feeling that this would not be a wise move, but instead his dad told him to go for it. So the producer hooked his friend up with an agent.

John Gavin's early movies include *Behind the High Wall* (1956) and *A Time to Love and a Time to Die* (1958). His reviews were lukewarm, but, tall and handsome, he continued to be a popular romantic lead. He worked hard at acting, an effort that paid off in his later movies, including *Midnight Lace* (1960), *Thoroughly Modern Millie* (1967), and *The Mad Woman of Chaillot* (1969). Among his other better-known films are *Imitation of Life* (1959), *Psycho* (1960), and *Spartacus* (1960). Gavin made his first Broadway appearance in *Seesaw* (1973), and his work on the stage brought critical notice. He also worked in the television industry, appearing in the series *Destry* (1964) and *Convoy* (1965). From 1971 to 1973 he served as president of the Screen Actors Guild.

In 1966 Gavin went on a USO tour to Vietnam, meeting with Navy personnel aboard ships on "Dixie Station," off the coast of South Vietnam. He also visited Army units ashore. Caught in several firefights, he was never injured.

During his tour, while on board the aircraft carrier USS *Oriskany* (CVA-34), he dreamed one night of a *Princeton* pilot's accident. His friend had bailed out of his stricken F4U Corsair and failed to get out of his parachute when he hit the water. An onrushing destroyer that was steaming to his rescue inadvertently came too close to him and drowned him in its churning bow waves. In the dream, the pilot urged Gavin to "get out of there."

The next day Gavin was scheduled to helicopter to other surface ships from the *Oriskany* or be flown to another carrier that was on the line, the USS *Franklin Delano Roosevelt* (CVA-42). Without giving thought to his dream, he chose to go over to the *FDR*. That same day a fire erupted beneath the *Oriskany*'s flight deck on the starboard side of the hangar bay, the result of an exploding magnesium parachute flare. The flames raced through five decks and claimed the lives of forty-four men, many of whom were veteran combat pilots who had flown raids over Vietnam just a few hours earlier. The ship was saved by the heroic efforts of her crew. The men jettisoned heavy bombs while working alarmingly close to the flames; others wheeled planes out of danger, rescued pilots, and helped extinguish the blaze during three hours of prompt, bold actions.

By the time of his USO tour, Gavin had already begun to make his mark in government service. His pleasant personality, intelligence, education, and linguistic abilities suited him ideally for working in diplomatic circles. In July 1961 he was appointed special adviser to Secretary General José Mora of the Organization of American States, tasked with garnering support for President John F. Kennedy's Alliance for Progress aid program for Latin America. During the Reagan administration he served as U.S. ambassador to Mexico (1981–86), and he has received decorations for his work in panamericanism from three foreign governments.

Gavin is married to actress Constance Towers. He has four children.

★

## APPENDIX A

# The Ladies Do Their Bit

Female stars enthusiastically contributed to the effort during the two world wars and Korea, even though they were not wearing service uniforms. They appeared at liberty and war-bond drives and on morale-building radio shows. They served doughnuts and coffee, danced and talked with U.S. servicemen at star-studded canteens in Hollywood, in New York City, and at USO recreational facilities. They entertained fighting men in battle zones as members of troupes led by Bob Hope, Bing Crosby, Jack Benny, and others, and visited the wounded in military hospitals. Glamour shots of beauties such as Betty Grable, Rita Hayward, Maureen O'Hara, Esther Williams, and, during Korea, Marilyn Monroe were on every ship and in every barracks. Especially for those who had no wife or girlfriend waiting for them, these actresses represented their own American dream girl who would be there when they got home.

The 6 February 1930 commissioning ceremonies of the USS *Pensacola* (CA-24) featured Ethel Merman presenting a goat to the crew as a mascot. (U.S. Naval Historical Center)

Betty Hutton entertained personnel at NAS Kaneho, Oahu, in June 1945. (U.S. Navy photo)

Mary Pickford Rogers spoke to the crew of the USS *Huntington* (CL-107) in Venice in 1948. The cruiser's CO, Capt. Arleigh A. Burke, stands behind her. (U.S. Naval Historical Center)

The Special Service Division of the Fleet Recreation and Morale Office staged USO shows throughout World War II. Carole Landis traveled with Jack Benny to Aiela Hospital, Oahu, in 1945. (U.S. Navy photo)

As a child, Margaret O'Brien was once Adm. Chester W. Nimitz's dinner partner. (U.S. Naval Historical Center)

Elizabeth Taylor visited the USS *Worcester* (CL-144) off Cannes, southern France, in 1949. (U.S. Naval Historical Center)

In 1952 Doris Day greeted the *Juneau* (CLAA-119), returning from the Far East. (U.S. Naval Historical Center)

Shirley Temple toured the Pearl Harbor Naval Base in 1950. (U.S. Naval Historical Center)

Jane Russell did her bit in World War II. (From the book *Movie Lot to Beachhead* [1945] by the editors of *Look* magazine)

## APPENDIX B

# Hedy Lamarr

Aside from selling a record-breaking seven million dollars' worth of war bonds in one day, one actress also made a technical contribution, one that at the time would have been expected only from a man. Screen siren Hedy Lamarr was one of two inventors of a communications system that is still in use today in an expanded, more refined form. But during World War II, both the concept and the U.S.-approved patent for the system belonged to Hedy Lamarr and George Antheil.

The daughter of a bank executive, Hedwig Eva Maria Kiesler was born in Vienna, Austria, in 1914. By age seventeen the future Hedy Lamarr was working at Sascha Studios as a script girl and had already appeared in small roles. Soon the spirited actress moved to Berlin, joining the Austro-German movie crowd. In 1933 she shocked her parents and society by appearing in the silent film *Extase,* in which she appeared nude in extremely suggestive scenes. Her husband (the first of six), Friedrich A. Mandl, a powerful munitions tycoon, tried to buy up all copies of the film but was unsuccessful, and the film can still be seen today. The scandal drove her from the European screen.

Friedrich Mandl's young bride, though lavished with every material possession a person could dream of, including gold dishes and a lodge in the Alps, was not happy. Mandl sold arms to the Nazis, but Hedwig hated everything the fascists stood for. After enduring the home atmosphere for three years, she fled to Paris in 1937. There she met American movie czar Louis B. Mayer, who could not help but notice both her looks and the fact that she had previous acting experience. He offered her a contract with MGM and, sending her off to Hollywood, suggested that she change her name to one probably inspired by silent screen star Barbara La Marr. Thus Hedy Lamarr came to America, and soon afterward she appeared in the successful film *Algiers* (1938, opposite Charles Boyer).

Two years later Lamarr attended a party at the home of actress Janet Gaynor, where she chatted with George Antheil, the famous composer and pianist. They arranged to meet and talk some more. The result of all this talking would be a collaboration in the development of a secret communications system that the two thought might prove helpful to the Allied cause. There was no notion of monetary reward for their invention; they considered it their patriotic duty. What they created was the concept of frequency-hopping.

Lamarr was not only dazzling physically, she was also very intelligent. While still married to Mandl, she had paid close attention to the endless dinner-table talk about war and weapons; Mandl had provided much not only to the Germans but also to Mussolini, helping him in his African campaigns. Hedwig listened as her husband's guests described the problems they were having with torpedoes, which were frequently lost during attack exercises. Target ships took evasive maneuvers, and ocean currents were ever-changing. All of this opened up numerous paths for speeding torpedoes. Radio-controlled torpedoes seemed to be the answer, but it was agreed that they could too easily be jammed. If Lamarr at that time thought of a way to solve the problem, she kept it to herself.

What she and Antheil designed was a system that could be adapted for radio control of a remote device such as a torpedo. By quickly changing frequencies in synchronization, the potential for unjammable radio-controlled torpedoes could become a reality. During a series of meetings between Lamarr and Antheil, the system was developed and roughly illustrated, and on 10 June 1941 they submitted an application (Serial No. 397,412) for a patent. On 11 August 1942, Lamarr and Antheil were granted U.S. Patent 2,292,387, for a "Secret Communication System." The owners were listed as Hedy Kiesler Markey (she was then married to screenwriter Gene Markey) of Los Angeles and George Antheil of Manhattan Beach, California. Their application explained in detail how the technology worked:

> Our system as adapted for radio control of a remote craft, employs a pair of synchronous records, one at the transmitting station and one at the receiving station which change the tuning of the transmitting and receiving apparatus from time to time, so that without knowledge

The ravishing Hedy Lamarr was one of two inventors of a communications system that is still in use today. (Photofest)

of the records an enemy would be unable to determine at what frequency a controlling impulse would be sent.

Furthermore, we contemplate employing records of the type used for many years in player pianos, and which consist of long rolls of paper having perforations variously positioned in a plurality of longitudinal rows along the records. In a conventional player piano record there may be 88 rows of perforations, and in our system such a record would permit the use of 88 different carrier frequencies, from one to another of which both the transmitting and receiving station would be changed at intervals. Furthermore, records of the type described can be made of substantial length and may be driven slow or fast. This makes it possible for a pair of records, one at the transmitting station and one at the receiving station, to run for a length of time ample for the remote control of a device such as a torpedo.

The two records may be synchronized by driving them with accurately calibrated constant-speed spring motors, such as are employed for driving clocks and chronometers. However, it is also within the scope of our invention to periodically correct the position of the record at the receiving station by transmitting synchronous impulses from the transmitting station. The use of synchronizing impulses for correcting the phase relation of rotary apparatus at a receiving station is well known and highly developed in the fields of automatic telegraphy and television.

Antheil credited Lamarr entirely with the invention, but his own contribution is impossible to miss. As a composer, he fully understood that synchronizing split-second hops between radio frequencies would be no different from synchronizing player pianos.

After patenting their discovery, Lamarr and Antheil promptly got back to their careers in the film and music worlds, but the War Department never put their concept to use during the war. It was not until 1962, three years after the Lamarr-Antheil patent had expired—the seventeen-year protection period had run out and not been renewed— that Sylvania implemented the system aboard Navy ships blockading Cuba.

In 1957, engineers at Sylvania's Electronic System Division in Buffalo, New York, had independently developed the same concept, and the company was granted a series of antijamming communications patents. Today the sophisticated electronically operated device is used in the U.S. Milstar communications satellite system. Lamarr and Antheil received no recognition for their invention for nearly three decades, but later patents in frequency-hopping have made reference to their work as the generic patent.

Following her brief technical foray, Hedy Lamarr made a series of films in the early and mid-1940s that did little to enhance her career. She turned down lucrative roles and in 1945 formed her own production company, which fared poorly. Finally, in 1949 Cecil B. de Mille cast her in *Samson and Delilah* (opposite Victor Mature), bringing her back into the limelight. Other successes followed, such as *Canyon* (1950), *My Favorite Spy* (1951), *Loves of Three Queens* (1954), *The Story of Mankind* (1957), and *The Female Animal* (1957).

She and her late husband George Antheil were finally honored for their invention in March 1997 by the Electronic Frontier Foundation in San Francisco. Until then they had never received so much as a thank you, not to mention a monetary return, for their significant technical contribution. And she could use a little extra money to supplement her current income. Still socially vigorous, she lives comfortably, if not lavishly, in Miami on her Screen Actors Guild pension and Social Security. She has three children.

★

APPENDIX C

# The Music Men

During World War II, music was the bridge of memories for Navymen around the world. A letter from home was, of course, the most prized gift a sailor could receive, but the strains of a familiar romantic song could remain in the soul and heart for many precious moments.

"I'll Walk Alone," "I Had the Craziest Dream," "There'll Be Blue Birds over the White Cliffs of Dover," "I'll Get By," and "I'll Be Home for Christmas" were just a few of the slower, more danceable numbers. For those who liked to "cut a rug" or jitterbug, there were "Don't Sit under the Apple Tree with Anyone Else but Me," "Straighten up and Fly Right," "Jersey Bounce," and "Kalamazoo."

Like the other services, the Navy had famous musicians in uniform who led both large orchestras and small bands in providing a little stardust for war-weary sailors. Although their civilian careers were grounded in music, many appeared on the silver screen.

## Eddy Duchin

One of the most interesting and talented musicians of the World War II era was socialite bandleader and pianist Eddy Duchin, father of musician Peter Duchin. Duchin's band, like other sophisticated musical groups of its time, played the top clubs in New York and gradually gained radio sponsorship, which gave it national notoriety. The band also made records and introduced myriad songs to the public, among them the classic "Stormy Weather."

Known as the Magic Fingers of Radio, Duchin appeared in two motion pictures with his orchestra in the late 1930s, *Coronado* (1935) and *The Hit Parade* (1937). Tyrone Power interpreted the talented musician's life in *The Eddy Duchin Story* (1956, opposite Kim Novak), but the movie missed Duchin's World War II Navy service.

For his service on the destroyer escort *Bates* (DE-68), Lt. Comdr. Eddy Duchin (second from right) received a Letter of Commendation, with authorization to wear the commendation ribbon and Combat V. (Peter Duchin collection)

Duchin reported for active duty in June 1942, his musical group having been disbanded, and was assigned to the Great Lakes Naval Training Station. Next he was sent to the Naval Reserve Midshipman's School at Northwestern University, after which he was ordered to the Section Base, Port Everglades, Florida, for brief duty on board the USS *Saluda* (IX-87). This wooden-hulled yawl-rigged converted yacht was used for experimental underwater sound operations.

Because he had perfect pitch and had no trouble telling the difference between various sounds, Duchin received training in the use of underwater detection devices at the Naval Training School at Northwestern University and at the Sub-Chaser School in Miami. After a series of brief tours on board patrol craft and then Fire Fighters School in Boston, Duchin reported to the precommissioning detail of the destroyer escort USS *Bates* (DE-68).

He was assigned as sound officer and senior watch officer aboard the *Bates* and was aboard the ship both during the Normandy assault and later in the Pacific, during the Iwo Jima and Okinawa campaigns.

For his "meritorious performance of duty" during his service on the *Bates*, Eddy Duchin received a Letter of Commendation from the secretary of the Navy, with authorization to wear the commendation ribbon and Combat V. His citation read:

> During the invasion of Normandy when the *Bates* supported a predawn reconnaissance landing off Utah Beach on D-Day, Lieutenant Commander Duchin rendered invaluable assistance to his Commanding Officer in carrying out this vital assignment. Participating in the pre-invasion reconnaissance and the landings of Iwo Jima and Okinawa, he succeeded in maintaining his department at a high state of combat efficiency thereby contributing materially to the success of his ship in completing its highly important missions.

Just a month after Duchin departed the *Bates*, the ship was mortally damaged by Japanese kamikaze attacks during patrol operations off the coast of Ie Shima, Okinawa. The destroyer escort capsized and sank in twenty fathoms of water while being towed into the Ie Shima anchorage, on 25 May 1945.

Between April and June 1945, Eddy Duchin was attached first to Commander Destroyers, Pacific Fleet and Pacific Fleet Schools, Camp Catlin, Hawaii, and then served on the staff of Commander Destroyer Squadron 64. Following a brief tour of duty in Washington, Duchin was relieved of all active duty on 15 December 1945.

Aside from the commendation ribbon with Combat V, Duchin was authorized to wear the American Area Campaign Medal, the European–Africa–Middle Eastern Area Campaign Medal, the Asiatic-Pacific Area Campaign Medal, and the World War II Victory Medal.

# Eddie Peabody

Playing thirty-plus stringed instruments, Eddie Peabody achieved international renown as "King of the Banjo." He appeared in three feature films and some twenty-five screen shorts, playing as well in vaudeville, on the radio, and in television programs. He made numerous records

Eddie Peabody served in both world wars, eventually reaching the rank of captain in the Naval Reserve. At Great Lakes, he trained over sixty bands for shore bases and ships afloat. While with Commander Submarine Force, Pacific Fleet, he put together and trained bands throughout the Pacific, overseeing at least six thousand shows. (U.S. Naval Historical Center)

and produced shows on both sides of the Atlantic. Eddie Peabody was also a Navyman who reached the rank of captain in the Naval Reserve.

After attending high school in Lynn, Massachusetts, in March 1917 Edwin Ellsworth Peabody enlisted in the Navy as an apprentice seaman. He was only fifteen years old, but by the time the Navy discovered this, he had served long enough to qualify for enlistment. During his enlisted service in World War I and following the Armistice, he served on board the battleship USS *Nebraska* (BB-14) and in submarine chasers and submarines. He completed his service in the submarine S-14. Peabody later explained that short guys—he was five feet five inches tall—were needed because of the cramped conditions in the early boats. He was discharged in 1921 at the rating of quartermaster second class.

Commissioned in the Naval Reserve as a lieutenant in 1935, Peabody dutifully met his periodic reserve training requirements until July 1941. Then he was called into active service as a band, music, and entertainment officer at the Naval Training Center at Great Lakes, Illinois, where he trained over sixty bands for shore bases and ships afloat, creating as well the radio program *Meet Your Navy.*

In June 1944 he was transferred to the staff of Commander Submarine Force, Pacific Fleet. There he put together and trained bands at all of the Pacific submarine bases, overseeing at least six thousand shows that were put on throughout the area's hospitals, bases, and ships. To express the Navy's appreciation, the chief of the Bureau of Naval Personnel wrote a letter commending Peabody for "outstanding performance of duty as Welfare and Recreation Officer on the Staff of Commander Submarine Force, Pacific Fleet during the period 14 July to 24 January 1945." The letter continued:

> Charged with the important morale building assignment of organizing and training Navy bands and entertainment groups at Pearl Harbor, Midway, Majuro, and Guam, and personally leading an entertainment troupe to practically every advance base in the Pacific including the Solomons, Australia, New Guinea, Leyte Gulf, Ulithi, etc., Commander Peabody rendered invaluable service during that difficult period. The example he set of tireless energy, constant personal attention to the welfare of others and cheerful acceptance of hardships and danger, as well as the excellent type of entertainment he provided, undoubtedly served to strengthen the morale of many thousands of men of all services.

Eddie Peabody was detached from duty in the Philippines in January 1945. He returned to Great Lakes, where he was released to inactive status the following month. He continued to serve in the Naval Reserve, reaching the rank of captain in March 1962, the same year he was transferred to the inactive retired list.

Captain Peabody wore not only his commendation ribbon but also the World War I Victory Medal, Fleet Clasp; the American Defense Service Medal; the American Area Campaign Medal; the Asiatic-Pacific Area Campaign Medal; the World War II Victory Medal; the Philippine Liberation Ribbon; and the Naval Reserve Medal.

## Artie Shaw

By the time he joined the Navy, bandleader and clarinetist Artie Shaw was already famous. He had recorded Cole Porter's acclaimed "Begin the Beguine" and had featured Billie Holiday's magnificent voice in his band. His recordings of "Stardust," "Frenesi," and "Indian Love Call," among others, together with his gift for playing jazz music, had marked him as one of the masters of his time. In 1939 he had appeared in his first movie, *Dancing Co-ed* (with Lana Turner, who briefly became one of his numerous beautiful-actress wives). *Second Chorus* (1941, starring Fred Astaire and Paulette Goddard) told the story of his turbulent career. He had had differences with members of both the music world and the press but had managed to stay afloat through it all.

Enlisting after the Japanese attack on Pearl Harbor, Shaw was initially stationed on Staten Island, New York. He trained on board a minesweeper for a short while and was then ordered to Newport, Rhode Island, where he was promoted to chief petty officer and put in charge of a mediocre band.

Having worked with some of the finest musicians in the business, Shaw was anxious to lead a "real" band. He persuaded the brass in Washington to permit him to recruit a first-rate musical group to tour the Pacific theater. The result was the first such group of its kind, and in the summer of 1943 Shaw and his band sailed from Pearl Harbor on board the battleship USS *North Carolina* (BB-55) for Pacific theater duty.

Their first stop was Noumea, New Caledonia, followed by the New Hebrides, the Solomons, and Guadalcanal. They played on makeshift stages in jungles, on board ships, in hangars, and out in the open, often without a public-address system—which meant that they had to play

After persuading Navy brass to let him put together the first top-notch Navy musical group to tour the Pacific theater, Chief Petty Officer Artie Shaw (center) often played with his band on makeshift stages in jungles and on board ships. (U.S. Navy photo)

harder in order to be heard. New Zealand was next on their schedule, and then Australia, where they spent months traveling back and forth across the continent, playing for service personnel.

By this time the band was near exhaustion from its nonstop heavy schedule. They had been through air raids and enemy fire while living and performing on the run. During their tour the band survived seventeen enemy air attacks on the ships that were transporting them. Even Radio Tokyo took notice of Artie Shaw. They played his records, lying (to make the boys homesick) that the band was currently appearing at the St. Francis Hotel, San Francisco—where the Americans would, of course, rather have been.

In fact, by this time Shaw and his band were spent. Even their instruments had begun to show the effects of the weather and the wear and tear of constant playing. Finally fatigue overcame the group, and they were sent back to the States. Shaw was hospitalized at the Naval Hospital at Oak Knoll, California, suffering from exhaustion. After a three-month stay, he was discharged from the Navy in 1944.

## Claude Thornhill

Jackie Cooper played drums in Chief Petty Officer Claude Thornhill's Navy band, and Ens. Dennis Day, the popular tenor from the Jack Benny radio show, was one of his vocalists. Thornhill and his group toured the Pacific playing for the troops, specializing in posts that had been recently taken from the enemy. A noted arranger and fine musician, Thornhill was appreciated by both friends and fellow musicians for his exceptional sense of humor and his unselfish spirit. Before joining the Navy in October 1942, he had already recorded such hits as "Sleepy Serenade," "Snowfall" (his theme song), and "A Sunday Kind of Love" (which launched the career of vocalist Fran Warren). He spent three years in the Navy.

## Rudy Vallee

The oldest of these troopers was Rudy Vallee, who had enlisted in the Navy in 1917 after dropping out of high school at age sixteen. However, he was soon discharged for being underage and returned to finish school, eventually graduating from Yale in 1927 with a Ph.B. (bachelor of philosophy). Having played in the Yale orchestra and making the country club and society dance circuit with the Vincent Lopez Band after graduation, he struck out on his own with an eight-piece group called the Connecticut Yankees.

The small group played its first engagement at the Heigh-Ho Club in New York and soon was picked by radio station WABC. Success was almost immediate. The band's distinctive style—no brass, two strings, two saxes, lots of piano, and a leader who announced, sang

By the end of World War II, Lt. Rudy Vallee (here, at his wedding to actress Bettejane Greer) was bandmaster for the Eleventh Naval District Coast Guard Band. (U.S. Coast Guard photo)

through a megaphone, and chatted with the audience about his music and songs—soon made Rudy Vallee the toast of the American music world. When radio listeners heard the familiar greeting "Heigh-ho everybody," they knew they were about to hear one of their favorite crooners.

Vallee went on to do weekly radio shows for Fleischmann's Yeast and the Sealtest Company and appeared in theaters and clubs throughout the country, introducing songs such as "The Vagabond Lover" and "Deep Night." He began appearing in movies in 1929 (in *The Vagabond Lover*), and during the following years he played in more than twenty, his last being *Won Ton Ton: The Dog Who Saved Hollywood* (1976). Others that featured his serenading included *Sweet Music* (1935) and *The Palm Beach Story* (1942; he played a smug millionaire opposite Claudette Colbert).

When the United States went to war in 1941, Vallee enlisted in the Coast Guard, rising to the rank of chief petty officer and eventually to that of full lieutenant, USCGR. By the end of the war he was bandmaster for the Eleventh Naval District Coast Guard Band, a forty-seven-piece military ensemble that was said to be one of the country's finest. The group provided entertainment at war-bond drives and military social gatherings.

## Paul Whiteman

Known as the King of Jazz for his popularizing of the genre in America and Europe, the beloved Paul "Pops" Whiteman was a bandleader, symphonic arranger, and conductor. He introduced to the public many composers, musicians, and singers who later became mainstays of the American musical fabric. Bing Crosby, Dinah Shore, Mildred Bailey, and Morton Downey all started with the Whiteman Orchestra, and Pops often waved his baton over an orchestra of virtuosos such as Jimmy and Tommy Dorsey, Red Nichols, Bix Beiderbecke, Lennie Hayton, Henry Busse, Jack Teagarden, and Roy Bargy. He commissioned George Gershwin's "Rhapsody in Blue" and conducted the first performance of the composition with Gershwin at the piano. The event was considered to be a major milestone in the history of jazz.

But before Paul Whiteman became a famous maestro, he was First Musician in the U.S. Navy during World War I, playing the saxophone and violin. A big man, Whiteman weighed in at over three hundred pounds, and when he first attempted to enlist in the Navy, the recruiters turned him down as unfit for combat duty. But he persisted, and in 1917, despite his off-the-chart weight, the Navy accepted him to lead a forty-piece marching band at Naval Station Mare Island, San Francisco. After finding a tailor who could make a big-enough uniform, he was ready to assume his naval duties.

His task was to put together and train an orchestra. Within four months the Mare Island Naval Training Camp Symphony Orchestra was performing not only at the station's church services but also throughout the Bay area, at theaters and events such as Red Cross, Liberty Loan, and Naval Relief Auxiliary drives.

First musician in the U.S. Navy during World War I, Paul Whiteman led a forty-piece marching band at Naval Station Mare Island, San Francisco. In 1942 he revisited Mare Island as a guest conductor. (U.S. Naval Historical Center)

Though successful at what he did best, Whiteman wanted to be one of those who went to sea and risked their lives. He applied for an operational assignment even though he feared the sea, but because of his lack of combat training and his fitness condition, he was turned down for an overseas assignment. He was ordered instead to a coastal submarine chaser off California. But shortly after he reported aboard, an explosion in the boiler room killed ten men, compounding Whiteman's phobia of the sea. Gratefully he returned to shore duty, and a week after he had resumed his bandmaster duties, the war ended.

Although Whiteman had found Navy life grilling, he had enjoyed the service's discipline. No flimsy excuses were tolerated: the musicians were expected to show up on time and carry out their assignments, a welcome experience for the band's conductor. He had had superiors to report to as well, of course, which he would later recognize as a useful learning experience. He had also enjoyed the like-clockwork pay, as well as the radio school he had been required to attend. That experience too would later come in handy, during recordings with his orchestra.

After the Navy, Paul Whiteman became one of the most popular orchestra leaders in the world, playing in major theaters at home and abroad. He conducted music on the radio for NBC and CBS starting in the early 1930s, continuing his on-the-air activities through the 1940s while conducting on the *Philco Radio Hall of Fame*. In 1946 he celebrated his twenty-one years as a maestro with a concert at Carnegie Hall.

Movie roles were also a part of his many theatrical achievements. He appeared in, among others, *Thanks a Million* (1935), *Strike up the Band* (1940), *Atlantic City* (1944), *Rhapsody in Blue* (1945), and *The Fabulous Dorseys* (1947, with Tommy and Jimmy Dorsey and Janet Blair).

★

# Jack Dempsey

One of the greatest American boxing champions, William Harrison Dempsey fought sixty-nine professional bouts and won fifty-five, forty-seven of them by knockout. The "Manassa Mauler" was heavyweight champion of the world from 1919 until 1926, when Gene Tunney defeated him in Atlantic City, New Jersey. In the seventh round of their rematch the next year, an exhausted Dempsey failed to move immediately to the neutral corner after downing his opponent, thus losing precious seconds before the referee began the count—the famous "long count." The match went on, and at the end of the tenth round, Tunney was declared the heavyweight champion.

Jack Dempsey turned his boxing talents to refereeing, traveling to important fights around the Americas. Known for his generosity and his ability to remember names and faces, he also became a businessman, a syndicated newspaper writer, the author of several books, boxing editor for the magazine *Liberty,* and a radio commentator. He got involved in political and social activities, raising money for various charities and hospitals and campaigning for President Franklin D. Roosevelt's reelection.

Dempsey was active in film as well. While still "the Champ," he had starred in the silent serial *Daredevil Jack* (1920) and appeared in boxing documentaries. Over the years he continued to turn up in movies such as *The Prizefighter and the Lady* (1933, in the company of Myrna Loy), *Off Limits* (1953, with Bob Hope and Mickey Rooney), and *Requiem for a Heavyweight* (1962, with Anthony Quinn and Jackie Gleason).

And, during World War II, Jack Dempsey joined the U.S. fighting forces. He held a reserve commission in the U.S. Coast Guard and was called to active duty as a lieutenant in June 1942. Initially he was assigned as director of physical education at New York's Manhattan Beach

Jack Dempsey's films included *Winning His Way* (1924), with Junior Coghlan (to the left of Dempsey). During World War II he served as a lieutenant in the U.S. Coast Guard. (Frank Coghlan collection)

Training Station, Brooklyn, and while there he made appearances at fights, camps, hospitals, and war-bond drives.

In September 1944 he was assigned temporary duty on the troop transport *Wakefield* (AP-21). He visited hospitals and forward-area camps throughout the European theater of operations, always cheerful. Dempsey was later sent to the central Pacific as a morale officer and toured combat areas across the western Pacific. In April 1945 he was on the transport *Arthur Middleton* (AP-55) during the invasion of Okinawa. Seeing the Champ being transported to the beach in a landing craft no doubt helped compose the nerves of many of the troops.

Commander Dempsey returned to the Manhattan Beach Training Station in July 1945 and was released from active duty in September. A month later he was called back to participate in a Victory Bond drive; he was released in December of that year. Jack Dempsey was honorably discharged from the Coast Guard Reserve in April 1952.

For outstanding performance of his wartime duties, Dempsey had been awarded the Navy commendation ribbon in 1946. He also had the American Area Campaign Medal, the Asiatic-Pacific Area Campaign Medal with one star, and the World War II Victory Medal.

He died in 1983; he was eighty-eight years old.

★

# And Others

This book is not, of course, all-inclusive. Many other actors wore blue during World War I, World War II, the Korean War, and afterward. Here are the names of a few of them:

Nick Adams (USCG)
Bob Arthur
Scott Brady
Lee Bonnell (USCG)
Beau Bridges (USCG)
John Bromfield
Raymond Burr
Sid Caesar (USCG)
Joseph Campanella
William Campbell
Harry Carey, Jr.
Richard Carlson
Gower Champion (USCG)
Kevin Conway
Bill Corey
Jeff Corey
James Daly
Billy de Wolfe
Paul Dooley
David Doyle
Jack Elam
Dana Elcar
Leif Erickson
Chad Everett
Larry French
Farley Granger

Fred Gwynne
Alan Hale, Jr. (USCG)
Lloyd Haynes
Earl Holliman
William Hopper
Robert Horton (USCG)
Jeffrey Hunter
Tab Hunter (USCG)
Claude Jarman, Jr.
Richard Kiley
Harvey Korman
Otto Kruger
John Larroquette
Harvey Lembeck
Bill Leslie
Jack Lord
Dewey Martin
Tony Martin
Vic Morrow
Robert Morse
George O'Brien
Richard Quine (USCG)
Jeff Richards
Harry Richman
Don Rickles
Jason Robards

Edward G. Robinson
Wayne Rogers
Robert Stevens (USCG)
McLean Stevenson
Larry Storch
Lawrence Tibbett

Tom Tryon
Lee Van Cleef
Jack Warden
Pat Wayne (USCG)
Dennis Weaver
Gig Young (USCG)

In a San Diego bar in May 1943, Aviation Ordnanceman Richard A. Boone, left, relaxed with some of his Torpedo Squadron Six buddies (including Naval Institute Press author of *Crossing the Line* Alvin Kernan, second from right). VT-6 was a member of Air Group Six, commanded at that time by naval aviator and air ace Lt. Comdr. Edward (Butch) O'Hare. Boone was assigned as an aerial gunner in TBF torpedo planes that flew from the decks of Pacific carriers. A distant relation to Daniel Boone, Richard sometimes sported a coonskin cap as he manned his rear turret during flight operations. He enlisted in the Navy in 1942 and remained in VT-6 until the end of the war, flying from the *Enterprise* (CV-6), *Intrepid* (CV-11), and *Hancock* (CV-19), and participating in numerous campaigns, including Wake Island, Gilbert, Marshall, Caroline Islands, Okinawa, and home island sorties against Japan.

It was after the war that Boone became famous, appearing on Broadway and in some sixty-five movies. He was the character Paladin in *Have Gun, Will Travel* (1957–63). (Alvin Kernan collection)

Douglas, Kirk. *The Ragman's Son*. New York: Simon and Schuster, 1988.

Ebsen, Buddy. *The Other Side of Oz*. Newport Beach, Calif.: Donovan, 1993.

Fairbanks, Douglas, Jr. *A Hell of a War*. New York: St. Martin's, 1993.

Fincher, E. B. *The War in Korea*. New York: Franklin Watts, 1981.

Ford, Glenn, and Margaret Redfield. *Glenn Ford, R.F.D. Beverly Hills*. Old Tappan, N.J.: Hewitt House, 1970.

Freedland, Michael. *Jack Lemmon*. New York: St. Martin's, 1985.

Gleichauf, John F. *Unsung Sailors: The Naval Armed Guard in World War II*. Annapolis, Md.: Naval Institute Press, 1990.

Graham, Michael B. *Mantle of Heroism: Tarawa and the Struggle for the Gilberts*. Novato, Calif.: Presidio, 1993.

Herbert, Solomon J., and George H. Hill. *Bill Cosby*. New York: Chelsea House, 1992.

Hirschhorn, Clive. *Gene Kelly: A Biography*. New York: St. Martin's, 1974.

Hodgson, Marion Stegeman. *Winning My Wings: A Woman Airforce Service Pilot in World War II*. Annapolis, Md.: Naval Institute Press, 1996.

Hoopes, Roy. *When the Stars Went to War: Hollywood and World War II*. Random House, 1994.

Hoyt, Edwin P. *McCampbell's Heroes*. New York: Van Nostrand Reinhold, 1983.

Hudson, Rock, and Sara Davidson. *Rock Hudson: His Story*. New York: William Morrow and Co., 1986.

*Jane's Fighting Aircraft of World War II*. London: Studio Editions, 1990.

Johnson, Carl. *Paul Whiteman: A Chronology*. Williamstown, Mass.: Williams College, 1976.

Kent, Zachary. *World War I: "The War to End Wars."* Hillsdale, N.J.: Enslow, 1994.

Kettlekamp, Larry. *Bill Cosby: Family Funny Man*. New York: Julian Messner, 1987.

Knox, Donald. *The Korean War, Pusan to Chosin: An Oral History*. New York: Harcourt Brace Jovanovich, 1985.

Lamparski, Richard. *Whatever Became of . . . ?* New York: Crown, 1982. (On John Howard)

Law, Jonathan, ed. *Brewer's Cinema: A Phrase and Fable Dictionary*. London: Cassell Wellington House, 1995.

*Lincoln Library of Sports Champions*. Vol. 5. Columbus, Ohio: Frontier, 1989.

Lloyd, Ann; Graham Fuller; and Arnold Desser. *The Illustrated Who's Who of the Cinema*. New York: Macmillan, 1983.

Maltin, Leonard. *Movie Encyclopedia*. New York: Penguin Books, 1994.

———. *1996 Movie and Video Guide*. New York: Penguin Books, 1995.

Morella, Joe, and Edward Z. Epstein. *Paul and Joanne: A Biography of Paul Newman and Joanne Woodward*. New York: Delacorte, 1988.

Morison, Samuel Eliot. *History of United States Naval Operations in World War II*. 15 vols. Boston: Little, Brown and Co., 1947–62.

Murphy, Edward. *Korean War Heroes*. Novato, Calif.: Presidio, 1992.

Nash, Jay Robert, and Stanley Ralph Ross, eds. *The Motion Picture Guide, 1927–1983*. Chicago: Cinebooks, 1986.

# Selected Bibliography

## Books

Albert, Col. Joseph H. *Utmost Savagery*. Annapolis, Md.: Naval Institute Press, 1995.

Allen, Thomas E., and Norman Polmar. *Code-Name Downfall*. New York: Simon and Schuster, 1995.

Baltake, Joe. *Jack Lemmon: His Films and Career*. Secaucus, N.J.: Citadel, 1986.

Benchley, Nathaniel. *Humphrey Bogart*. Boston: Little, Brown and Co., 1975.

Benny, Jack, and Joan Benny. *Sunday Nights at Seven*. New York: Warner Books, 1990.

Benny, Mary Livingstone; Hilliard Marks; and Marcia Borie. *Jack Benny*. New York: Doubleday and Co., 1978.

Bergeron, Barbara, and Chuck Bartelt, project eds. *Variety Obituaries*. New York and London: Garland, 1988–.

Blair, Clay. *The Forgotten War*. New York: Times Books, 1987.

Bogart, Stephen Humphrey. *Bogart: In Search of My Father*. New York: Dutton, 1995.

Brooks, Tim, and Earle Marsh. *The Complete Dictionary of Prime Time and Cable TV Shows*. 6th ed. New York: Ballantine Books, 1995.

Brown, David. *Warship Losses of World War II*. Annapolis, Md.: Naval Institute Press, 1995.

Carpenter, Dennis, and Joseph Dorinson. *Anyone Here a Sailor? Popular Entertainment and the Navy*. Great Neck, N.Y.: Brightlights Publications, n.d.

Churchill, Winston S. *The Second World War: The Hinge of Fate*. Boston: Houghton Mifflin, 1950.

Clark, Tom. *Rock Hudson: Friend of Mine*. New York: Pharos Books, 1990.

Coghlan, Frank, Jr. *They Still Call Me Junior*. Jefferson, N.C.: McFarland and Co., 1993.

Cooper, Jackie, and Dick Kleiner. *Please Don't Shoot My Dog*. New York: William Morrow and Co., 1981.

Crystal, David. *The Cambridge Biographical Encyclopedia*. Avon: Cambridge University Press, 1994.

*Current Biography Yearbook*. New York: H. W. Wilson, 1941–96.

Curtis, Tony, and Barry Paris. *Tony Curtis: The Autobiography*. New York: William Morrow and Co., 1993.

Davidson, Bill. *Spencer Tracy: Tragic Idol*. New York: Kensington, 1987.

*Dictionary of American Naval Fighting Ships*. 8 vols. Washington, D.C.: Government Printing Office, Naval History Division, 1959–81.

Nowlan, Robert A., and Gwendolyn W. Nowlan. *Film Quotations*. London: McFarland and Co., 1994.

Nuwer, Hank. *Strategies of the Great Football Coaches*. New York: Frank Watts, 1988.

O'Brien, Pat. *The Wind at My Back: The Life and Times of Pat O'Brien*. New York: Doubleday and Co., 1964.

O'Donnell, Monica M., ed. *Contemporary Theatre, Film, and Television*. Vol. 1. Detroit, Mich.: Gale Research, 1984.

Osborne, Robert. *65 Years of the Oscar: The Official History of the Academy Awards*. New York: Abbeville, 1994.

Parish, James Robert, series adviser. *Spencer Tracy: A Bio-Bibliography*. Westport, Conn.: Greenwood, 1994.

Parish, James Robert, and Don E. Stanke. *The Debonairs*. New York: Arlington House, 1975.

Parish, James Robert, and Vincent Terrace. *The Complete Actors' Television Credits, 1948–1988*. Metuchen, N.J., and London: Scarecrow, 1989.

Potter, E. B. *Sea Power: A Naval History*. Annapolis, Md.: Naval Institute Press, 1981.

Rogers, Mary Pickford. *Sunshine and Shadow*. Garden City, N.Y.: Doubleday, 1955.

Roscoe, Theodore. *Destroyer Operations in World War II*. Annapolis, Md.: Naval Institute Press, 1953.

———. *United States Submarine Operations in World War II*. Annapolis, Md.: Naval Institute Press, 1949.

Rosenberg, Robert. *Bill Cosby: The Changing Black Image*. Brookfield, Conn.: Millbrook, 1991.

Roskill, S. W. *The War at Sea, 1939–1945*. Vols. 1–3. London: Her Majesty's Stationery Office, 1956.

Schneider, James G. *The Navy V-12 Program: Leadership for a Lifetime*. Boston: Houghton Mifflin, 1987.

Shale, Richard, ed. *The Academy Awards Index: The Complete Categorical and Chronological Record*. Westport, Conn.: Greenwood, 1993.

Shaw, Artie. *The Trouble with Cinderella*. New York: Farrar, Straus and Young, 1952.

Showell, Jak P. Mallmann. *The German Navy in World War II*. Annapolis, Md.: Naval Institute Press, 1979.

Siegel, Scott, and Barbara Siegel. *The Encyclopedia of Hollywood*. New York: Facts on File, 1990.

Simon, George T. *The Big Bands*. New York: Schirmer Books, 1981.

Smith, Ronald L. *Cosby*. New York: St. Martin's, 1986.

Stack, Robert, with Mark Evans. *Straight Shooting*. New York: Macmillan, 1980.

Steirman, Hy, ed. *Harry Belafonte*. New York: Hillman Periodicals, 1957.

Teichmann, Howard. *Fonda: My Life as Told to Howard Teichmann*. New York: New American Library, 1981.

Thomas, Bob. *Golden Boy: The Untold Story of William Holden*. New York: St. Martin's, 1982.

Tillman, Barrett. *Hellcat: The F6F in World War II.* Annapolis, Md.: Naval Institute Press, 1979.

Toland, John. *In Mortal Combat: Korea, 1950–1953.* New York: William Morrow, 1991.

Vaeth, J. Gordon. *Blimps and U-Boats.* Annapolis, Md.: Naval Institute Press, 1992.

Vallee, Rudy. *My Time Is Your Time.* New York: Ivan Obolensky, 1962.

Wayne, Jane Ellen. *Robert Taylor.* New York: St. Martin's, 1973.

West, Selden. Forthcoming authorized biography of Spencer Tracy, to be published by Alfred A. Knopf, 1997.

Widener, Don. *Lemmon.* New York: Macmillan, 1975.

## Periodicals

In addition to the specific articles listed below, the authors also consulted various wartime and other period newsclips and press releases on actors, including Capt./Comdr./Lt. Comdr. Robert Montgomery, Lt. Robert Taylor, and others.

*All Hands* (Navy magazine), November 1945, 48. (On the USS *Metha Nelson*)

Boswell, Day, and Robert Scheina. "Coast Guardsman Romero 'One of Us Guys.'" *Commandant's Bulletin,* 14 September 1984, 12–13.

Brady, James. "In Step with Ernest Borgnine." *Parade* magazine, 1 October 1995.

"Comdr. Glenn Ford." *Philadelphia Inquirer,* 7 February 1967.

*Dallas Morning News,* 17 September 1989, 45A, 50A, 51A. (On Ed Begley)

Demaris, Ovid. "I'm Available: At 70, Glenn Ford's Still Raring to Go." *Parade* magazine, 9 November 1986, 4.

Great Lakes Naval Training Center Public Affairs Office staff. "80 Years . . . Great Lakes, a Great Place." *Lakeland Newspapers* (Grayslake, Ill.), November 1991.

"'A Hell of a War': An Interview with Douglas Fairbanks, Jr." *Naval History* magazine, October 1993, 21–24.

Monroe, Alexander G., Capt., USNR. "Henry Fonda and the U.S. Navy." *Naval History* magazine, Spring 1991, 10.

Morgan, Allen E. "Navy Reserve Aviation Base, Long Beach, 1929–1942: Part I, The Early Years." *American Aviation Historical Society Journal* (Ojai, Calif.) 16, no. 4 (1971).

Morris, Mrs. Wayne. "My Husband Is Home." *Photoplay* magazine, April 1945, 32–33, 115–16.

Morrow, Tom, PA1. "Victor Mature, Former CG BMC, Remembers World War II Years." *Scan* (USCG periodical), June 1979.

"NNMC Sports Personality." *National Naval Medical Center News,* 23 December 1957. (On Bill Cosby)

Schemeligian, Bob. "Romero Maintains Dashing Image." *Las Vegas Sun,* 27 September 1991, 3D.

Silverman, Stephen M., and Ron Arias. "Day-O Reckoning: A Bout with Prostate Cancer Couldn't Slow down Harry Belafonte's Comeback at Age 69." *People* magazine, 26 August 1996, 61.

Slutsker, Gary. "I Guess They Just Take and Forget about a Person." *Forbes* magazine, 14 May 1990, 136–38. (On Hedy Lamarr)

Tillman, Barrett. "Wayne Morris: Actor, Naval Aviator, and Fighting 15 Ace." *The Hook,* Summer 1984.

"Wallace Beery Seriously Ill." *Morning Telegraph,* 29 October 1929.

"The War That Was." *People* magazine, 7 August 1995.

*Washington Post,* 8 January 1967. UPI photos and captions covering Glenn Ford's thirty-day tour of duty in the Naval Reserves.

Winchell, Walter. "Hollywood Joins the Navy." *Photoplay–Movie Mirror* (Hollywood), 1942. Reprinted in *Hollywood and the Great Fan Magazines,* edited by Martin Levin. New York: Arbor House, 1970.

## Official Records and Archival Sources

In addition to the specific sources listed below, the authors consulted official U.S. Navy biographies, award citations, fitness reports, notices of separation, transcripts of naval service, and other records and documents held by the Bureau of Naval Personnel, Navy Department, Washington, D.C.; the National Personnel Records Center (Military Personnel Records), St. Louis, Mo.; the Operational Archives, Naval Historical Center, Washington, D.C.; the Ships' History Division, Naval Historical Center, Washington, D.C.; and the U.S. Coast Guard Historian's Office, Washington, D.C.

Commander Air Group 15. Action report, 27 October 1944, "Report of Air Operations conducted by Carrier Air Group Fifteen during period 6 September to 24 September 1944." Operational Archives, Naval Historical Center, Washington, D.C.

Commander Task Group 38.3 (Commander Carrier Division 1). Action report, 2 December 1944, "Battle of the Philippines, 24–25 October 1944." Operational Archives, Naval Historical Center, Washington, D.C.

"Eddie Albert: Pacific War interview, May 1993." Nimitz Museum oral history tape no. 259. Nimitz Museum, Fredericksburg, Tex.

Fowler, Walter E., Comdr., USNR. "History of Air Ferry Squadron Three," 1 December 1944. Operational Archives, Naval Historical Center, Washington, D.C.

"History of Underwater Demolition Team Seventeen." Operational Archives, Naval Historical Center, Washington, D.C.

Letter from Logan Ramsey to his mother, September 1945. (An edited version of this letter appeared in the *Saturday Evening Post,* 12 January 1946.)

Letter from Marion Stegeman (class of 1943 WASP, Avenger Field, Sweetwater, Tex.) to her mother, 31 May 1943. Marion Stegeman Hodgson collection.

Marine Corps Historical Center files. U.S. Navy Yard, Washington, D.C.

"A Narrative Account of the Operations of Cruiser Covering Force, Home Fleet, Designated to cover the passage of the Russian Convoys, 'PQ-17' and 'QP 13,' through the Greenland and Barents Sea, by D. E. Fairbanks, Jr., Lieutenant, USNR Flag Lieutenant and Aide to Commander Task Force 99." Operational Archives, Naval Historical Center, Washington, D.C.

Office of the troop commander, USS *Sheridan*, at sea. Correspondence dated 30 November 1943. Addressed to commanding officer, USS *Sheridan*. Subject: Performance of duty, report of in the case of certain personnel [Eddie Albert], USS *Sheridan*.

"Radio-Controlled Hellcat—First Standard Military Plane to Fly without Pilot." Navy Department release, 12 October 1945.

*Register of Commissioned and Warrant Officers of the United States Naval Reserve*. Washington, D.C.: Government Printing Office, 1944.

"The Role of the Naval Air Transport Service in the Pacific War." Naval Air Transport Service document, 1945. Operational Archives, Naval Historical Center, Washington, D.C.

Torpedo Squadron 99. Naval aviation log, July 1944–June 1945. Naval Historical Center, Washington, D.C.

———. War diary, 6 September 1945. Naval Historical Center, Washington, D.C.

"Turning toward Victory: 1943." Admiral Nimitz Museum symposium, Fredericksburg, Tex., 3–5 May 1993.

*United States Submarine Losses, World War II*. Appendix, "Axis Submarine Losses, German U-Boats, Japanese I- and RO-Boats, Italian Submarines." Washington, D.C.: Naval History Division, 1963.

University of Kansas alumni association biographical information on Buddy Rogers.

U.S. Coast Guard Public Information Division biography. USCG Headquarters, Washington, D.C.

U.S. Patent Office. Patent No. 2,292,387, issued 11 August 1942, to Hedy Kiesler Markey, Los Angeles, and George Antheil, Manhattan Beach, Calif.

USCGC *Storis* (WMEC-38). Change of command brochure, 18 July 1984. Ships' History Division, Naval Historical Center, Washington, D.C.

USS *Admiral H. T. Mayo* (AP-125). Log book, 1945. National Archives, College Park, Md.

USS *Block Island* (CVE-106). Ship's history, undated. Ships' History Division, Naval Historical Center, Washington, D.C.

USS *Endicott* (DD-495). Action report, 23 August 1944. Operational Archives, Naval Historical Center, Washington, D.C.

USS *Hollandia* (CVE-97). Muster rolls, August–September 1945. National Archives, College Park, Md.

USS *Marshall* (DD-676). Ship's history, undated. Ships' History Division, Naval Historical Center, Washington, D.C.

USS PC-1139. Action report, 7 February 1944. Operational Archives, Naval Historical Center, Washington, D.C.

———. Log, 18 November 1943–31 May 1944. National Archives, College Park, Md.

USS *Satterlee* (DD-626). Deck log, 1943. National Archives, College Park, Md.

USS *Sheridan* (APA-51). Action report, 29 November 1943, "Activity of Salvage Boat No. 13." Operational Archives, Naval Historical Center, Washington, D.C.

"USS *Stewart* Was Only Combatant Navy Ship Captured and Used by Japanese." Navy Department press and radio release, 2 March 1946.

USS *Taussig* (DD-746). Deck log. National Archives, College Park, Md.

———. Report of changes to muster roll, 14 March 1945. National Archives, College Park, Md.

USS YMS-24. Action report, 26 August 1944. Operational Archives, Naval Historical Center, Washington, D.C.

———. War diary, August 1–16, 1944. Operational Archives, Naval Historical Center, Washington, D.C.

Wallace Beery file (newsclips, aircraft owned). Research Department, Smithsonian Air and Space Museum, Washington, D.C.

## Interviews and Telephone Conversations (All with Jim Wise)

Begley, Ed., Jr. (Ed Begley's son): August 1996.

Cox, Mrs. John (John Howard's wife): November, December 1995.

Coghlan, Frank "Junior": throughout 1995.

Gavin, John: April 1995.

Ford, Peter: 2 August 1996.

Howard, Dale (John Howard's son): April 1995.

Madison, Bridget (Guy Madison's daughter): April 1995.

Newman, Paul: 8 March 1997.

Ramsey, Logan: October–November 1996.

Ramsey, Mary Ann (Logan Ramsey's sister): October–November 1996.

Rogers, Beverly (Charles "Buddy" Rogers's wife): throughout 1995 and 1996.

## Letters (All to Jim Wise)

Albert, Eddie: 20 February, 20 August 1996.

Bitterly, Joseph (John Howard's former shipmate): November, December 1995.

Coghlan, Frank "Junior": ongoing, 1995–96.

Cooper, Jackie: 22 September 1995.

Cox, Mrs. John (wife of John Howard): November, December 1995.

Douglas, Kirk: 10 December 1995.

Duchin, Peter (Eddy Duchin's son): 17 April 1996.

Ewell, Marjorie (Tom Ewell's wife): throughout 1996.

Fairbanks, Douglas, Jr.: 31 May 1996.

Ford, Peter (Glen Ford's son): 17 April, 12 August 1996.

Gavin, John: throughout 1996.

Howard, Dale (John Howard's son): November, December 1995.

Lenkeit, Dutch (Guy Madison's former stationmate): 27 April 1996.

Madison, Bridget (Guy Madison's daughter): throughout 1996.

Morris, Pat (Wayne Morris's wife): throughout 1996.

Newman, Paul: 8 February 1996.

Posner, Jules (U.S. Army veteran who met John Howard during World War II in Naples): November, December 1995.

Ramsey, Logan: 14 October 1996.

Ramsey, Mary Ann (Logan Ramsey's sister): throughout 1996.

Romero, Eduardo (Cesar Romero's brother): 18 September 1995.

Stack, Robert: 27 May 1996.

West, Seldon (official biographer of Spencer Tracy): throughout 1996.

# Index

# About the Authors

James E. Wise, Jr., became a naval aviator in 1953 following graduation from Northwestern University. After naval intelligence school he served as an intelligence officer aboard the USS *America*, and later served as the commanding officer of various naval intelligence units. Since his retirement from the U.S. Navy in 1975, Captain Wise has held several senior executive posts in private-sector companies. He has previously published two books, *Shooting the War: Memoirs of a World War II U-boat Officer*, with Otto Giese (Naval Institute Press, 1994); and *Sole Survivors of the Sea* (Baltimore: Nautical and Aviation Publishing Co., 1994). A third is forthcoming in 1997 from Kent State University Press: *Sailors' Journey into War*. He is also the author of many historical articles in naval and maritime journals. Captain Wise and his wife live in Alexandria, Virginia.

Anne Collier Rehill has worked in publishing for twenty years in several capacities, including in production at the *Village Voice*, as an editor and writer at *Us* magazine, and as an acquisitions editor at the Naval Institute Press. She has previously published articles in periodicals and two book translations of the original French (*Unmentionables*, by Claire Paillochet, co-translated with Christel Petermann; and *Brigitte Bardot*, by Raymond Boyer and François Guérif. New York: Delilah Books, 1983), with a third forthcoming in 1997 (*Thérérèse de Lisieux: A Life of Love*, by Jean Chalon. Ligouri, Mo.: Ligouri Books). Ms. Collier Rehill holds an M.A. in French literature and has taught French or English at several colleges. She currently works as a writer, editor, and translator from her home near State College, Pennsylvania, where she lives with her husband.

The **Naval Institute Press** is the book-publishing arm of the U.S. Naval Institute, a private, nonprofit, membership society for sea service professionals and others who share an interest in naval and maritime affairs. Established in 1873 at the U.S. Naval Academy in Annapolis, Maryland, where its offices remain today, the Naval Institute has members worldwide.

Members of the Naval Institute support the education programs of the society and receive the influential monthly magazine *Proceedings* and discounts on fine nautical prints and on ship and aircraft photos. They also have access to the transcripts of the Institute's Oral History Program and get discounted admission to any of the Institute-sponsored seminars offered around the country.

The Naval Institute also publishes *Naval History* magazine. This colorful bimonthly is filled with entertaining and thought-provoking articles, first-person reminiscences, and dramatic art and photography. Members receive a discount on *Naval History* subscriptions.

The Naval Institute's book-publishing program, begun in 1898 with basic guides to naval practices, has broadened its scope in recent years to include books of more general interest. Now the Naval Institute Press publishes about 100 titles each year, ranging from how-to books on boating and navigation to battle histories, biographies, ship and aircraft guides, and novels. Institute members receive discounts of 20 to 50 percent on the Press's nearly 600 books in print.

Full-time students are eligible for special half-price membership rates. Life memberships are also available.

For a free catalog describing Naval Institute Press books currently available, and for further information about subscribing to *Naval History* magazine or about joining the U.S. Naval Institute, please write to:

Membership Department
U.S. Naval Institute
118 Maryland Avenue
Annapolis, MD 21402-5035
Telephone: (800) 233-8764
Fax: (410) 269-7940
Web address: www.usni.org